Successful Negotiations

Marc Helmold · Tracy Dathe · Florian Hummel

Successful Negotiations

Best-in-Class Recommendations for Breakthrough Negotiations

Springer

Marc Helmold
Berlin, Germany

Tracy Dathe
Holzkirchen, Germany

Florian Hummel
Berlin, Germany

ISBN 978-3-658-35700-9 ISBN 978-3-658-35701-6 (eBook)
https://doi.org/10.1007/978-3-658-35701-6

This book is a translation of the original German edition "Erfolgreiche Verhandlungen" by Helmold, Marc, published by Springer Fachmedien Wiesbaden GmbH in 2019. The translation was done with the help of artificial intelligence (machine translation by the service DeepL.com). A subsequent human revision was done primarily in terms of content, so that the book will read stylistically differently from a conventional translation. Springer Nature works continuously to further the development of tools for the production of books and on the related technologies to support the authors

This Springer imprint is published by the registered company Springer Fachmedien Wiesbaden GmbH part of Springer Nature.
The registered company address is: Abraham-Lincoln-Str. 46, 65189 Wiesbaden, Germany

Preface

The book "Successful Negotiations—Best-in-Class Recommendations for Breakthrough Negotiations" describes how to conduct international negotiations in a structured, professional and successful manner. The experience of the authors and negotiation experts Professor Marc Helmold, Dr. Tracy Dathe and Professor Florian Hummel from intercultural negotiations in the most diverse areas and industries has been incorporated here. Numerous other experts from important industries and from the most diverse cultural areas have contributed directly or indirectly to this publication through their experience. Last but not least, individual results from applied research in the context of project and final theses at Master's and doctoral level have also contributed to the topicality of this guide to negotiation.

This book provides a comprehensive overview of negotiations and successful negotiation breakthroughs. It systematically and logically brings together aspects that were previously perceived as separate, such as negotiation preparation, negotiation execution, negotiation psychology and negotiation success in a national, international and intercultural context. In addition to the structured approach in six steps, psychological and non-verbal tools are explained in a practical and clear manner, which will lead the negotiator to a successful negotiation conclusion. Furthermore, intercultural and international elements are ideally integrated into the work.

The focus here is on practical relevance, whereby the authors' concrete experience from industry, teaching, research and business is combined with theoretical elements, enabling a concise and comprehensible presentation of the content. Enriched with numerous practical examples and country-specific recommendations for action, this negotiation guide has numerous unique selling points.

This reference book is particularly interesting for employees in the areas of sales, purchasing or marketing who have to negotiate performance characteristics of products and services such as specifications, performance descriptions, quality characteristics, prices with customers or suppliers. In addition, the book also provides recommendations for employees from areas such as development, quality management, production, human resources, finance or logistics, who are directly or indirectly involved in the value chain through their function. Executives and project managers also belong to the circle of interested parties, especially when intercultural peculiarities and elements come into play in negotiations with business partners. Furthermore, entrepreneurs, owners of smaller companies or start-ups belong to the target groups who want to initiate or maintain business relations in an international or national context. Furthermore, the symbiosis of theory and practice enables the application in higher education, so that this work also focuses on professors, teaching staff and students in an international context. Finally, the book is aimed at public sector clients and local authorities who wish to develop their project management and procurement staff into experts in negotiation. The target group includes small and medium-sized enterprises as well as international corporations.

This book closes the gap in literature and practice with the A-6 model in six steps on how negotiators succeed not only in conducting successful negotiations, but also in maintaining successful business relationships and implementing projects economically. The valuable recommendations for action specifically link practical and conceptual aspects with cultural and theoretical components based on the authors' many years of negotiating experience in multi-million euro projects. Furthermore, intercultural country elements, job interviews and special negotiations in the service sector or project management are described in detail. As former executives, all authors conduct workshops and negotiation trainings for companies and support well-known companies conceptually or actively in negotiations for purchasing and sales activities.

The book provides knowledge on how international and intercultural elements can be effectively taken into account in negotiations. It is academically demanding, but at the same time comprehensible and compact, the structure of the work thus follows a decidedly application-oriented concept.

Although job interviews, politics and special topics (negotiating in the service sector or in complex projects) are also covered, the focus of the book is on negotiating business partners in the global exchange of goods and in commercial transactions. Examples are given from a company perspective from purchasing, sales as well as other company functions in a practical manner. Terms such as negotiating partner, negotiating opponent or the negotiating counterparty are used neutrally and synonymously.

Chapter 1 deals with the special features, elements and characteristics of negotiations in an international context, in politics or in job interviews. In addition to current negotiation concepts and issues, intercultural peculiarities are dealt with in detail.

Chapter 2 summarizes three important negotiation concepts from Harvard, Schranner and Professor Helmold. Although there are other concepts, the presentation here is limited to three fundamental models because almost all other concepts contain essential features of these three concepts. The chapter summarizes key differences among the three concepts at the end.

Chapter 3 provides recommendations for systematic preparation and the actual conduct of negotiations. Analysis and conduct of negotiations are elementary prerequisites for result-oriented and successful negotiations.

Chapter 4 delves into the six steps of Professor Marc Helmold's successfully used A-6 model for negotiations in an international context. This chapter is rounded off with recommendations for action and the intercultural peculiarities already briefly described. Interesting in this context are numerous practical examples that enable the reader to successfully conduct his or her own negotiations.

In Chap. 5, useful tools from teaching and practice such as the industry analysis consisting of five dimensions, the strength-weakness analysis or the margin enhancement and profitability improvement plan are discussed with examples from practice.

Chapter 6 deals with the psychology of negotiation and non-verbal communication elements in negotiations through body language, gestures or facial expressions. Practical examples in this chapter show what to look out for and how behavioural patterns of the negotiating counterparty can be used specifically in negotiations.

Chapter 7 presents international and intercultural characteristics of countries and regions. This is unique in the literature as it describes interculturally successful and failing strategies for countries such as Germany, the United States, India or China. Economic strength and trade relations with Germany were taken into account in the selection of a total of 13 country examples. Therefore, in addition to the ten strongest economies, neighboring countries such as the Netherlands are also listed. In addition, Saudi Arabia in the Arab region ideally rounds off this intercultural chapter. Results and recommendations are based on a literature research combined with applied research results and the practical experiences of the authors in the mentioned countries and regions.

Chapter 8 describes negotiations in claim management. Subsequent claims or supplements arise due to deficiencies and deficiencies in performance on one of the negotiating sides. Frequently, deficiencies and defects in quality, condition or specification lead to considerable financial losses, which result in renegotiations in the context of claim management.

Chapter 9 shows the phases that occur when financial difficulties arise. In order for companies not to fall into insolvency, compelling, sustainable and proactive measures are necessary in the event of financial difficulties. Lastly, this chapter provides important recommendations on what restructuring measures and related negotiations need to be implemented as a company in the event of financial difficulties so that a financial crisis and insolvency can be averted.

Chapter 10 provides information on the special features to be taken into account in negotiations in complex projects. Usually interdisciplinary teams are involved here, which almost always also have different motives and interests. Here, too, the chapter ends with practical recommendations for action for project members and project managers.

Chapter 11 focuses on negotiations in the services sector. Services are intangible goods in the economic sense and are characterized by intangibility, perishability and uniqueness (individuality), so that special aspects have to be taken into account in negotiations. In addition to the 7P and the 3R concept, special features of negotiations in the service sector are presented.

Chapter 12 concludes the book with a summary of eleven negotiation principles and specific recommendations for action for negotiations within the value chain and between business partners in a national or international context. In addition, key competencies and success factors that make negotiations successful are mentioned, supplemented with numerous country examples and intercultural peculiarities of 13 countries and regions. The extensive and up-to-date bibliography invites further study. In particular, the country specifics, which have been defined on the basis of the authors' practical experience, a detailed literature review and through university research, make this book "Successful Negotiations—Best-in-Class Recommendations for Breakthrough Negotiations" unique in its kind.

The last Chap. 13 contains useful tools and appendices that can be used to support negotiations.

Thanks are due to the numerous negotiation professionals and international business partners who have indirectly supported this publication with their experience. The authors hope that their wide-ranging experience in this negotiation guide will provide companies with ideal assistance in building long-term bridges with international business partners. For the authors, diversity, appreciation of other cultures and openness to the world are among the current and future key factors for successful and sustainable negotiations. Finally, the three authors would like to thank Stefanie Winter and the Springer team for the friendly, competent and professional handling of this negotiation guide.

Berlin, Germany; Hiroshima, Japan — Marc Helmold
Holzkirchen, Germany; Frankfurt am Main, Germany — Tracy Dathe
Hamburg, Germany; Berlin, Germany — Florian Hummel
December 2021

Contents

About the Authors

Marc Helmold is a professor at the IU International University of applied Sciences at the Campus Berlin for Business Administration, Strategic Management, Negotiations in an International Context and Supply Chain Management (SCM). Prior to his appointment as professor, he held various management positions at well-known companies in the automotive and railway industries. From 2002 to 2006, he worked as an executive in the context of a global cooperation for a leading automobile manufacturer in Japan and conducted negotiations in the higher three-digit million euro range. In addition to working in the automotive industry, from 2010 to 2017 he worked for a manufacturer of commuter trains, trams, regional and express trains. Here he was head of the main purchasing and supply chain management (SCM) department with a purchasing budget in the higher three-digit million euro range. In China, he was responsible for the international purchasing office (English: IPO, International Procurement Organization) and for the distribution of spare parts in China at the same company from 2013 to 2016 as Managing Director of China Activities. Especially in Asia, the sustainable consideration of intercultural elements was necessary in all negotiations. The project volumes here were also in the three-digit million euro range. The purchasing office had about 70 employees at five locations in China. He completed his PhD at the University of Gloucestershire in supplier management. In 2016, he was appointed professor at the IUBH in Berlin. In parallel, he founded his own consulting company in process optimization. As part of this work, Professor Helmold conducts training for practitioners and academics in the field of negotiations.

Tracy Dathe is a professor at Macromedia University in Berlin. She is an experienced financial expert and university lecturer in the field of multinational manufacturing SMEs. From 2012 to 2016, as CFO at the Erich Jaeger Group in the automotive supply industry, she was responsible for the overall commercial management at the German headquarters as well as for the subsidiaries in China, France, Italy, Sweden, Czech Republic, Turkey as well as in the USA. From 2014 to 2016, she was appointed Italian Branch Manager of the Erich Jäger Group. Dr. Tracy Dathe started her career at Hochtief AG/Philipp Holzmann AG Sino-German Ertan Joint Venture in Southern China. After working in various countries such as Lesotho in South Africa and Greece, Dr. Dathe joined Ina Schaeffler KG. She began her academic career at Chongqing University and continued it with business studies at the Fernuniversität Hagen. In her subsequent doctoral studies at the University of Gloucestershire in Cheltenham/UK, she analyzed the impact of performance-related pay in medium-sized companies in China, Germany and the Czech Republic. Today, Dr. Dathe supports medium-sized companies with her company Dr. Dathe Consulting & Trading and works part-time as a lecturer in the fields of financial management and international communication at various German universities, including the Frankfurt School of Finance & Management in Frankfurt am Main, the International School of Management (ISM) and the University of Trier. She owes her expertise in international cooperation with China not least to her many years of practical experience in industry and her Chinese origin.

Florian Hummel is Professor and Prorector at IU International University of applied Sciences. Professor Hummel studied at the University of Brighton (BA honours, Travel Management), Cranfield University (MSc, Air Transport Management) and the University of Sheffield (Doctor of Education). He received his first appointment as Professor from Cologne Business School in 2013. He looks back on positions in airport management and the international car rental business before he has now been active in the management of private universities for 15 years. As managing director of two private educational institutions, he has promoted the international orientation of these institutions in particular, negotiating and establishing a large number of international university cooperations of various types, from dual and joint degrees to the establishment and operation of campus locations of foreign universities in Germany. In addition to his current role as academic director of IUBH International University of Applied Sciences in Berlin, Hamburg, Erfurt and Hannover, he is an external evaluator for the Dublin Institute of Technology and honorary director of marketing for the European arm of CHRIE, the Council on Hotel, Restaurant and Institutional Education. His teaching and research interests lie in intercultural management and business strategy, particularly in the service sector in the areas of tourism/hotels and private higher education.

Abbreviations

3R	Retention, Related Sales and Referrals
7P	Product, Price, Place, Promotion, Physical Evidence, People, Process
AAA	American Arbitration Association
AG	Aktiengesellschaft (Public Limited Company)
AHK	Aussenhandelskammer (Chamber of Commerce Abroad)
BATNA	Best Alternative to a Negotiated Agreement
BME	German Association for Materials Management, Purchasing and Logistics
CIF	Cost, Insurance, Freight
CISG	United Nations Convention on Contracts for the International Sale of Goods
CJV	Corporation Joint Venture
DAP	Delivered at Place
DDP	Duty, Delivery paid
DR	Doctor
EUR	Euro
EXW	ExWorks
FAS	Free Alongside Ship
FCA	Free Carrier
FIE	Foreign Invested Enterprise
FOB	Free on Board
GmbH	Gesellschaft mit beschränkter Haftung
ICC	International Chamber of Industry and Commerce
IFM	Institute for Medium-Sized Business Research
IHK	Chamber of Industry and Commerce
IPO	International Procurement Organisation
IUBH	International University Bad Honnef
JIT	Just in Time
JV	Joint Venture
LdO	Least desired Outcome
MaHeLeanCon	Dr. Marc Helmold Lean Consulting
M.B.A.	Master of Business Administration

MdO	Most desired Outcome
MEP	Margin Enhancement Plan
NGO	Non-governmental organization
NPO	Non-profit organization
ÖPNV	PublicTransport
PESTEL	Political, Economic, Social, Technological, Environmental, Legal Aspects
QCD	Quality, Costs, Logistics
QCDT	Quality, Costs, Logistics, Technology
ROP	Risks and Opportunities
SCM	Supply Chain Management
SME	Small and Medium-sized Enterprises
SWOT	Strengths and Weaknesses Analysis
UN	United Nations
VMI	Vendor Managed Inventory
WFOE	Wholly Foreign Owned Enterprise
ZoMA	Zone of Mutual Agreement

List of Figures

List of Tables

Introduction to the Negotiations 1

If one is not patient in small things, one brings about the failure of great undertakings Confucius. (551 B.C.-479 B.C.)

Contents

M. Helmold et al., *Successful Negotiations*,
https://doi.org/10.1007/978-3-658-35701-6_1

Summary

Negotiations are a form of communication, usually in the form of a conversation, about a controversial issue that is characterized by conflicting needs, interests and motives. Basically, negotiations aim to balance interests by weighing positions and intensity of needs to reach a conclusion (Obrien, Negotiations for Procurement Professionals, Kogan Page, Croyden, 2016). All people have interests, wants and needs. These needs may be of different nature but have same characteristics. Buyers have a desire and need to obtain the lowest purchase price in a transaction, whereas sellers strive for the highest selling price. Internal company demands for a higher budget are also needs that have to be enforced in internal company negotiations (Helmold and Terry, Lieferantenmanagement 2030, Springer Gabler, Wiesbaden, 2016a). In a company, for example, there may be a desire for additional sales staff in order to expand into other countries and markets. Job interviews also involve desires and needs of the parties involved, namely to find the suitable employee or position. In addition to the actual job, there are numerous elements in job interviews, such as salary, fringe benefits or social benefits, that are part of the negotiations.

1.1 Negotiations: Definition and Delimitation

Negotiations are a form of communication, usually in the form of a conversation, about a controversial issue, which are characterized by conflicting needs, interests and motives. Basically, negotiations aim to balance interests by weighing positions and the intensity of needs to reach a conclusion (Obrien 2016). All people have interests, desires, motives, and needs that they want to realize. These needs may be different in nature but have the same characteristics and expressions (Obrien 2016). Buyers have the desire and need to obtain the lowest purchase price in a transaction, whereas sellers strive for the highest selling price. Both sides aim for the best price for their own side (Obrien 2016). Intra-company demands for a higher budget are also needs that have to be enforced in intra-company negotiations (Helmold and Terry 2016a). For example, in a company, there may be a desire for additional salespeople to expand into other countries and markets. Job interviews also involve wants and needs of the parties involved, namely to find the appropriate employee or position. In addition to the actual job, there are numerous elements in job interviews, such as salary, benefits, or perks, that are part of the negotiation. Not only in companies, but also in personal life, there is a plethora of needs that end up in negotiations. For example, a daughter may want her father to take her to school by car instead of using public transportation. Or a family negotiating where to go on vacation. All of these needs and wants represent negotiations over controversial issues and usually lead to a more or less consensual outcome. Negotiations are interactions between two or more parties about a specific issue with the fundamental interest of the parties to reach an agreement. These are characterized by an envisaged reconciliation of interests and a negotiated outcome (Obrien 2016). Negotiations are diverse, as all authors describe, and take place in every conceivable area of life (Helmold 2018; Dathe and Helmold 2018; Schranner 2009; Obrien 2016). Examples of negotiations are:

- Commercial discussions and agreements between buyers and sellers in commercial transactions

- Technical agreements on product performance characteristics between customer and supplier
- Agreements between supplier and customer on the performance and specification characteristics of services
- Coalition negotiations between parties to form a government after the last federal elections
- Online auctions of the purchasing department of a large corporation for the scope of a major project
- Haggling with the seller at the flea market with the subsequent purchase of an antique piece of furniture
- Students who have an oral final exam and answer questions from professors.
- Applications and interviews for a position with personnel and technical department about salary
- Requesting a salary increase from an employee to his supervisor due to good performance
- Agreement of employee goals within the framework of the annual appraisals by the supervisor and employee
- Arrangements of freelance consultant about project scope and workload with the commissioning customer
- Application of an honorary lecturer to a university to lecture to students of economics and business studies
- Discussion between parents and children about which restaurant the family goes to in the neighbourhood
- Children asking their parents for sweets at the checkout while shopping in a supermarket
- Hostage-taking and assertion of the hostage-takers' claims with the police, e.g. getaway car

The term negotiation originally comes from the Latin stems "Neg" (German: Nein, keine) and "Otsia" (Freizeit), i.e. "no leisure time". Unlike the nobility, the patricians, the citizens of Rome had no leisure time as part of their daily trading and work. In the seventeenth century, the term has been modified in the French language towards the meanings such as "business transaction, agreement, and resolution of a conflict" (Cambridge Dictionary 2018). Obrien defines negotiation as the process and reaching of an agreement on a particular matter by at least two parties (Obrien 2016). In this context, all parties aim at balancing interests and eliminating conflict, through common ground (Obrien 2016; Abdel-Latif 2015). Negotiations are therefore characterized by the following attributes and properties:

- At least two or more parties must be involved
- The objective of the parties must be to reach an agreement
- The effort of the parties must be to resolve a conflict amicably
- There must be a willingness to give and take from all parties

- A desired balance of interests must be achieved
- All parties must take initiatives to find a solution

If these attributes are only partially fulfilled or not fulfilled at all, one does not speak of negotiations, as Obrien states (Obrien 2016). In addition to the attributes of negotiations, numerous authors describe that certain success factors are necessary for positive negotiations. Negotiations need to be effective, efficient and take place in the right environment (Obrien 2016). According to Obrien, the following success factors can be summarized in order to successfully conduct negotiations (Obrien 2016):

- Effectiveness in negotiations (quality)
- Efficiency in the process of negotiations (time management)
- Climate of negotiations (relations)
- Balance of power of the negotiating partners (equality)
- Agreement on the points of negotiation (communication)
- Shared benefits (fairness)
- Formulation of objectives (clarity)
- Profit orientation (value creation)

1.2 Competencies and Characteristics for Negotiations

We humans have needs and negotiate on a daily basis. Negotiations arise on the basis of these human needs and can take place in private life, in companies, between companies or in politics (Helmold and Terry 2016a). Negotiations are based on different interests and motives of at least two or more negotiating parties and are usually interactive (Obrien 2016). Differing interests therefore automatically lead to demands and positions of the negotiating counterpart, which cannot be accepted by the negotiating parties and therefore have to be rejected. In turn, we as negotiating partners, on the other hand, have to convince the opposing negotiating party of our own arguments and assert them as best we can. These aspects therefore require various skills and traits of the negotiators to successfully achieve the negotiation breakthrough (Helmold 2018). The traits include persistence, strategy knowledge, result orientation, persuasiveness, patience, flexibility, self-confidence, sustainability, competence, cultural understanding, solution orientation, catalytic thinking, process orientation, perseverance, and facilitation skills, as Fig. 1.1 shows. Although not all of the above competencies need to be equally present, a balanced possession of these competencies is a condition for successful negotiation (Helmold and Terry 2016b). Professionally trained negotiators can successfully influence the company's outcome, whereas a lack of competencies will lead to diminutions in the outcome (Helmold et al. 2017). Especially due to the increasing international trade, these competence requirements will be of central importance for companies in the future, as the authors Helmold, Dathe and Büsch state in their study (Helmold et al. 2017). Other authors and negotiation consultants

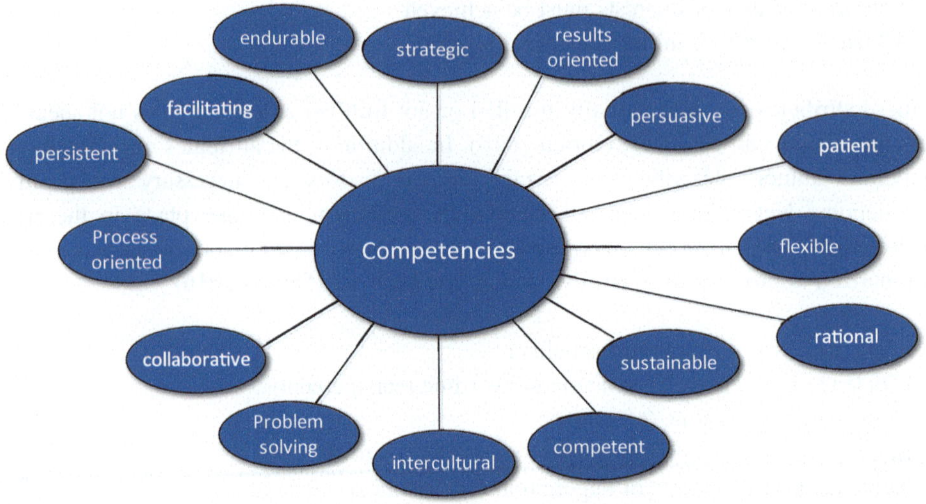

Fig. 1.1 Competence requirements in negotiations. (Source: Own representation, Marc Helmold)

such as Schranner or Obrien also point to deficits and weaknesses of companies in international and intercultural negotiations (Schranner 2015; Wilkes 2016; Obrien 2016). As a necessary consequence, companies must therefore offer their employees competent and professional training in negotiation techniques and conflict management, both internally and externally, in order not to suffer a competitive disadvantage (Wilkes 2016). Furthermore, the advancing internationalization is a trigger for companies to train employees interculturally and internationally (Obrien 2016). This includes language skills as well as cultural specifics in international negotiations, which are described in Chap. 7 (Helmold et al. 2017). Figure 1.1 shows the necessary competencies that are mandatory for international negotiations.

1.3 Negotiations as Part of the Corporate Strategy

In the competition for customers and markets, companies have to make countless strategic, operational and tactical decisions every day in order to secure or expand competitive advantages and their own market position (Johnson and Scholes 1997; Porter 1985). In this context, strategic management provides methods and tools that enable them to develop and implement strategies to achieve long-term success (Johnson and Scholes 1997; Mintzberg et al. 1998). Strategic management, understood as conscious, logically structured action, concerns decisions that influence the fundamental direction of a company. They serve the goal of securing the long-term success of the company by generating competitive advantages (Mintzberg et al. 1998). Means for this are the positioning in the market and the design of the resource base of the company (Johnson and Scholes 1997).

Fig. 1.2 Phase model in strategic management—strategic triangle. (Source: Own representation based on Johnson and Scholes 1997)

Strategic decisions of a company require tactical and operational implementation. Negotiations with a wide variety of stakeholders can come into play here, e.g. negotiations with government bodies, with consultants, with the owners on the strategic direction, with important customers or suppliers, or with the works council. The ideal typical process of strategic management consists of the steps of strategic analysis, strategic selection and strategic implementation, as Fig. 1.2 shows. These three phases are known as the Strategic Triangle according to Johnson and Scholes (Johnson and Scholes 1997):

1.3.1 Strategic Analysis

Step one begins with the strategic analysis (Johnson and Scholes 1997). This serves as a comprehensive information gathering as a basis for strategy formulation. It mainly consists of analysis and forecasting of the company's environment, i.e. macro-framework conditions, industry, customers and competition (external analysis) and analysis and forecasting of the company itself (internal analysis) (Johnson and Scholes 1997). Analyses within this stage include the environment, expectations, capabilities, competencies and resources (Johnson and Scholes 1997). The environmental analysis, which is described in Appendix 7, (PESTEL, Political, Economic, Social, Technological, Environmental and Legal), is an appropriate tool in the international context (Helmold and Terry 2016a). Other tools such as the industry or strengths and weaknesses analysis are also suitable as a means of preparing for negotiations (see Chap. 5).

1.3.2 Strategic Selection

To formulate the strategy, first of all, based on the analyses in the previous phase "strategic analysis", strategy alternatives and options are developed that appear suitable for generating competitive advantages. These alternatives are then evaluated on the basis of evaluation criteria, whereby the evaluation criteria must reflect the company's goals. Among the alternatives, the one that promises the best possible achievement of the company's goals is now selected; it represents the future corporate strategy (Johnson and Scholes 1997). Porter recommends selecting either cost leadership or performance leadership as the strategy option (Porter 1985). These generic strategies can be industry-wide or focused only in one industry (Porter 1985). Where cost leadership focuses on optimal costs, performance leadership focuses on unique selling points in quality or other areas from the customer's perspective (Porter 1985).

1.3.3 Strategic Implementation

Once a strategy has been chosen, it must be successfully implemented, i.e. translated into concrete actions that steer the company in the direction of the formulated strategy (Porter 1985). To do this, it is first necessary to operationalize the strategy to such an extent that management at all levels associates it with goals that correspond to their respective areas of responsibility. This hierarchical breakdown of goals is often reflected in strategic and operational planning, which serves to control resources in line with the strategy (Porter 1985). For strategy to be lived in a company, it must harmonize with the structures and systems in the company (Porter 1985). Therefore, strategic implementation must always be accompanied by an appropriate design of organization, processes, management information systems and incentive systems, as Johnson & Scholes point out (Johnson and Scholes 1997). In addition to these prerequisites, employees must be attracted and enthused to implement the strategy (Johnson and Scholes 1997). Information, motivation and qualification of employees, i.e. change management, play an important role here. The last important element in strategy implementation is systematic control. This refers to the progress of the implementation, the effectiveness of the measures and the success of the strategy for the company (Johnson and Scholes 1997). Also a form of control is the continuous monitoring of the premises of the chosen strategy. If conditions in the company's environment change, the strategy may need to be readjusted. Premise control is identical to strategic analysis, which shows that strategic management is a continuous process. Strategic management takes place at several levels. At the corporate level, the main focus is on issues related to the management of the portfolio in business areas. In particular, corporate strategy must ensure that the overall company is worth more than the sum of its individual businesses (Johnson and Scholes 1997). If a company comprises several business units, strategic management also takes place at the business unit level. The focus of the business strategy is the behavior of the company in the respective market and competitive environment. It is therefore often referred to as competitive strategy (Porter 1985). In connection with the overall strategy, the concepts of mission, vision and mission statement are often referred to as well as strategic management. Sub-strategies or strategic objectives (sales strategies, procurement strategies, in-house or external production strategies, marketing strategies, financial strategies, etc.) are defined as subordinate and must be implemented tactically (in the medium term). In this context, negotiations with internal or external stakeholders are necessary. Stakeholders are all groups that are indirectly or directly involved in the company's performance (Johnson and Scholes 1997), such as customers, suppliers, banks, the tax office or other groups (Johnson and Scholes 1997).

1.3.4 Shaping the Strategic Direction: Strategic Pyramid

A helpful tool for negotiations is the strategic pyramid (see Fig. 1.3) according to Johnson and Scholes (1997). In this context, strategy means the long-term positioning as well as the decision of the company which business areas are to be successfully conquered with which strategies (Johnson and Scholes 1997). Strategy is therefore "the fundamental, long-term orientation and design of a company to achieve competitive advantages in a changing environment through the use of resources and competencies and to realize the long-term goals of the stakeholders" (Johnson and Scholes 1997). This orientation is described in the mission, which describes the long-term and overall purpose of the company. The definition

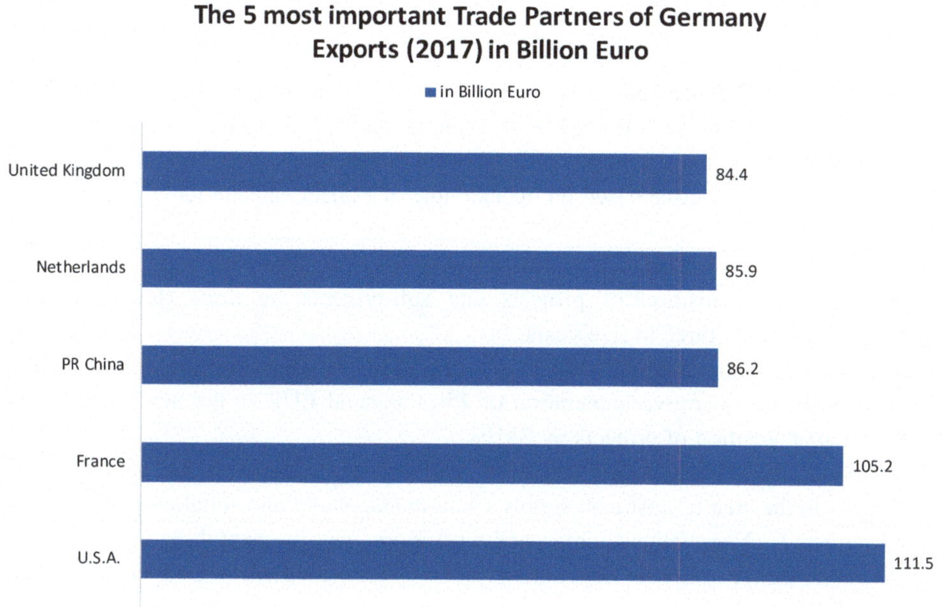

Fig. 1.3 Strategic pyramid. (Source: Own representation based on Johnson and Scholes 1997)

of the mission is followed by the vision, which manifests the desired future status of the company. The time frame here can be assumed to be between two and five years. In the example of the consulting firm of the author Professor Marc Helmold, MaHeLeanCon, the mission and vision are as follows:

1.3.4.1 Mission and Vision

Mission and vision comprise the long-term purpose of the company and the strategic intent of the company (Johnson and Scholes 1997). For Professor Helmold's MaHeLeaCon company, these elements look as follows (IUBH 2018):

Example

Mission: To create value by advising small and medium-sized enterprises (SMEs) from Germany or China with the aim of supporting them in entering the Chinese market or vice versa in Germany and to successfully design and implement the market entry. In addition, companies are prepared and supported in process improvements and in negotiations with customers or suppliers. In particular, successful negotiations with business partners from different countries in an international context, taking into account cultural elements, are one of the main pillars of the company and mission.

Vision: The vision or strategic intent can be defined as follows: Acquisition and support of ten to 15 customers (SMEs) in the areas of market entry, negotiations and process improvements, and generation of a turnover of up to EUR 500 thousand in the next four to five years (IUBH 2018).

1.3.4.2 Generic Objectives

The mission and vision are followed by the generic and specific goals. Generic goals are not quantified and are more general, while specific goals are quantified and more concrete (IUBH 2018). The objective based on the example of MaHeLeanCon looks like this:

Example

Generic goals: Acquisition of projects and sub-projects by three (few) important customers in the next three to five years.

Subproject A: Support of an SME in entering the Chinese market through consulting and sales activities. Turnover generation of 150 thousand EUR in the next three to five years. Initial acquisition of projects by SMEs.

Subproject B: Process improvement of a global company with the acquisition of subprojects in the area of upstream supply chain management and supplier quality.

Sub-project C: Negotiation training and workshops over the next three years. Generation of a competence centre for negotiations and conflict management. Cooperation with at least five SMEs and creation of an excellence concept for buyers and sellers.

In addition, further goals are the successful implementation of five to ten negotiation trainings as well as the implementation of intercultural workshops for companies.

1.3.4.3 Quantified Targets

The next step is the quantification of the generic goals. The scientists Johnson & Scholes distinguish between longer-term and generic (goals) as well as shorter and quantified objectives for the company (Johnson and Scholes 1997). Quantified goals can basically include sales, financial, quality, logistics, cost and alpha goals (Helmold and Terry 2016a).

1.3.4.4 Core Competencies

The core competencies are absolutely necessary for the implementation. These describe the resources, the skills or the knowledge that lead to a competitive advantage. In the example of MaHeLeanCon, these competencies are an extensive and worldwide network, the many years of experience as well as the expertise in the respective areas. As part of the alignment process, companies need to conduct a detailed analysis of their core competencies. Johnson & Scholes define core competencies as a competitive advantage over competitors through which companies can distinguish and differentiate themselves (Johnson and Scholes 1997).

1.3.4.5 Strategic Implementation of the Objectives

After determining the mission, vision, goals and core competencies, the translation into strategic goals follows. The long-term implementation of these elements is defined as strategic goal setting. Negotiations come into play in the implementation of the strategic goals. In the example of MaHeLeanCon these are mainly in the agreements about hourly rates and effort with the customers, but also about scope, time and quality of consulting and services.

1.3.4.6 Infrastructure

Infrastructure in the sense of strategic management includes not only buildings, machines, plants, offices, resources or employees, but also knowledge and innovations of the company that ensure long-term success (Helmold and Terry 2016a). For this, facilities, buildings, factories or offices are needed, which represent the strategic infrastructure. In addition, other success criteria such as resources, knowledge, experts, name recognition, network or innovations are also of key importance. In the case of MaHeLeanCon, there are offices in Berlin and Munich, and the establishment of an office in China is also being considered. At the moment the company concept refers to a few customers who want to have the expert knowledge and instruments of the consulting company at their disposal. Particularly in areas such as value chain management, supplier management or intercultural management, MaHeLeanCon has been able to secure several unique selling points with an international network of experts (Helmold and Terry 2016b).

1.3.4.7 Performance Review and Execution (Target/Actual Analysis)

The last element of the strategic pyramid is the control of success (control and execution) and a target-performance comparison. A suitable tool for this step is the Balanced

Scorecard (BSC) or an action plan. The instrument of the BSC was already developed in 1992 by the professors Norton & Kaplan. A BSC is an instrument in strategic management and contains four categories (Johnson and Scholes 1997):

- Customer satisfaction
- Financial category
- Internal processes and improvements
- Learning organization

In practice, companies adapt or extend the original four dimensions according to their specific needs (Helmold and Terry 2016a).

Example
In MaHeLeanCon consulting, there are a total of five categories that build on the Norton & Kaplan model but incorporate client-specific aspects for MaHeLeanCon success. The five categories are:

- Customer satisfaction and volume of orders (repeat orders)
- Quality and degree of fulfilment targets (degree of fulfilment in time, costs and resources)
- Cost and financial targets (sales targets, savings, process costs, effort and benefit)
- Resource deployment targets (days, number of employees, cost of employees)
- Internal improvement targets (efficiency improvement and unique selling propositions)

1.4 Negotiations in an International and Intercultural Context

Negotiations in an international context are becoming more important than ever for companies, given the balance of trade in Germany (Federal Statistics Office 2018; Dathe and Helmold 2018). Furthermore, the authors Dathe and Helmold state that internationalisation will continue to advance, especially in countries such as China, Japan or South Korea (Dathe and Helmold 2018). Looking at imports and exports in 2016 and 2017, it becomes clear that Germany was the world export champion in both years. In 2017, more than 1279 billion EUR worth of goods and commodities were exported from Germany to other countries (Federal Statistical Office 2018). The most important countries for exports are the United States of America, France, the People's Republic of China, the Netherlands and the United Kingdom (Federal Statistical Office 2018) (Fig. 1.4). In contrast, goods and commodities worth 1034 billion EUR were imported (Fig. 1.5). Again, in addition to Italy, the United States of America, France, the People's Republic of China and the Netherlands are among the top five countries. As the Federal Statistical Office (Statistisches Bundesamt 2018) further reports on the basis of preliminary results, German exports in 2017 were thus 6.3% higher and imports 8.3%

Fig. 1.4 Germany's five most important trading partners—exports. (Source: Federal Statistical Office (2018). Press release No. 039 of February 8, 2018: German exports in 2017: +6.3% on 2016. Exports and imports reach new record levels. Retrieved 2018-03-15. https://www.destatis.de/DE/PresseService/Presse/Pressemitteilungen/2018/02/PD18_039_51.html)

higher than in 2016. Exports and imports in 2017 exceeded the previous highs of 2016, when goods worth 1203.8 billion EUR were exported and goods worth 954.9 billion EUR were imported. The foreign trade balance ended 2017 with a surplus of more than 244.9 billion EUR. In 2016, the balance of foreign trade had reached 248.9 billion EUR, the highest level ever in Germany's history. In 2016, Germany's current account balance had shown an asset balance of 259.3 billion EUR. The foreign trade balance closed with a surplus of 18.2 billion EUR in the month of December 2017. Adjusted for calendar and seasonal effects, the foreign trade surplus in December 2017 was 21.4 billion EUR (Federal Statistical Office 2018).

Figure 1.6 shows the possibilities of internationalization through own or external resources (Dathe and Helmold 2018). Resources in this sense are buildings, machines or plants. If a company decides to produce outside the borders of Germany within the framework of its own resources, this is referred to as international in-house production (red border). If a company outsources and purchases products or services from suppliers, this is referred to as global sourcing or international outsourcing (Dathe and Helmold 2018).

Figure 1.7 shows the managing director of Midas, Mr. Li, and Dr. Marc Helmold in front of the company's logo in China. Midas is a producer of aluminium profiles for the

Fig. 1.5 Germany's five most important trading partners—imports. (Source: Federal Statistical Office (2018). Press release No. 039 of February 8, 2018: German exports in 2017: +6.3% on 2016. Exports and imports reach new record levels. Retrieved 2018-03-15. https://www.destatis.de/DE/PresseService/Presse/Pressemitteilungen/2018/02/PD18_039_51.html)

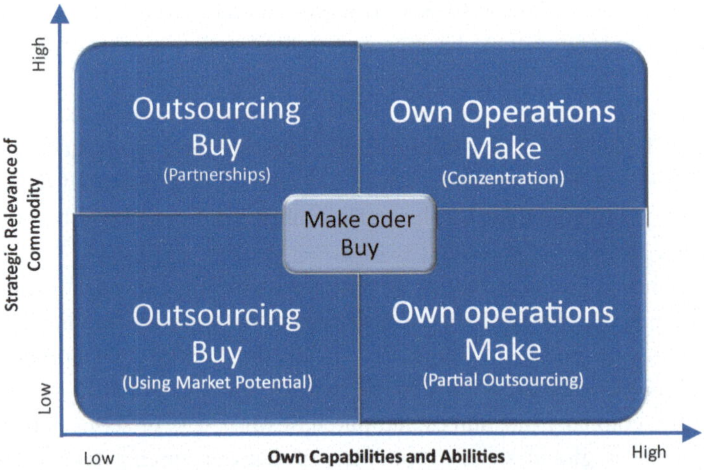

Fig. 1.6 In-house and outsourced production in an international context. (Source: Own illustration based on Dathe and Helmold 2018)

Fig. 1.7 Managing directors Mr. Li and Dr. Marc Helmold. (Source: Marc Helmold (2018). The picture shows the managing director Mr. Li (Midas) and managing director Dr. Marc Helmold, Bombardier Transportation. Midas is one of the market leaders for the sale of aluminium profiles for the construction of trains)

railway, construction and automotive industries, which are sold worldwide. The company has been able to significantly increase sales through a very strong internationalization and expansion of the business (Huang 2017).

1.5 The Win-Win Illusion in Negotiations

In numerous negotiation books and seminars, the win-win concept has been described and offered by trainers for the resolution of conflicts for decades. This concept comes from game theory and is also known in the field of negotiation as the "Harvard concept" and in conflict mediation as "conflict resolution without losers" (Helmold 2018). The principle states that it would be possible to find outcomes through which both parties emerge as winners despite initial conflicting interests (Bauer-Jelinek 2007). Further, the win-win strategy is based on the willingness of negotiators to reach common and lasting solutions by not insisting on superficial positions but revealing their underlying motives. In order to achieve this, all participants must have a high level of communication skills and the atmosphere must be reasonably trusting and harmonious. Even proponents of the theory qualify that win-win is all the more likely to work if the parties' differences in interests are not too great (Helmold 2018). However, the experience of the authors Dr. Helmold and Dr. Dathe shows that when there are conflicts of interest in business or politics, both parties try to get the respective maximum for themselves, there is rarely a chance for a real win-win for both sides (Bauer-Jelinek 2007). Particularly in the case of budget constraints or projects with several interested parties and providers, negotiating positions are often adopted that are not considered win-win but win-lose. In contrast to the win-win principle, in the win-lose concept there is a negotiating party that is not a winner (Helmold and Terry 2016a).

As long as there are enough people who are not exclusively concerned with their own advantage, but who value a fair balance of interests in negotiations, their attitude can be used on a large scale to assert their own interests. Those who want to extract the maximum (negotiators-maximizers) for their objective drive a deceptive maneuver by appealing to mutual gain (Polwin-Plass 2016). The maximum (lat.: the most) implies the greatest possible negotiation success and the maximum achievement of the negotiation objectives for the negotiator or negotiation maximizer (Bauer-Jelinek 2007). While the fair-minded negotiator is still searching for common ground, the negotiator-maximizer has already presented his positions. And if he is good at the win-win technique, the "do-gooder" only realizes much later that his gain is worth nothing or less (Bauer-Jelinek 2007).

Example

The following case study is intended to explain this situation in more detail (Bauer-Jelinek 2007). An employee in procurement or sales has worked in a company for two years and has achieved significant success in reaching his budget targets. The savings have fundamentally improved the department's bottom line. The employee has several years of work experience, but has been with the company for two years. As part of his performance review, the employee expects to receive a bonus or salary increase as a result of his savings. He expects the supervisor to approach him, but the supervisor does not approach the employee. As a result, the employee decides to approach the supervisor, but the supervisor has his own goals in mind and wants to appease the employee with a "win-win deal." With the budget savings, a new sales employee is hired to handle the heavy workload. The supervisor puts the employee off until better times and the next fiscal year. He also talks about how additional resources would ensure job security in tough economic times. In his conversation, he emphasizes common interests, especially the well-being of the company in the long run, and ends the conversation amicably. The employee is now in a dilemma. Should he renounce his motive and agree to the offer so that new resources can be hired, or should he continue to press for a raise? Real-life examples like the one just mentioned show that the win-win situation is usually just an illusion. In this case, the supervisor has won the negotiations for himself. Savings and budget achievement help him to further expand his department, while the employee receives no benefit at all (Bauer-Jelinek 2007). His job has not really become more secure and due to his very good performance the individual targets for the following business year may even be increased further (Helmold and Terry 2016a).

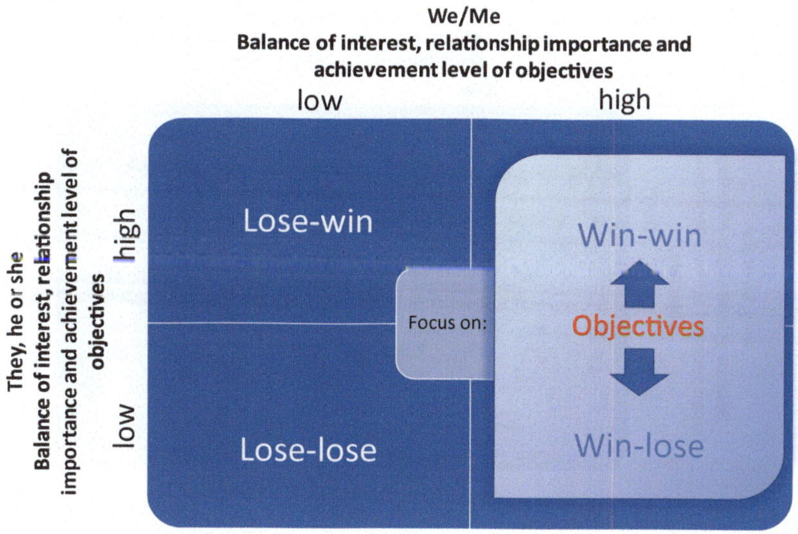

Fig. 1.8 Negotiation concepts win-win, win-lose, lose-win, lose-lose. (Source: Marc Helmold's own representation)

Figure 1.8 shows the respective concepts win-win, win-lose and lose-win in negotiations. If there is a high balance of interests between both parties and a high degree of goal achievement by both sides (ME and HE/SHE as negotiating partners or opponents), a win-win situation has been achieved. However, if one of the parties is not completely satisfied because the objectives have not been achieved to full satisfaction, this is referred to as a win-lose or lose-win situation.

Often the boundaries between the concepts are fluid and target achievement levels can underlie dynamic, macro- or micro-economic changes.

Example

In a multi-million EUR project in the transport sector, which had dragged on for several months in terms of negotiations, the contract was awarded to the company of the author Dr. Marc Helmold. In the final stages of the negotiations, the customer, a state-owned company, reduced the bid price by more than ten percent and the product launch was scheduled for a minimum period of a few years. The agreement meant that the project had to be bid below cost (long-term price floor). Had the author's company not agreed to these demands, the project would have gone to a competitor from the Far East. Despite winning the bid, one could not really speak of a win-win, especially due to the drastic financial losses. However, a "not all lost" lose-win could be achieved from a "total" lose-win, although the project was below the price floor (Helmold 2018). However, it was possible to use existing capacity that would otherwise have been underutilized, which in turn would

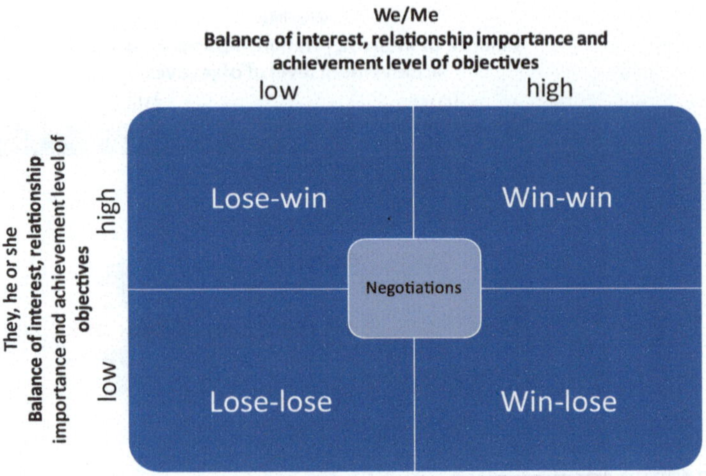

Fig. 1.9 Win-win or win-lose at the heart of negotiations. (Source: Marc Helmold's own representation)

have freed up staff. Furthermore, it was possible to work with an efficiency program and stakeholders on cost optimizations in the value chain. The authors therefore recommend targeting a negotiated outcome that takes into account one's own needs and focuses on one's own goal achievement (Dathe and Helmold 2018). Figure 1.9 shows the target corridor of negotiations with the aspiration to put one's own points and interests in the foreground (Helmold and Terry 2016a).

1.6 Negotiations in Different Cultures

In the course of globalization and liberalization of markets, the exchange of goods and services has steadily increased, as shown in Figs. 1.4 and 1.5 with imports to and exports from Germany (Dathe and Helmold 2018). This has also led to cross-national and cross-cultural business contacts. Successful communication and negotiation are already complicated in one's own culture. When it comes to cross-cultural negotiations with different foreign partners, this fact is amplified even more (Dathe and Helmold 2018). This is because each culture has its own peculiarities, its own methods of negotiation, its own rules of the game, which are foreign, unknown or perhaps even incomprehensible to us. That is why intercultural competence plays a prominent role in international negotiations, alongside rhetorical and argumentative skills. There are enough examples of negotiations failing because there was a lack of understanding of culturally specific business behaviour. In order to reduce misunderstandings and intercultural pitfalls, it is therefore imperative to get to know and understand the mentality and business culture of the other party. In international business transactions, preparing for a negotiation not only

Fig. 1.10 Negotiation strategies in different cultures. (Source: Marc Helmold's own representation)

requires dealing with the product, the market situation and the supplier. Often expectations and negotiation goals are different, so these aspects need to be analyzed in detail at an early stage (Lanz 2018). Also, relationships, good or bad, or relationship building in an international context are also understood differently, as Liker & Choi state (Liker and Choi 2004). They also have to deal with the country itself and with the customs and cultural conditions there in order to be successful (Helmold et al. 2017). Chapter 7 shows which traps (icebergs) and opportunities (icebreakers) exist in different countries such as Germany, the United States of America, Great Britain, India, China, Japan or France. Figure 1.10 gives recommendations on how to proceed in international negotiations. If both partners have detailed and in-depth knowledge, negotiations can be successfully conducted on an equal footing. However, if neither side has any experience or knowledge of the other culture, it is advisable to involve experts.

Culture, according to Hofstede, is "the collective programming of the mind that distinguishes members of one group or category of people from another" (Hofstede 1991). Following Geertz, culture is the way in which people communicate, transmit and develop their knowledge of attitudes towards life. Attitudes are based on determinants such as language, values, norms or other aspects. Culture is the pattern of meaning-making within which people interpret their experiences and guide their actions (Geertz 1973). Culture is an important phenomenon and element in international negotiations, as Dathe & Helmold state (Dathe and Helmold 2018). All people live in and develop a specific culture. Culture structures a field of action specific to the population, ranging from objects created and used to institutions, ideas and values. Culture always manifests itself in a system of orientation typical of a nation, society, organization or group. This orientation system is formed from specific symbols (e.g. language, religion, norms, rules, gestures, facial expressions, clothing, greeting rituals) and is handed down in the respective society, organisation or group, i.e. passed on to the next generation. The orientation system defines

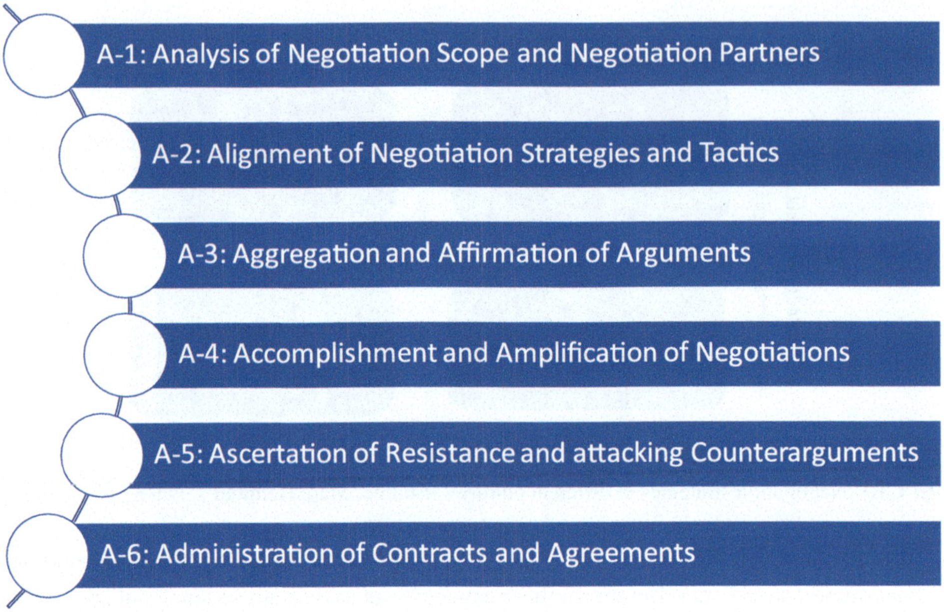

Fig. 1.11 Cultural elements in international negotiations. (Source: Marc Helmold's own representation based on Hofstede 1991)

for all members their belonging to the society or group and enables them to cope with their own environment. Culture influences the perception, thinking, values and actions of all members of the respective society. In the international context, cultural understanding and sensitivity are important aspects. In Asian countries such as Japan, it is not advisable to talk about personal matters, and people should address each other by their last names. A pat on the back, a greeting kiss or even a handshake are not customary in Japan. What is correct is a slight bow with a straight back. There are subtle differences: Those lower in the hierarchy bow lower. Older people are above younger people, guests are above hosts, men are above women. In business, usually only the seller bows, the buyer may limit himself to a nod. Failure to do so usually leads to an unsatisfactory negotiation outcome. The most important elements are shown in Fig. 1.11 and will be presented more clearly and country-specifically later on (based on Helmold 2010):

- Language
- Values
- Standards
- Understanding equality and diversity
- Religion
- Customs
- Laws

- Understanding time
- Emotionality and rationality
- Group understanding

1.6.1 Hofstede's Understanding of Culture

The Dutch cultural researcher Geert analysed extensive empirical data from the employees of IBM in 74 countries between 1967 and 1976. Based on this database, he later developed a cultural model called VSM (value survey model), in which he defined the dimensions of cultures using statistical methods (Hofstede 1980, 2007). This model is still frequently used today in academic research in the field of intercultural communication as well as in business practice (Dathe and Helmold 2018).

Hofstede's understanding of culture is described as *"the collective programming of the mind"* that divides people into the different cultural groups and considers cultural values as the core elements of cultures (Hofstede 1980, 2007). These can be divided into the following dimensions in the VSM model:

- Power distance
- Individualism vs. collectivism
- Masculinity vs. femininity
- Uncertainty avoidance
- Long-term orientation
- Indulgence vs. restraint (Hofstede 1980, 2007).

1.6.1.1 Power Distance

Power in a society is always distributed unequally. The power distance stands for the difference in the power position of individuals that is accepted by those members of society with little influence. This measure describes the extent to which society is willing to accept general inequality (Hofstede 2007). In a culture with low power distance, there is always an attempt to minimize inequality among people. In contrast, in cultures with high power distance, inequality is seen as normality. Behaviour against the hierarchical rules is seen as a violation of the social rules and is punished.

In a culture with a small power distance (this includes Germany), managers in companies tend to involve employees in operational decisions and strive for equal treatment of all employees.

In contrast, in cultures with large power distance, a hierarchical structure can be observed in almost every sphere of life. Although it is well known that unchecked power leads to abuse of authority or corruption (Chia et al. 2007; Lee and Oh 2007), the power of formal authorities remains unchallenged in people's minds. Corporate rules such as unpaid overtime are also rarely questioned. In companies, managers are seen as decision makers for the general interest. Decisions are usually made without direct involvement of employees. The authority of superiors is not openly challenged, i.e. not only their formal decisions but also their statements at meetings are not questioned, especially in public. Status-related highly unequal pay is also generally accepted (Dathe and Helmold 2018). In business negotiations, it is therefore advisable to (1) identify the decision-maker as soon as possible and (2) treat the decision-maker with more formal respect or special attention, for example, the gift presented to the decision-maker should be somewhat more lavish compared to the others. Disagreements should be well packaged. Direct contradictions should be avoided as far as possible.

1.6.1.2 Individualism Vs. Collectivism

In an individualistic society, individuals strive for self-determination. In a collectivist society, on the other hand, individuals tend to identify with their social positions. For the common good of the group, members are often willing to accept certain inconveniences in their own lives or to "bend the rules".

Another consequence of collectivism is shorter interpersonal distance. Sometimes the curious questions border on an invasion of privacy for the more individualistically minded. For good intercultural communication, however, it is advisable not to react harshly in such cases, but to give information with tact in the "harmless questions" in favour of building a good personal relationship, or to skilfully sidestep the "unpleasant questions" without offending the other person.

1.6.1.3 Masculinity Vs. Femininity

Traditionally, professional success is seen as a masculine virtue and caring for each other in society is seen as a feminine virtue. This cultural dimension describes whether a society is dominated by masculine or feminine values (De Mooij and Hofstede 2010).

In contrast to a masculine society, in which individual success often has a high priority, interpersonal cohesion plays a significant role in a feminine society. Such feminine values can be observed above all in the family circle or in unofficial group formations in professional life. The members of such groups often do their utmost to gain advantages for each other, for example in the allocation of jobs, promotions and salaries, or adopt a common defensive position in conflicts with non-members of the group. This phenomenon could go so far that employees in the company do not seek out those in charge when problems arise, but rather, if possible, those close to the person in charge who are known (Dathe and Helmold 2018).

From this one can deduce: (a) the confirmation of the successes of the negotiating partners promotes the mood of the conversation and (b) good relationships are often particularly valuable to invest in.

1.6.1.4 Uncertainty Avoidance

Many Germans feel uncomfortable when the consequences of their actions are unclear. In other words, German culture exhibits a high degree of uncertainty avoidance (Hofstede and Hofstede 2011; Dathe and Helmold 2018).

In a culture with high uncertainty avoidance, a conscientious way of working is also valued, but this does not mean that one can always expect formulated rules and formalities for the completion of one's tasks (Hofstede and Hofstede 2011; Dathe and Helmold 2018). In terms of negotiation, it means that business partners from these cultural backgrounds are not solely concerned with technical data, but there are a number of other factors that influence their business decisions, such as adaptability as well as a willingness to be accommodating with the potential business partner.

Although the ambiguity of information often causes stress among Germans, patience is sometimes indispensable for success on the international market. It should not be ignored that the low uncertainty avoidance also results in positive effects such as higher acceptance of new technologies.

1.6.1.5 Long-Term Orientation

Long-Term Orientation describes the willingness to invest in one's own future (Hofstede and Hofstede 2011). In cultures with a long-term orientation, entrepreneurs attach great importance to long-term business relationships. For a promising business relationship, business partners are often willing to take higher risks (Dathe and Helmold 2018). Such a gesture is often portrayed as personal and should be met with a corresponding gesture of appreciation.

1.6.1.6 Indulgence Versus Restraint

In a society with a high IRV (indulgence) value, individuals often extrovert their joy and other human emotions. There is a more lenient approach to morality. Pleasure, idleness and a rather relaxed approach to one's own physicality characterize the society.

In a society with a low IRV value (restraint), on the other hand, a high value is placed on a sense of duty. On the other hand, there is less tolerance for human desires and impulses. Professional duties clearly take precedence over private life. In order to help the family achieve a higher status through financial achievement, millions of Chinese migrant workers leave their homes to work in a factory in a distant city. This leads to social problems for the family members left behind, such as child neglect and loneliness among the elderly.

1.6.2 Cultural Understanding According to E. T. Hall

In this section, Chinese culture is further outlined in the cultural model of the American anthropologist and ethnologist Edward Twitchell Hall Jr. In his research in the field of intercultural communication, Hall describes cultures in the following facets:

- Context orientation
- Monochronic vs. polychronic understanding of time
- Spatial awareness.

1.6.2.1 Context Orientation

Context orientation is Hall's way of describing the communication style of information acquisition or information processing. In cultures with a weak contextual orientation, information is communicated explicitly. The communication participants interact directly with each other and try to provide information as precisely as possible, while personal relationships do not play a significant role. In general, German culture is considered to be a culture with weak contextual orientation (Hall, Beyond culture 1976).

In a strongly contextual culture, much of the information is not explicitly encoded in the linguistic messages, but is assumed to be common knowledge through the relationships of the communication participants. The contextual factors such as the personal relationships, the facial expressions of the interlocutors or the circumstances of their encounter are among important carriers of information (Hall, Beyond culture 1976).

To illustrate the contextual relevance in communication, some situations in communication with British people are listed in Table 1.1.

Table 1.1 Examples of contextual reference: Communication with British people (English)

What the British say	What the British mean	What foreigners understand
I hear what you say	I disagree and do not want to discuss it further	He accepts my point of view
With the greatest respect	You are an idiot	He is listening to me
That's not bad	That's good	That's poor
That is a very brave proposal	You are insane	He thinks I have courage
Quite good	A bit disappointing	Quite good
I would suggest	Do it or be prepared to justify yourself	Think about the idea, but do what you like
Oh, incidentally/by the way	The primary purpose of our discussion is	That is not very important
I was a bit disappointed that	I am annoyed that	It doesn't really matter
Very interesting	That is clearly nonsense	They are impressed
I'll bear it in mind	I've forgotten it already	They will probably do it
I'm sure it's my fault	It's your fault	Why do they think it was their fault?
You must come for dinner	It's not an invitation, I'm just being polite	I will get an invitation soon
I almost agree	I don't agree at all	He's not far from agreement
I only have a few minor comments	Please rewrite completely	He has found a few typos
Could we consider some other options	I don't like your idea	They have not yet decided
WHAT THE BRITISH SAY	WHAT THE BRITISH MEAN	WHAT FOREIGNERS UNDERSTAND

Source: http://www.telegraph.co.uk (The Telegraph 2017)

One can see that contextual reference in communication can easily mislead strangers.

If a culture is strongly characterized by a high degree of context orientation, an abundance of unspoken rules or information applies in communication. It may even be the case that key business strategies are agreed over an informal lunch among selected participants rather than in formal meetings with the people responsible for the organisation. For long-term business success in such cultures, it is important to develop a good sense of context in the partner companies and to behave accordingly.

1.6.2.2 Monochronic Or Polychronic Understanding of Time

German culture is considered to be a typically monochronic culture. This means that it is common practice in Germany to complete work steps one after the other. In doing so, one strives to adhere to a predetermined schedule (Hall 1983).

In polychronic cultures, however, people are more accustomed to carrying out several activities at the same time. On the one hand, this has the consequence that one is susceptible to distractions, but on the other hand it makes one react quickly to changes. In contrast to monochronic cultures, for a polychronic culture the schedule is merely a reference (Hall 1983).

These contrasting characteristics of cultures often lead to conflict or frustration in international cooperation. A good solution is to understand the reason for the counterpart's actions and to show understanding. Only with friendly intention and patience can it be possible to make the counterpart understand one's own point of view.

1.6.2.3 Understanding of Space

For Hall, there exists an invisible, circular space around each person that is perceived as their privacy. The extent of this space varies from culture to culture. If the perceived, appropriate distance is undercut by the counterpart without permission, this usually triggers discomfort in communication. But if the distance is clearly exceeded, this can be interpreted negatively, for example as a lack of trust or even hostility (Hall 1966).

A related concept to Hall's understanding of space is the concept of territory, that is, the places or the objects that a person considers his or her personal property, an extended private sphere. The intrusion of territory can trigger hostile reactions (Hall 1966). Territory can vary widely across cultures. Knowledge of the negotiating partners' understanding of space is important in order to avoid misunderstandings, especially in international communication.

1.7 Negotiations in Business: Buyer-Seller Relations

1.7.1 Buyer and Seller: Customer and Supplier

The majority of negotiations take place in national or international trade between companies (Helmold and Terry 2016a). When the customer's purchasing and the supplier's sales face each other, the aim is to transfer a product or a defined service under the best possible conditions (Helmold and Terry 2016a). By their nature, the respective "optimal conditions" from the perspective of a buyer are different from those from the perspective of a seller, so that controversies usually arise that are to be resolved in the course of negotiations. It is therefore imperative for procuring and selling companies to acquire skills and knowledge in order to optimally place and implement their position and demands. Figure 1.12 shows the buyer-seller relationship with the aim of both parties to reach a negotiation conclusion with the best possible outcome for each party.

1.7.2 Negotiation Objectives

Targets between trading partners usually refer to the sales price. However, there are other important determinants besides the sales price. These include, in addition to the price, i.e. the purchase or acquisition costs for the buyer, quality, delivery performance and technical aspects (Q-K-L-T = quality-cost-delivery-performance-technology). Within this classification, the most important goals can be defined. Should other objectives be of interest in addition, one speaks of the alpha (Q-K-L-T + α). Alpha is the first Greek letter α in the Greek alphabet. Alpha elements can be, for example, ethics requirements that the supplier must meet in order to be allowed to sell goods and services to a customer. Other aspects may be employee training or the implementation of specific information systems for connectivity (Helmold and Terry 2016a). Figure 1.13 shows the categories that are central to business negotiations. Figure 1.14 lists subcategories as examples and describes them in detail in Sects. 1.7.3, 1.7.4, 1.7.5, 1.7.6, and 1.7.7.

It is of importance for the vendor to consider the most important trends in purchasing and the requirements they necessitate. In a survey with purchasing managers and decision-makers in supplier management, five important trends were identified (Helmold and Terry 2016a):

- Centralization
- Internationalization
- Rotation principle
- Digitisation (e.g. online auctions)
- Strategic supplier management

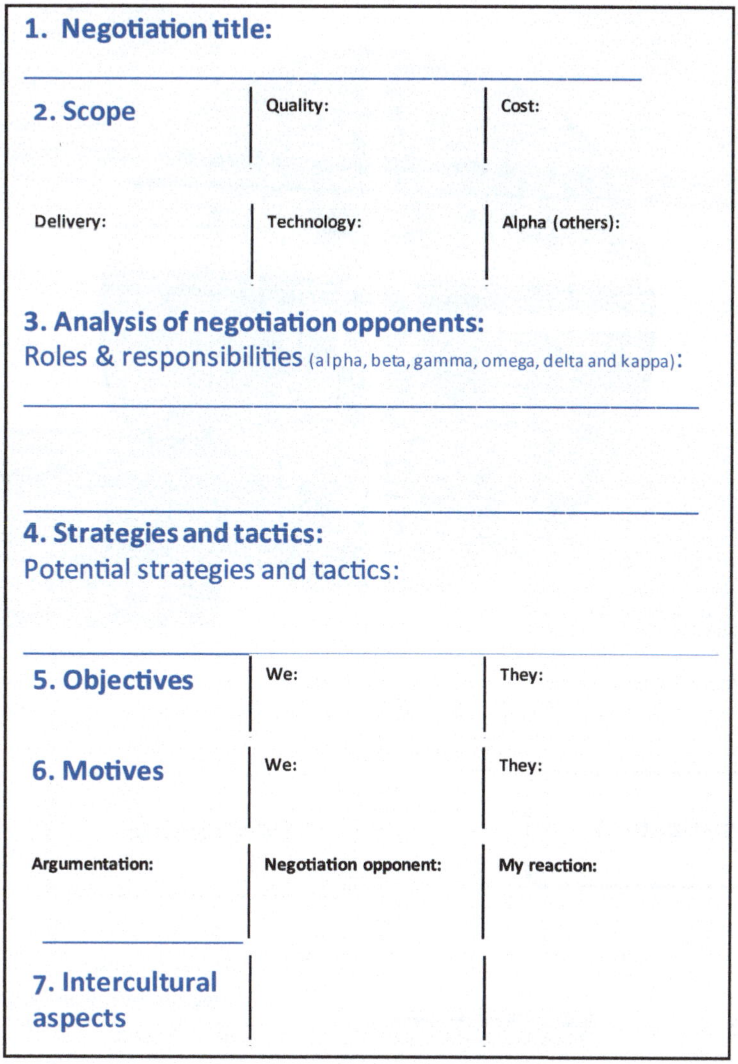

Fig. 1.12 Buyer-seller relationships. (Source: Marc Helmold's own representation)

The rotation in purchasing is intentionally very high. Many a buyer does not sit in his post for more than two years. Then he changes the category and the suppliers with whom he has business relations. Because otherwise he could build up an emotional bond with the supplier and possibly no longer only look at the price. But the sales department on the supplier side often relies on this emotional bond.

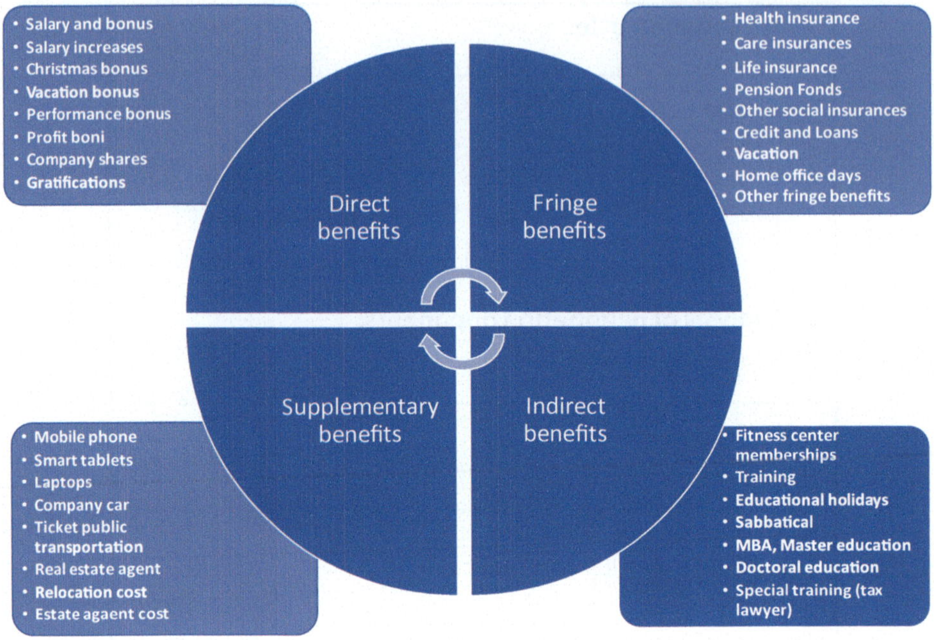

Fig. 1.13 Bargaining leverage in business negotiations: Q-K-L-T plus alpha. (Source: Marc Helmold's own representation based on Helmold 2010)

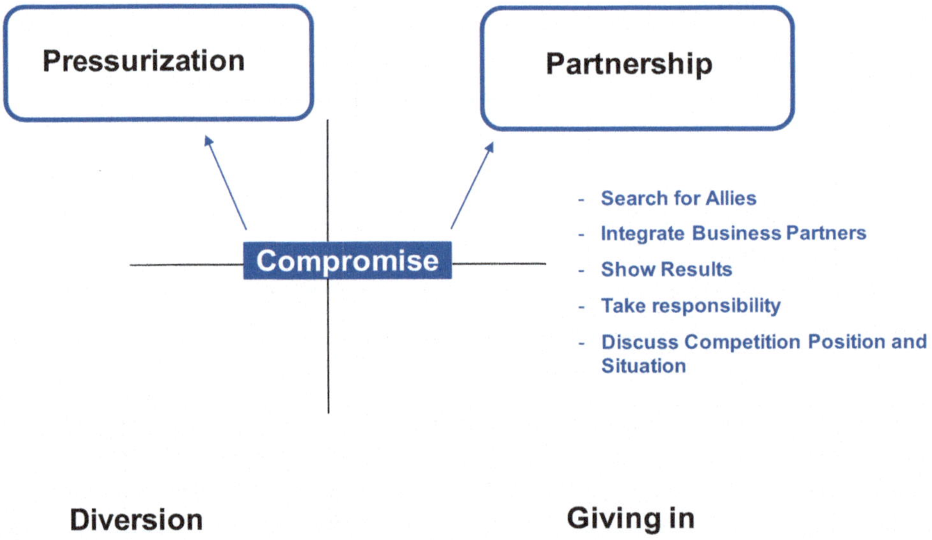

Fig. 1.14 Q-K-L-T typology in negotiations. (Source: Marc Helmold's own representation based on Helmold and Terry 2016a)

1.7.3 Quality Objectives

Quality targets must be clearly defined in contracts. As a rule, a distinction is made here between delivery quality and quality in the field or at the customer's premises within the scope of the warranty.

1.7.3.1 Delivery Quality

Quality and condition of the goods upon delivery. By law, the buyer (customer) is obliged to randomly check the delivery quality upon receipt of the goods.

1.7.3.2 Field Quality

Quality level of goods and products that are with the customer. Companies usually measure this on the basis of voluntary or statutory warranty claims.

1.7.3.3 Defective

Number of bad parts in relation to all parts and goods delivered.

1.7.3.4 Quality Management Systems

A quality management system includes external certification by authorized certifiers (e.g. Technical Inspection Agency, TÜV). Many new customers insist on this certification (e.g. DIN EN ISO 9001:2015) from their suppliers, which can involve costs in the higher six-figure range.

1.7.4 Cost Targets

Cost targets include all expenses that are necessary for the procurement of goods and services (Helmold and Terry 2016a). In addition to direct procurement costs (unit price), there are indirect expenses (qualification, construction of a machine) that are closely linked to procurement.

1.7.4.1 Escalation

Escalation are annual cost increases on the part of the supplier. Mostly, these are justified with inflation and higher operational costs over the project duration.

1.7.4.2 Running Costs

Acquisition and support of 10 to 15 customers (SMEs) in the areas of market entry and process improvements and generation of a turnover of up to 500 thousand EUR in the next four to five years.

1.7.4.3 Payment Targets

A payment term is the agreed time of payment for the delivery of goods and services. The payment term has a direct impact on the liquidity (cash flow) of the company. Very good companies have very short payment terms with their customers (payment on delivery) and longer terms with their suppliers, e.g. 60 days.

1.7.4.4 Qualification Costs

Cost of qualifying a supplier to understand the customer's quality system, customer requirements, specification and processes.

1.7.5 Logistics Objectives

Logistics components can account for more than 40% of the unit price of goods deliveries, especially in international freight transport (Helmold and Terry 2016a). Transport, packaging and customs clearance must therefore be taken into account in negotiations. In addition, logistics concepts exist to ensure delivery performance, e.g. vendor managed inventory (VMI), where suppliers are responsible for inventory management (Helmold and Terry 2016a).

1.7.5.1 Packing

Costs for packaging the goods. Packaging primarily serves to protect the goods from damage.

1.7.5.2 Transport and Logistics Costs

Costs for packaging, transport service, storage and customs clearance.

1.7.5.3 Logistics Concepts

Customers expect high delivery reliability and usually have delivery concepts such as just-in-time (JIT). This delivery flexibility will also have an impact on the cost structure.

1.7.6 Technical Objectives

Much of the negotiating mass is negotiated at a very early stage. At this stage, it is important to consider technical elements that have a direct impact on the budget and costs (Helmold and Terry 2016a).

1.7.6.1 Development Services

Commissioning of external companies for the complete or partial development of products with performance features of the customer.

1.7.6.2 Technical Changes

In most cases, engineering changes entail cost increases that have to be negotiated. Usually, the discussions take place between the engineer or technician and an experienced sales manager. In this context, it is advisable to also train technicians and engineers through sustainable training.

1.7.6.3 Design-to-Cost

Contracting of external companies for the complete or partial development within the framework of a set budget and target price.

1.7.7 Alpha Goals

Alpha goals are any goals that do not fall into the category of quality, cost, delivery performance, or technology.

1.7.7.1 Ethics Goals

Corporate ethics (Corporate Social Responsibility, CSR) includes universally valid norms and values of a company, according to which companies want to act, especially by acting responsibly towards society. The company transfers these principles to employees and other stakeholders such as suppliers. Ethical principles often aim at respecting human rights, creating reasonable and safe working conditions, protecting the environment and sustainable business (Helmold 2010).

1.7.7.2 Competence Goals

Competence goals encompass the skills of employees through a systematic and structured corporate culture of lifelong learning.

1.7.7.3 Other Alpha Targets

Alpha goals are multifaceted and can be developed from a wide variety of negotiators' motives for negotiating (Helmold 2010).

1.8 Interviews as Negotiations

Even if every interview proceeds differently, many patterns can be identified among HR professionals. The interview can be divided into eight phases (Köhler 2007). Personnel managers are usually not trained negotiators, so they proceed according to a standardized procedure. Furthermore, HR managers are not the decision makers but only the influencer in job interviews. The decision makers are the budget managers and division managers, although depending on the size of the company, decisions may also be delegated to middle management. An interview usually lasts one to two hours. The interview usually includes a

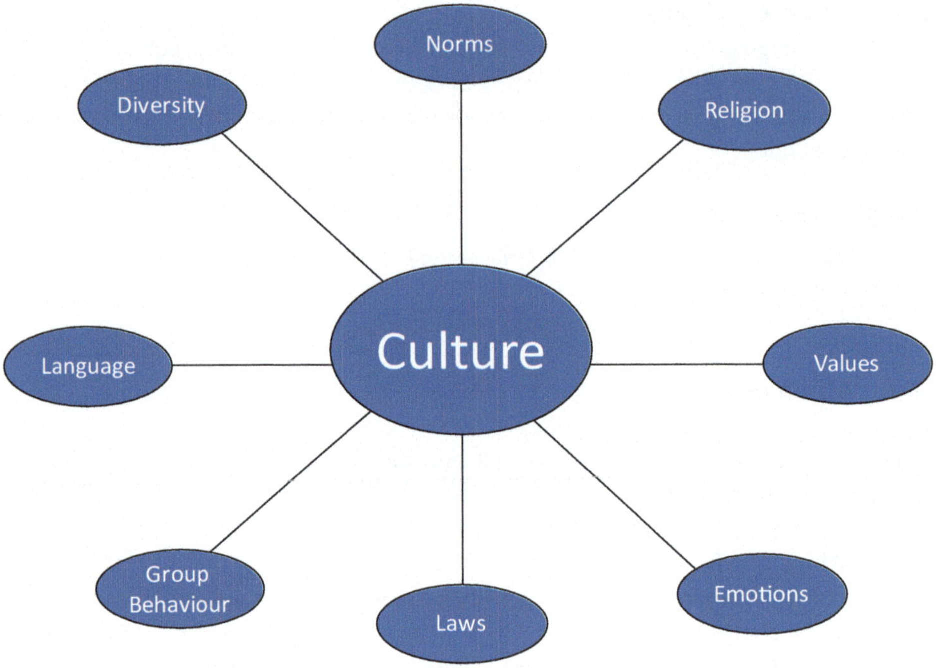

Fig. 1.15 Phases of an interview. (Source: Marc Helmold's own representation based on Köhler 2007)

pre-selection of suitable candidates by the division manager. Figure 1.15 shows the eight stages of an interview.

1.8.1 Phase 0: Market Intelligence and Research

When invited to an interview, the applicant should have obtained information from the other party. This includes participants and functions, in particular the specialist departments and the people taking part. Furthermore, backgrounds and responsibilities can also be found through relevant networks. In addition to people, current projects, customers and markets should be researched that could be related to the task and position. An applicant for a purchasing position should, for example, know the procurement scope and procurement countries of the tendering company in order to sell himself/herself in the best possible way. Opening up new markets can bring potential and opportunities for advancement. Finally, one should know one's market value, and possible fringe benefits such as company cars or further training can be explored in this preliminary phase (Köhler 2007; Fig. 1.16).

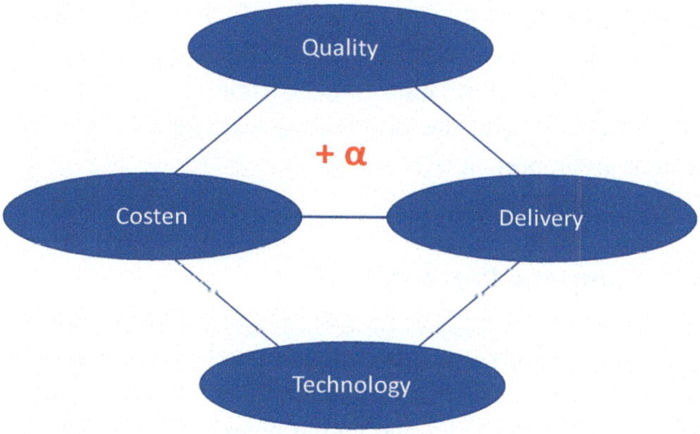

Fig. 1.16 Aspects to research before the interview. (Source: Marc Helmold's own representation)

1.8.2 Phase 1: Welcome and Start of Negotiations

Job interviews and other negotiations begin with the "warm-up" and the greeting. Usually the candidate is assigned a seat and offered a drink. In this phase, getting to know the candidate and the first assessment take place. Usually in the form of a small talk, the first "feeling out" takes place, the first assessment of how the interview partners appear to each other, whether they like each other, a positive (or negative) first impression is created. Typical questions in this phase are, for example (Köhler 2007):

- "Did you find your way here well?", "Did you arrive by train or car?". Always answer positively, because of course you have prepared well and confidently found the way.
- "How do you like our city, our region, our new building?" Answer positively, without exaggerating.
- "Would you like something to drink?" You should agree to this question, alcoholic beverages are taboo.

As soon as you meet the recruiter, you introduce yourself briefly by shaking hands and saying your name. You ask the applicant, for example, "How was your journey?", "Did you find your way here okay?" or "Such nice weather today, isn't it?". Here you should answer with friendly words and chat a little—on the one hand for sympathy points and on the other hand to relax yourself (Köhler 2007). According to a study, it is decided in the first 90 s whether a candidate comes across as likeable and emphatic or not (Köhler 2007).

1.8.3 Phase 2: Own Idea

In the phase of one's own introduction, one is predominantly asked to introduce oneself in a few minutes. Since everyone has usually been able to see the CV, an introduction with the most important milestones of five to ten minutes is sufficient. The classic opening for this phase is the phrase, "Why don't you tell us something about yourself?" The interviewer should be given only the information that is important to them. Qualifications, achievements, project results, and the professional experiences that are relevant to the position being sought are important (Köhler 2007).

1.8.4 Phase 3: Company Presentation

In principle, your own introduction is followed by a brief description of the company, the department in which the job has been advertised and the vacant position. In this context, experts recommend listening carefully and taking notes. This information can be used in the self-presentation, because requirements and expectations will be discussed during the interview. Since the candidate must have learned about the company beforehand, one can also carefully interject information into the negotiation. During the company presentation one can score points and shine with special knowledge about projects, information or other developments (Köhler 2007).

1.8.5 Phase 4: Core Negotiation and Motivation

After the warm-up and introductions, the most important phase is the core negotiation. Answers to questions should be brief and thoughtful. Typical questions are, for example:

- Why did you apply for this job?
- What qualifies you for this position?
- Why do you want to work in our company?
- What do you know about our company?
- Why do you want to change jobs?

You should be well prepared for these questions and have a good rationale, as Table 1.2 shows. Trained recruiters use different interview and questioning techniques in the interview. Even if the interviewer asks closed questions (yes/no questions), you should still give reasons for your answer. Answers should be short and structured. In addition to professional qualifications and goals, a recruiter is also interested in the applicant's personality. It is not only important to be able to fill the position competently, but also to fit into the existing team and the company culture.

1.8.6 Phase 5: Negotiations on Material and Organisational Elements

After the discussion on suitability, drive and aptitude, the negotiation on salary, fringe benefits and organisational elements follows in phase 5. The golden rule is to always quote

Table 1.2 Questions and answers in job interviews

Question	Good answer
What interests you about the advertised position?	The tasks and challenge
Why is the company interesting for you?	Excellent and great company, exciting customers
What qualifications do you bring to the job?	Study and experience with examples and successes
Why does this job suit you and your previous career?	Point out experience. Point out possible further training and qualifications

Source: Marc Helmold's own representation based on Köhler (2007)

Table 1.3 Questions and answers in phase 5

Question	Good answer
What are your salary expectations?	Between 75,000 EUR and 80,000 EUR
Do you have any other ideas besides salary?	Company car, paid training, company telephone
When can you start?	Point out notice period and answer with counter question, "when would you like me to start?"
Do you have any other questions or comments?	Refer to a familiarisation plan

Answers to material and organisational questions
Source: Marc Helmold's own representation based on Köhler (2007)

a range from to when stating the salary, as Table 1.3 shows. The analysis of the range according to position, experience, industry and region plays a central role here.

Figure 1.17 shows the possible objectives such as salary benefits, intangible benefits, fringe benefits and additional benefits. In principle, everything may be negotiated and regulated in the employment contract. In most cases, the employer has no right to order further training at the employee's expense without such a regulation, and in principle the employer is in turn not obliged to finance private further training of his employee, even if this presents itself or can present itself as so-called added value for the employment relationship.

Basically, employers as well as employees are interested in the work being done as efficiently as possible. For this reason, many employers also assume the costs of further training for the employee without much discussion or pay subsidies for this. Large companies offer their employees an additional budget from which the employees can finance their own further training in addition to other motivational benefits. The framework conditions of these cost transfers can vary with regard to the travel costs that are often incurred. The employer can claim these further training courses as costs for tax purposes, so that there is an interest on the employer's side. Continuing education can include training with and without a degree. For example, in the context of employment, the costs of training

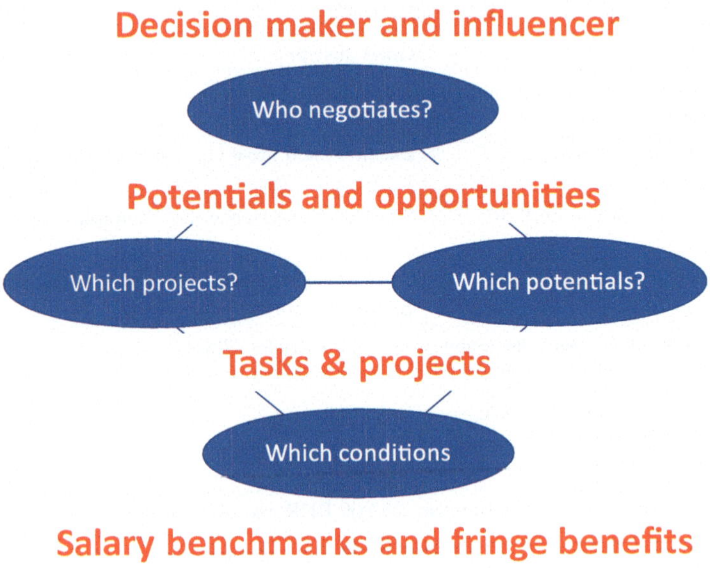

Fig. 1.17 Negotiation goals in job interviews. (Source: Marc Helmold's own representation)

in negotiation techniques, a Master of Business Administration (M.B.A.) or a Six Sigma expert can be included in the negotiations. For executives, it is common to include a bonus, company car and elements of a company pension plan in the negotiation. The values of these elements can amount to more than 50% of the current annual gross salary (Püttier and Schnierda 2014).

1.8.7 Phase 6: Questions and Termination of Negotiations

Even before the negotiations for the vacant position, it is advisable for the candidate to write three to five questions that should be asked when prompted (Püttier and Schnierda 2014). One should not ask questions about aspects that have long been said or clarified in the interview or that one can answer oneself. Also, questions about working hours or vacation time as well as special benefits and salary increases should not be asked (at least in the first interview), because this questions one's own motivation. These things should be secondary or at least initially treated as such (Püttier and Schnierda 2014).

1.8.8 Phase 7: Adoption and Decision of the Outcome of the Negotiations

If you notice that the interview is coming to an end, you should set deadlines and milestones for further action. You can also find out what happens next in the selection process and when you can expect feedback. Once this has been clarified and there are no more questions, the recruiter will thank the candidate and say goodbye. The candidate should thank you for the invitation and say goodbye. In some cases, questions related to travel reimbursement should also be asked. Based on the authors' experience, travel reimbursement should be clarified in advance. If deadlines are not met, it is acceptable to make an inquiry with the HR manager about the status (Püttier and Schnierda 2014).

1.9 Negotiations in the Political Arena and with Non-Profit Organisations

According to the Duden dictionary, politics is defined as "action by governments, parliaments, parties, organisations or similar aimed at achieving certain goals in the state sphere and shaping public life" with the aim of enforcing positions. In the process, tactics are used in negotiations (Duden 2018). Political negotiations, unlike negotiations in business, can also involve threats by different governments to resolve conflicts militarily, as the negotiations between the United States of America and North Korea have shown (Helmold 2018). Political negotiations are not always subject to the same laws as economic negotiations, so the same tactics and strategies cannot generally be used. However, strategies and tactics similar to those used in economics can often be seen (Helmold 2018). Political negotiations are often influenced by an internal or external set of opinions and interdependencies of numerous stakeholders, for example interests of party members or voter groups, whereas companies can usually only implement their own interests. Examples of political negotiations in a national and international context are shown in Table 1.4 (Fetsch 2006).

In politics, negotiations are traditionally conducted by government officials or government representatives who have been mandated to achieve a certain target corridor in order to reach a negotiated outcome. To this end, national and international conferences often

Table 1.4 Examples of negotiations in politics

National negotiations	International negotiations
Coalition negotiations between various parties	Negotiations on the budget of the NATO defence alliance
Struggle over refugee quota by coalition parties	Negotiations between the EU and the USA on punitive tariffs
Negotiations on the use of a surplus in the budget	Negotiations of the free trade agreement with Japan
Negotiations on contentious domestic policy positions	Negotiations between Germany and France on a common foreign policy
Negotiations for important offices within a party	Negotiations on refugee agreement

Examples of negotiations based on Helmold (2018)

serve as lateral venues (Fetsch 2006). This type of conference diplomacy is usually organized by international organizations and results in more or less permanent events with a large number of participants. Besides lateral negotiations, there are also bilateral negotiations between two groups, countries or parties (Fetsch 2006). Negotiations at the political level are usually influenced by opinions, stakeholders, voters, lobbyists or the public, so that negotiation results in politics are often misinterpreted, as Brost describes in his interview with M. Schranner (Brost 2017). Negotiations in politics recently also often include organizations from the non-governmental sector in conferences (Fetsch 2006). These so-called non-governmental organizations are non-profit and socially oriented organizations (NGO, Non-Governmental Organizations; NPO, Non-Profit Organizations) that have humanitarian or charitable motives (Fetsch 2006).

Non-profit organisations are not profit-oriented. This means that no profits are paid out to members or shareholders. They try to operate in such a way that all costs are covered. NPOs can be divided into public and private non-profit organisations (Fetsch 2006):

- Associations
- Associations
- Foundations
- Clubs
- Charities
- Churches

Public NPOs are public enterprises as well as public administrations. Between public and private, cooperatives and chambers can be found as NPOs. Good management is also important for NPOs in order to use scarce resources such as manpower or financial resources as effectively as possible. An NGO is usually internationally oriented, an NPO rather regionally. Thus, an NGO has a wider reach and often represents political issues (e.g. development cooperation, human rights, etc.). Especially in this context, negotiations with governments or political organisations are of central importance, as Fetsch states (Fetsch 2006). An NPO is financed by self-generated financial resources, an NGO by membership fees and donations from parties, governments or stakeholders. The work of an NGO pursues the mission of improving the world. The work of an NPO offers services and goods within the framework of a business (Fetsch 2006).

References

Abdel-Latif, A. (2015). Nicht verblüffen lassen. Schützen Sie sich vor den zehn dreckigsten Verhandlungsfallen. Abgerufen am 1.4.2018. https://www.focus.de/finanzen/experten/adel_abdel-latif/nicht-bluffen-lassen-schuetzen-sie-sich-vor-den-zehn-dreckigsten-verhandlungsfallen_id_4772172.html.

Brost, Marc (2017). Verhandlungen. Tipps für eine erfolgreiche Verhandlungsstrategie. Mehr fordern, als man will. Interview mit M. Schranner. In: Die Zeit. Abgerufen am 11.7.2018. https://www.zeit.de/2017/43/verhandlungen-politik-training-matthias-schranner.

Bauer-Jelinek, Ch. (2007). Die geheimen Spielregeln der Macht und die Illusionen der Gutmenschen. Ecowin Verlag Salzburg.

Cambridge Dictionary (2018). Definition: Negotiation. Abgerufen am 15.3.2018. https://dictionary.cambridge.org/de/worterbuch/englisch/negotiation.

Chia, H.-B., Egri, C., Ralston, D., Fu, P. P., Kuo, M. C., & Lee, C. (2007). Four tigers and a dragon: Values differences, similarities, and consensus. Asia Pacific Journal of Management, S. 24.

Dathe, T. & Helmold (2018). Erfolg im Chinageschäft. Handlungsempfehlungen für kleine und mittlere Unternehmen (KMU). Springer Wiesbaden.

De Mooij, M., & Hofstede, G. (2010). The Hofstede model. International Journal Of Advertising, pp. 29(1), pp. 85–110.

Duden, 2018. https://www.duden.de/rechtschreibung/Politik#Bedeutung2. Abgerufen am 15.5.2108.

Federal Statistics Office (2018). https://www.destatis.de/DE/Home/_inhalt.html.

Fetsch, F. R. (2006). Verhandeln in Konflikten: Grundlagen – Theorie – Praxis (German Edition). Verlag für Sozialwissenschaften Wiesbaden.

Geertz, C. (1973). The Interpretation of Cultures: Selected Essays by Clifford Geertz (1973-10-25). Basic Books Group.

Hall, E. (1966). The Hidden Dimension. New York: Garden City.

Hall, E. (1976). Beyond culture. New York: Garden City.

Hall, E. (1983). The Dance of Life: The Other Dimension of Time. New York: Anchor Books.

Helmold, M. (2010). Best-in-Class Lieferantenmanagement in der Automobilindustrie. Shaker Aachen.

Helmold, M. (2018). Erfolgreiche Verhandlungen und Best-in-Class Empfehlungen für den Verhandlungsdurchbruch. Manuskript und Workshopunterlagen im Master- und MBA-Studium.

Helmold, M. & Terry, B. (2016a). Lieferantenmanagement 2030. Springer Gabler Wiesbaden.

Helmold, M. & Terry, B. (2016b). Global Sourcing and Supply Management Excellence in China. Springer Singapur.

Helmold, M. & Dathe, T. & Büsch, M. (2017). Praxisbericht aus der Bahnindustrie – Bombardier Transportation. Veränderte Anforderungen durch Global Sourcing. In: Beschaffung aktuell. 4.5.2017. Abgerufen am 17.5.2018. https://beschaffung-aktuell.industrie.de/einkauf/veraenderte-anforderungen-durch-global-sourcing/.

Hofstede, G. (1980). Culture's Consequences: International Differences in Worked-Related Values. Beverly Hills: Sage Publication.

Hofstede, G. (1991). Cultures and Organizations: Software of the Mind. McGraw-Hill Maidenhead.

Hofstede, G. (2007). Asian management in the 21st century. Asia Pacific Journal of Management 24 (4):411–420.

Hofstede, G., & Hofstede, G. J. (2011). Lokales Denken, globales Handeln: Interkulturelle Zusammenarbeit und globales Management. 5. ed. Munich DTV.

Huang, C. (2017). Midas posts 76.3% jump in FY16 profit on acquisition's contribution. Abgerufen am 30.3.2018. http://www.businesstimes.com.sg/companies-markets/midas-posts-763-jump-in-fy16-profit-on-acquisitions-contribution.

IUBH (2018). Vorlesungsunterlagen für M.B.A.-Veranstaltungen. Prof. Dr, Marc Helmold. Negotiations in the international context.

Johnson, G. & Scholes, K. (1997). Exploring Corporate Strategy. Text and Cases. 4th Edition. Prentice Hall London.

Köhler, D. (2007). Stressfrei ins Vorstellungsgespräch. 16.7.2007. Abgerufen am 15.5.2018. https://www.akademie.de/wissen/vorstellungsgespraech-vor-nachbereitung/gespraechsverlauf-in-acht-phasen.

Lanz, H.P. (2018). Der Kuchen ist größer als du denkst. Wirtschaftsmediation. Frankfurt. Abgerufen am 25.3.2018. https://www.wirtschaftsmediatoren-ihk.de/f%C3%BCr-hilfesuchende/beitr%C3%A4ge-zum-konfliktmanagement/teil-3-der-kuchen-ist-gr%C3%B6%C3%9Fer-als-du-denkst/.

Lee, S.-H., & Oh, K. (2007). Corruption in Asia: Pervasiveness and arbitrariness. In: Asia Pacific Journal of Management, 24(1), S. 97–114.

Liker, J. K., & Choi, T. Y. (2004). Building deep supplier relationships. In: Harvard Business Review, 82 (12), 104–113 + 149.

Mintzberg, H., Quinn, J.B. & Ghoshal, S. (1998). The Strategy Process. Revised European Edition. Prentice Hall London.

Obrien, J. (2016). Negotiations for Procurement Professionals. 2nd Edition. Kogan Page Croyden.

Polwin-Plass, L. (2016). Checklisten für den Vertrieb. Verhandlungsstrategie. 22.9.2016. In: Die Vertriebszeitung. Abgerufen am 20.3.2018. https://vertriebszeitung.de/verhandeln-im-grenzbereich-strategien-und-taktiken-im-vertrieb/.

Porter, M.E. (1985). Competitive Advantage. Creating and sustaining superior Performance. Free Press New York.

Püttier, Ch. & Schnierda, U. (2014). Das überzeugende Vorstellungsgespräch für Führungskräfte: Wie Sie Headhunter, Personalprofis und Top-Manager überzeugen. Campus Frankfurt.

Schranner, M. (2009). Verhandeln im Grenzbereich. Strategien und Taktiken für schwierige Fälle. 8. Auflage. Econ München.

Schranner, M. (2015). 7 Prinzipien für erfolgreiches Verhandeln. BME-Keynote Matthias Schranner gibt sieben Tipps für zielführende Verhandlungen. 15.1.2015. Abgerufen am 20.3.2018. https://www.bme.de/7-prinzipien-fuer-erfolgreiches-verhandeln-888/.

Statistisches Bundesamt (2018). Pressemitteilung Nr. 039 vom 08.02.2018: Deutsche Exporte im Jahr 2017: +6,3% zum Jahr 2016. Exporte und Importe erreichen neue Rekordwerte. Abgerufen am 15.3.2018. https://www.destatis.de/DE/PresseService/Presse/Pressemitteilungen/2018/02/PD18_039_51.html;jsessionid=86A76343A81D3E6B58E2A4A4716DC45E.InternetLive2.

The Telegraph (2017). http://www.telegraph.co.uk.

Wilkes, K. (2016). Was bewegt Matthias Schranner? Zehn Millionen mehr, bitte! Die Zeit Online. 22.6.2016. Abgerufen am 17.5.2018. https://www.zeit.de/2016/22/matthias-schranner-verhandlungsfuehrer-regierung-geiselnahme.

Negotiation Concepts

2

He who speaks so as to be understood speaks well
—Molière (1622–1673)

Contents

Summary

Negotiations, according to Obrien (Negotiations for Procurement Professionals. 2nd Edition. Kogan Page Croyden, 2016), are interactions of multiple parties about a specific issue with the aim of all parties to achieve a result. Negotiations are characterized by an envisaged reconciliation of interests and a negotiated settlement (Obrien, Negotiations for Procurement Professionals. 2nd Edition. Kogan Page Croyden, 2016). This is considered in all existing negotiation concepts. Probably the best known negotiation concept is the Harvard concept, which was developed by Fisher and Ury. In addition to the Harvard concept, the Schranner concept is discussed as a

M. Helmold et al., *Successful Negotiations*,
https://doi.org/10.1007/978-3-658-35701-6_2

negotiation model for difficult negotiations. However, the focus of the publication is on the A-6 concept, which was developed by Dr. Marc Helmold and has been successfully applied in practice.

2.1 Gap between Practice and Theory

Negotiation techniques or conflict management in an international context are still not represented as an independent discipline in science and at universities. Few universities or business schools offer negotiation techniques or conflict management in an intercultural context (IUBH 2018; Helmold and Terry 2017). This is due to the fact that not many experts in higher education institutionss have conducted international negotiations, so that expertise in negotiations, especially in the international arena, focuses on general behavioural patterns and recommendations. Furthermore, it can be observed that usually larger companies send their employees from the sales, marketing, supplier management or purchasing departments to trainings or they offer trainings internally (IUBH 2018). However, studies show that the topic of global procurement and thus also international negotiations is of central importance for many medium-sized companies (BME 2018).

2.2 Negotiation Concept According to Harvard

According to Obrien, negotiations are interactions of several parties about a concrete issue with the aim of all participants to achieve a result. Negotiations are characterized by an envisaged reconciliation of interests and a negotiated settlement (Obrien 2016). This is reflected in all existing concepts of negotiation. Probably the most commonly taught and referred to negotiation concept is the Harvard concept. It is the method of fact-based negotiation. The principle behind it was formulated by the American legal scholar Fisher in 1981 together with Ury in the book "Getting to Yes". In this book both authors describe how to negotiate constructively and efficiently (Fisher and Ury 1981). Fisher & Ury state that negotiation is a constant part of our lives. In all situations, agreements need to be reached that are appropriate to the complexity of the situation and the various interests involved. The use of power and leverage usually leads to ineffective and unsatisfactory results. According to the Harvard concept, on the other hand, it is better to seek solutions using a constructive negotiation method (Fisher and Ury 1981). A good negotiation outcome is transparent, that is, unambiguous in its interpretation, implementable, that is, the realistic implementation is fair, all parties can accept it. It is expedient, it benefits me and all parties, balancing interests and adding value (Fisher and Ury 1981). In the Harvard concept, negotiation is not only about factual issues and outcomes, but also about the personal relationships between the actors. Similarly, both authors identified that emotional elements such as trust or distrust determine the success or failure of the negotiation (Fisher and Ury 1981). For a long time, there was a dispute between two "schools" of negotiation

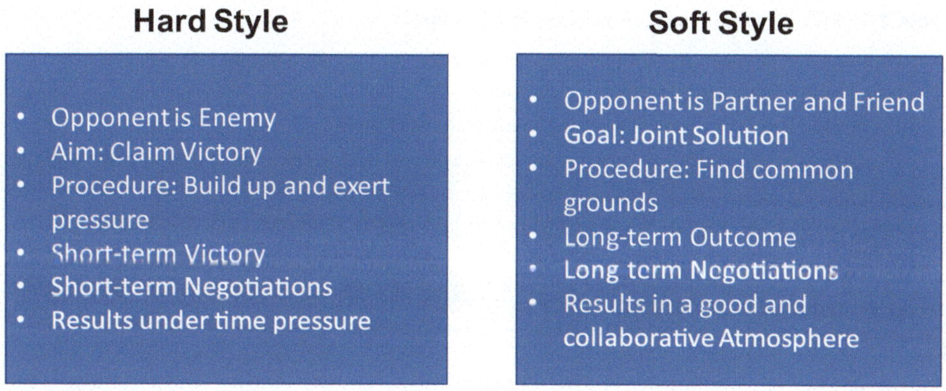

Fig. 2.1 Harvard soft and hard style concept. (Source: adapted from Fisher and Ury (1981))

on how to conduct negotiations successfully: Some believed that one should negotiate "hard," that is, seek one's own success on the merits at any cost and "defeat" the other side by any means; others recommended negotiating "soft," that is, protect one's good relationship with the other side at all costs and be rather generous on the merits so as not to strain the relationship (Fisher and Ury 1981). Figure 2.1 shows soft and hard negotiation elements (Fisher and Ury 1981).

In response to the controversial opinions on how to negotiate properly, Professors R. Fisher and W. Ury founded the Harvard Negotiation Concept in 1979. Thus, their scientific results have been incorporated into a generally accepted concept. In this scientific project, the professors evaluated numerous negotiations from areas such as business, politics or mediation and examined which success factors lead to a successful negotiation result. Based on this research, the book "Getting to Yes" was published in 1981, in which the basic principles of professional and factual negotiation are explained. This book is still the world's best-selling book on the subject of negotiation and the concept presented in it (Wermke et al. 2013). The answer of the Harvard negotiation concept to the dispute between "hard" and "soft" negotiation theory is: in order to negotiate successfully, one must negotiate hard on the substance and soft on the relationship level. The Harvard concept, therefore, is a method of cooperative negotiation that is firm on the merits but, for the sake of success, emphasizes mutual respect between the negotiating parties and focuses on their legitimate interests. The Harvard negotiation concept is based on five basic principles (Wermke et al. 2013). Fisher and Ury recommend as a golden rule of the Harvard concept, in addition to careful preparation for the negotiation, not only to identify one's own interests, but also to set priorities. Table 2.1 shows the basic principles of the Harvard concept.

Which interests are most important, what would also be important but is not absolutely necessary? On the basis of these clear priorities, it will be easier to evaluate proposals and not lose sight of one's own objectives. Instead of confrontation and the resolution of differences, the Harvard concept is about cooperative and consensual problem solving.

Table 2.1 Five basic principles of the Harvard concept

1	Differentiate between the subject of the negotiation on the one hand and the relationship between the negotiating partners on the other!
2	Do not focus on positions, but on the interests behind them
3	Develop as many options as possible first, evaluate and decide later which option is the optimal one.
4	Use standardized, universally accepted norms and criteria as objective decision-making criteria.
5	Decide for or against a negotiated agreement by comparing it with your best alternative on the basis of the objective decision criteria for it

Source: based on Wermke et al. (2013)

Therefore, care should be taken to ensure that no one entrenches themselves in positions that they cannot relinquish without losing face. One should, for this reason, always present proposals as options, as one of several ways of solving problems, not as ultimate demands (Fisher and Ury 1981). Examples include:

- "Would that be a compromise for you?"
- "Would that be an acceptable negotiated outcome?"
- "I would imagine that a good solution might be for us to . . ."
- "What do you think of that? Do you see any other possibilities?"
- "Does that sound interesting to you?"
- "What possibilities do you see?"
- "What alternatives do you see for a successful negotiation?"
- "What alternative courses of action can you think of?"
- "How can we agree?"

2.3 Schranner's Negotiation Concept: Negotiations for Difficult Cases

2.3.1 The Approach to Difficult Cases

In Schranner's concept "Negotiating at the Boundary" a total of seven principles or laws for difficult negotiations are presented (Schranner 2009). According to his website, Matthias Schranner can demonstrably show successful negotiation techniques that can be directly applied in business life. In various articles, Schranner is seen as the expert in negotiating difficult cases (Schranner 2018). Schranner's website states that in 95% of all cases, clients are able to negotiate themselves, but that in difficult cases, which account for about 5%, his approach can come into play (Schranner 2018). Schranner identifies three different types of actors in conflict situations (Polwin-Plass 2016):

1. Escape types
2. Attack types
3. Mixed types

2.3.1.1 Escape Types

Escape types are described by Schranner as individuals who tend to avoid or not make an appearance in critical situations (Schranner 2018; Polwin-Plass 2016). These usually withdraw in critical situations to avoid conflict. While this prevents conflict, the problem remains unresolved. In international negotiations, especially in Asian countries such as China, Japan or South Korea, one will ostensibly encounter escape types who will avoid open conflict (Helmold and Terry 2017). This will be discussed in detail further on.

2.3.1.2 Types of Attack

In addition to escape types, there are individuals who are confrontational and direct in their approach to negotiations (Schranner 2018; Polwin-Plass 2016). Schranner calls this type "attack type". They go for confrontation and thus solve problems in the short term. They very often destroy relationships in the long term, as they often say rash and emotional things (Schranner 2018; Polwin-Plass 2016). Especially in critical and dangerous negotiation situations, according to Schranner, attack types talk too much and too rashly, so that they very often betray confidential information when not matched (Polwin-Plass 2016). If attack types interculturally meet escape types or people who act rather reserved and passive, this can lead to a strong loss of face and the final failure of the negotiations (Dathe and Helmold 2018). In the context of international negotiations, however, it is advisable to wait and let the negotiating adversary talk for the time being (Helmold 2018).

2.3.1.3 Mixed Types

According to Schranner, there are individuals who display both characteristics of the first two categories (escape and attack types) to varying degrees (Polwin-Plass 2016). These are called "mixed types". Depending on the typification of the negotiating opponent, one's own tactics and strategy must be developed in a targeted manner (Polwin-Plass 2016).

2.3.2 Important Steps in Schranner's Concept

Schranner's concept includes seven important rules and focuses on difficult negotiations (Schranner 2015) Schranner sees the following steps and elements as focal points for negotiations in very difficult cases:

- Never give in
- Do not compromise
- Do not play for time and do not postpone
- Never say no

- Caution with threats
- Help the negotiating partner save face
- If the call is terminated, withdraw the offer
- Setting the anchor
- Clarifying the agenda
- Increase in receivables
- Creating summaries

Schranner likes to compare difficult sales negotiations in his seminars with negotiations from his professional life as a police officer and negotiator in criminal cases and explains what can be learned and applied from them for business life.

Example
For example, during a hostage situation, a man threatened a woman with a gun and announced that he would shoot his victim if the police did not leave the room immediately (Polwin-Plass 2016). This leads to different alternative courses of action according to Schranner. In the first step, there are the following alternative actions based on this real example (Polwin-Plass 2016):

- Give in to the aggressor's wish and leave the room
- Make a threat
- Offer a compromise
- Crack a joke to lighten the situation
- Appeal to the conscience of the hostage-taker
- Say "no"

Negotiations become difficult especially when the negotiating parties are convinced that they are right in one or all aspects of the negotiation (Polwin-Plass 2016). Even a criminal and hostage-taker has a justification for his act based on his conviction, even though his behaviour does not conform to the law (Polwin-Plass 2016). When negotiating with a hostage taker as well as in a sales negotiation, it is important according to Schranner not to be irritated or obviously respond to irritation (Polwin-Plass 2016). Displeasure and anger elicit stress, this stress in turn costs energy and stressed people become active and thus offensive (Polwin-Plass 2016). In this regard, Schranner recommends (Polwin-Plass 2016) to negotiate carefully so as not to jeopardize the conversation. Similarly, his advice is to never give in, especially when strategies and tactics Sect. 4.3 come into play (Polwin-Plass 2016). According to Schranner, giving in is by far the worst tactic in terms of negotiation. Giving in without reciprocation leads to even higher demands and is a sign of weakness (Polwin-Plass 2016; Schranner 2009). Suppose a protracted negotiation is in its final stages, the seller is under quite a bit of pressure, and now the only thing standing in the way of signing is the price. However, the buyer and customer now wants another price reduction in the multi-digit range. An escape type in this situation would try to escape from this situation, as Schranner describes (Polwin-Plass 2016; Schranner 2009). This behavior poses great risks for future negotiations, because the customer would demand an even higher discount in the next negotiation with the successful strategy of exerting pressure. Therefore, Schranner says: "Concessions are allowed, but only with demands in return. You have to weigh up the demands carefully, summarise them several times and then offer cooperation with consideration. This is how goals are achieved and mutual respect is worked out" (Polwin-Plass 2016).

Especially in price negotiations, you should never compromise. According to Schranner, compromises convey two dangerous risks. Firstly, the buyer would be confirmed in his strategy ("There's still something there.") and secondly, the impression would be created that exerting pressure is a successfully applied strategy ("By exerting pressure, we always succeed.") (Polwin-Plass 2016).

A compromise is a quick way out of a conflict, but it does not lead to a sustainable solution. A conflict must therefore be fought out and: "A negotiation is a conflict. To compromise would mean to respond to the middle of the negotiating partner, not to one's own. This leads to the counterpart setting the bar inherently higher next time. You have to be able to withstand pressure in order to be able to raise your own demands. It is important to emphasize common ground" (Schranner 2009). Schranner therefore recommends making concessions only in return for consideration and not compromising at all (Polwin-Plass 2016; Schranner 2009). Another recommendation involves ending negotiations with staying power and no adjournments (Polwin-Plass 2016; Schranner 2009). Polwin quotes Schranner: "When one plays for time, one hopes to be able to take a more optimal starting position at a later point in time. But if both negotiating partners are playing for time, it becomes problematic, because the possibility of getting into a better position dwindles. So adjourning is no use either, because in the meantime both negotiating partners become even more sure of their case and the next negotiation becomes even more difficult" (Polwin-Plass 2016; Schranner 2009).

Furthermore, the identification of the negotiating partner's room for manoeuvre plays a central role, setting a maximum and a minimum price with a pain threshold. According to Schranner, there are always two prices in price negotiations: the obvious price and the invisible price. The invisible one is significantly more important than the visible one, and the seller must approach it carefully (Polwin-Plass 2016; Schranner 2009).

Power and relationship are two important elements in Schranner's concept of negotiation, who recommends the display of power but considers pressure as a critical tool in negotiations (Polwin-Plass 2016; Schranner 2009). Pressure and counter-pressure lead to escalation and a mere clarification of power relations without a willingness to cooperate (Polwin-Plass 2016; Schranner 2009). Negotiation professionals should therefore avoid statements such as "no" or "rejection" in order to continue to flexibly retain all options (Polwin-Plass 2016; Schranner 2009).

A suitable tactic is the introduction of different demands with different prioritisations (Polwin-Plass 2016; Schranner 2009). The introduction of demands creates room for manoeuvre for one's own negotiating side. Schranner recommends asking questions in the subjunctive to include demands: "For example, could you imagine buying or doing this or that in addition so that we can accommodate you here and there?" (Polwin-Plass 2016;

Table 2.2 Recommendations for action according to Schranner

Negotiate carefully so as not to jeopardise the conversation
Identification of the scope for negotiation
Concessions only with consideration
Never give in, especially when tactics come into play
Avoid rejections and "no's
increases in own claims
Increase of the demand of the negotiating partner serve the information procurement
Caution with threats
Saving face is a key component
If the call is terminated, withdraw the offer

Source: based on Polwin-Plass (2016) and Schranner (2009)

Schranner 2009) Further, demands should not be communicated through threats (Polwin-Plass 2016; Schranner 2009). Saving face is an integral part of any negotiation, as the negotiating adversary will need support if they make concessions and deviate from their maximum goal (Polwin-Plass 2016; Schranner 2009).

Breaking off a negotiation can also be understood as a tactic, but in this situation one should revoke the concessions made so far (Polwin-Plass 2016; Schranner 2009). This means that when negotiations resume, the original starting point serves as the basis (Polwin-Plass 2016; Schranner 2009). Breaking off negotiations can be useful to buy more time. It is advisable to obtain the termination yourself (Polwin-Plass 2016; Schranner 2009).

Negotiations should always end on a positive note, for example, with comments such as: "We have come a long way" or "Financially, we have not yet been able to reach an agreement, but we have achieved a lot" (Polwin-Plass 2016; Schranner 2009). This is because if the negotiating partner returns to the negotiating table after some time has passed, he or she must explain with a plausible excuse that he or she is re-entering the negotiations (Polwin-Plass 2016; Schranner 2009). Table 2.2 summarizes the recommendations for action of the Schranner negotiation concept, based on (Polwin-Plass 2016; Schranner 2009).

2.4 Negotiation concept A-6 According to Dr. Marc Helmold

Dr. Marc Helmold has held various management positions in the automotive and railway industries since the late 1990s. In these positions, he has conducted negotiations with national and international customers and suppliers in the higher three-digit million range. Projects in the billion euro range were won as a manufacturer of trams, suburban trains, regional trains and express trains. These projects also always involved difficult and usually lengthy negotiations. Since 2016, he has been a professor of business administration, strategic management and supply chain management (SCM). In addition to teaching and

Fig. 2.2 A-6 negotiation concept by Dr Marc Helmold. (Source: own representation Marc Helmold)

research, he advises companies on international and cross-cultural business transactions and complex negotiations. Within this function and due to the deficits and weaknesses of existing negotiation concepts in the intercultural context, he has developed the A-6 negotiation concept (Helmold 2018) Chapter 4.

This concept is interculturally oriented, innovative, up-to-date, sustainable, unique and has already been successfully implemented in various projects. The practical and easy-to-use concept includes six steps from A-1 to A-6, which must be considered in every negotiation to achieve optimal success (Helmold 2018). In addition to its practical application, cross-cultural specifics are also described in Chap. 4, which come into play in international transactions in countries such as the United States of America, China, France, India, or other countries. Although the model is focused on business negotiations, other negotiations, for example, political negotiations, negotiations between private persons, negotiations about alimony, etc., can also be carried out within the framework of these six steps. Last, the A-6 concept is an inherently logical construct, which sequentially consists of six steps that build on each other. Figure 2.2 shows the six steps from analysis to respect and compliance with the agreement. After the detailed analysis, a selection of appropriate strategies and tactics takes place. The basis here is the script or manuscript, which is described in the context of this chapter. The strategies and tactics determine the argumentation and the structure of the negotiations (Eckert and Tarnowski 2017; Schulz 2017; Godeck 2017). Once one has completed these steps, one can move into the actual negotiation. This is where the radius of action is determined. Within the strategy and argumentation, possible counter-arguments of the other side and resistances have been identified as well as tactics to successfully break these resistances without the negotiating partner losing face. As a final step, the shaping of the negotiation outcome and the adherence to the negotiation agreements are crucial (Helmold 2018).

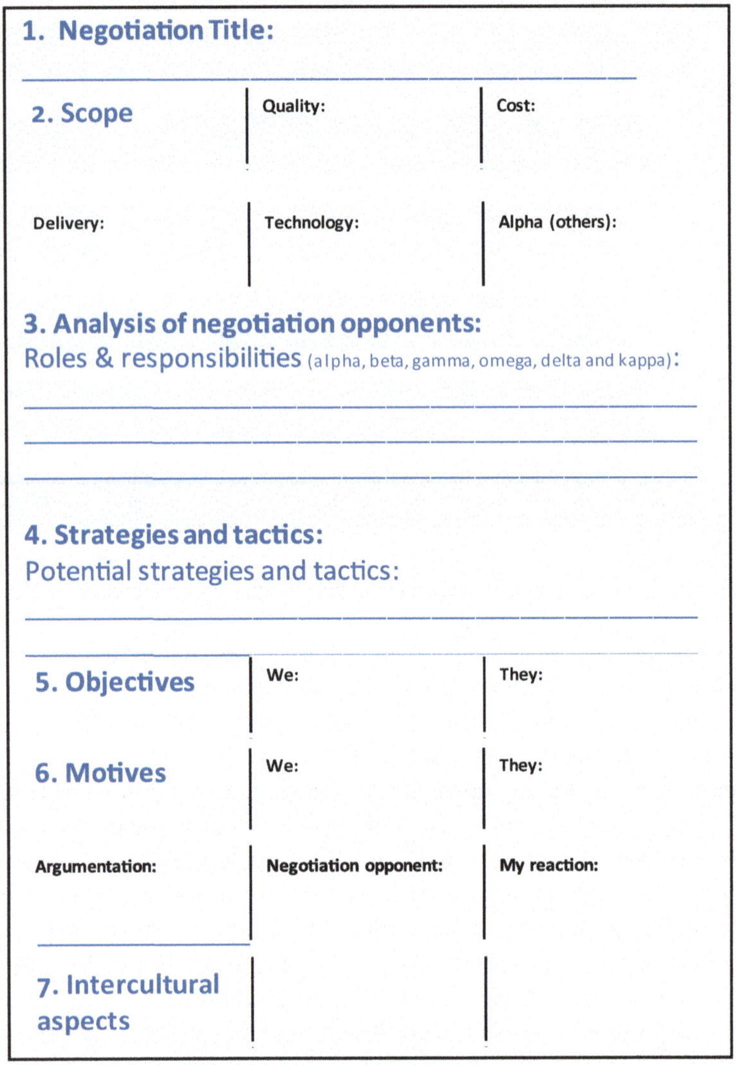

Fig. 2.3 Script/negotiation manuscript (section Annex 2). (Source: own representation Marc Helmold)

The script or negotiation manuscript plays a central role in the A-6 concept as a negotiation tool. The manuscript is the result of the individual steps, whereby the sequence should be seen as dynamic and flexible (not static) (Helmold 2018). Dynamic in this context means being very well prepared and anticipating behavioural patterns of the other side. Dynamism in negotiations equally means being agile and flexible in responding to advances from the negotiating counterparty. Figure 2.3 shows the script/negotiation manuscript as a preparation with significant elements such as key words of the

Table 2.3 Recommendations for action according to Dr. Marc Helmold

Acquiring competence through continuous training in the field of negotiations in an international context. Section 1.2
Systematic planning and structured analysis of key elements such as scope of negotiations, objectives, people and motives. Section 4.2
Consideration of intercultural elements in international negotiations. Section 1.6
Quantification of own objectives and presentation of value. Section 4.2.5
Determination of the negotiating scope with minimum and maximum targets in negotiating categories. (Q-K-L-T plus alpha. Section 4.2.5)
Using non-verbal techniques to achieve negotiation success. Chapter 6
Definition of appropriate strategies and tactics. Section 4.3
Argumentation and negotiation with prioritisation and the A-6 structure. Section 4.1
Use of suitable tools. Chapter 5
Attention to the conclusion of negotiations. Section 4.7
Saving face at all stages of negotiations. Section 4.6.5

Source: based on Helmold (2018)

negotiations, the analysis of the negotiating partners, the possible strategies and tactics and the minimum and maximum targets. The A-6 negotiation concept is described in detail in Chap. 4.

Table 2.3 shows the most important recommendations for action of Dr. Marc Helmold's concept. In addition to systematic preparation and analysis, international specifics are the focus of this model (Helmold 2018). Tools used and proven in practice are integrated in such a way that their implementation in fast and easy (Helmold 2018).

2.5 Differences and Characteristics of the Three Concepts

The three negotiation concepts described have different characteristics and emphases, as Table 2.4 shows. Harvard's concept Sect. 2.2 is basically developed for all types of negotiations, whereas Schranner's Sect. 2.3 focuses on difficult negotiations (Fisher and Ury 1981; Schranner 2009). Dr. Helmold's concept Sect. 2.4, Chap. 4 focuses on negotiations between trading partners in an international context and offers cross-cultural recommendations for action (Helmold and Terry 2016). All three concepts suggest detailed preparation, with Dr. Helmold's concept targeting the scope of the negotiation, motives, roles, and types of people negotiating (Helmold 2018). The preparation can be perceived with the standardized and in practice proven form Fig. 2.3. The Harvard concept recommends a precise preparation with the determination of the best possible alternative (BANTA, Best Alternative to a Negotiated Agreement). Schranner's concept, on the other hand, offers not only a negotiation preparation document, the script, but also a well-founded analysis of the motives and the roles (e.g., decision-maker).

Table 2.4 Comparison and characteristics of the negotiation concepts

	Harvard concept	A-6 concept by Dr. Helmold	Concept according to Schranner
Main focus	Basically all negotiations	Customer-supplier negotiations in an intercultural context	Difficult negotiations
Preparation	Analysis of interests, not positions	Scope analysis consideration of cultural elements, motives and interests. Analysis of persons on the opposite side of the negotiation	Typing of persons on the negotiatingcounterparty concentration on motifs
Methodology	Focus on interests, not positions Win-Win	Systematic, rationally emotionally applied negotiation. 6-phase model Win without the other person losing face	7 successful steps to negotiation success. Critical negotiations Win
Objective	Consensual outcome, Fair exit	Winning without the negotiating partner losing face	Win
Internationality	No	Important recommendations for action for many countries	Global presence of the Schranner Negotiation Institute
Intercultural recommendations	No	Yes	No
Emotionality	No	Yes, but: Rational emotionality	Yes
Nonverbal communication	No	Yes	Conditionally
Criticism of the model	Fairness not always givendifferent perspectives. International peculiarities not taken into account	Interculturally and internationally successfully applied concept. Concentration on commodity transactions (Business Negotiations).	Focus on difficult negotiations. International peculiarities not taken into account.

Own illustration based on Helmold (2018)

There are key differences in the negotiation methodology of the three concepts presented. Harvard suggests a focus on interests and fact-based negotiations in order to achieve a result that can be seen as a win-win for both parties. Drs. Helmold and Schranner have divergent suggestions from this because often an opposing party in a negotiation only aims to come out of the negotiation as a winner (Helmold and Terry 2017; Schranner

2009). Therefore, emotions can also be used purposefully and rationally to achieve the best possible negotiation outcome. Dr. Helmold's concept further targets international negotiations through the representation of country-specific characteristics (Helmold 2018; Geertz 1973; Helmold et al. 2017).

References

BME (2018). Bundesverband Materialwirtschaft, Einkauf und Logistik. Mittelstandspreis geht an Jokey. 10.11.2017. Abgerufen am 18.5.2018. https://www.bme.de/jokey-group-gewinnt-den-bme-innovationspreis-2017-2330/.

Dathe, T. & Helmold, M. (2018). Erfolg im Chinageschäft. Handlungsempfehlungen für kleine und mittlere Unternehmen (KMU). Springer Wiesbaden.

Eckert, M. & Tarnowski, T. (2017). Stress- und Emotionsregulation: Trainingsmanual zum Programm Stark im Stress. Mit E-Book inside und Arbeitsmaterial. Beltz Nordhausen.

Fisher, R. & Ury, W. (1981). Getting to Yes. Penguin Group London.

Geertz, C. (1973). The Interpretation of Cultures: Selected Essays by Clifford Geertz (1973-10-25). Basic Books Group.

Godeck, M. (2017). Die 10 wichtigsten Kennzahlen im Einkauf. In: Technik und Einkauf. Abgerufen am 1.5.2018. https://www.technik-einkauf.de/ratgeber/die-wichtigsten-kennzahlen-im-einkauf/.

Helmold, M. (2018). Erfolgreiche Verhandlungen und Best-in-Class Empfehlungen für den Verhandlungsdurchbruch. Manuskript und Workshopunterlagen im Master- und MBA-Studium.

Helmold, M. & Terry, B. (2016). Lieferantenmanagement 2030. Springer Gabler Wiesbaden.

Helmold, M. & Terry, B. (2017). Global Sourcing und Lieferantenmanagement in China. DeGruyter Berlin.

Helmold, M., Dathe, T. & Büsch, M. (2017). Praxisbericht aus der Bahnindustrie – Bombardier Transportation. Veränderte Anforderungen durch Global Sourcing. In: Beschaffung aktuell. 4.5.2017. Abgerufen am 17.5.2018. https://beschaffung-aktuell.industrie.de/einkauf/veraenderte-anforderungen-durch-global-sourcing/.

IUBH (2018). Negotiations in the international Context. Master-Studiengänge. Abgerufen am 18.5.2018. https://www.iubh-fernstudium.de/modul/negotiation-dlmnege/.

Obrien, J. (2016). Negotiations for Procurement Professionals. 2nd Edition. Kogan Page Croyden.

Polwin-Plass, L. (2016). Checklisten für den Vertrieb. Verhandlungsstrategie. 22.9.2016. In: Die Vertriebszeitung. Abgerufen am 20.3.2018. https://vertriebszeitung.de/verhandeln-im-grenzbereich-strategien-und-taktiken-im-vertrieb/.

Schranner, M. (2009). Verhandeln im Grenzbereich. Strategien und Taktiken für schwierige Fälle. 8. Auflage. Econ München.

Schranner, M. (2015). 7 Prinzipien für erfolgreiches Verhandeln. BME-Keynote Matthias Schranner gibt sieben Tipps für zielführende Verhandlungen. 15.1.2015. Abgerufen am 20.3.2018. https://www.bme.de/7-prinzipien-fuer-erfolgreiches-verhandeln-888/.

Schranner, M. (2018). Schranner Negotiations Institute. Abgerufen am 19.5.2018. https://www.schranner.com/de/institute/matthias-schranner-ceo.

Schulz, U. (2017). Verhandeln und Auseinandersetzen Die deutsche und die schwedische Art auf einen Nenner zu kommen. Abgerufen am 20.3.2018. http://www.schwedenkammer.de/fileadmin/user_upload/3_Business_interkulturell/SA2_12_verhandeln_und_auseinandersetzen.pdf.

Wermke, Ch. et al. (2013). AnwaltsBasics. 2. Auflage Hemmer Verlag Würzburg.

Preparation and Conduct of Negotiations

3

What you tell me, I forget. What you show me, I remember. What you make me do, that I understand. *Confucius (551 BC - 479 BC)*

Contents

Summary

The profound preparation of a negotiation in business transactions, in politics or in other conflicts is important for a successful negotiation outcome and represents the foundation of every negotiation. The time required for this can correspond to the planned duration of the negotiation, in some cases the preparation phase even takes more time. Only if the negotiator is informed about every detail of the negotiation and the other party and has derived a suitable approach and strategy from this, can the desired result of the negotiation be achieved. Sufficient knowledge and analysis of the negotiating partners, the positioning of one's own side, the anticipation of the motives of the opposing side and the possible arguments of the opposing side are decisive elements in the preparation phase, as explained in detail in the A-6 negotiation concept developed by Dr. Marc Helmold. The aim of the preparation is to strengthen one's own security in the subsequent negotiation. The aim is to ensure quick-wittedness and the ability to react to the negotiating partner.

M. Helmold et al., *Successful Negotiations*,
https://doi.org/10.1007/978-3-658-35701-6_3

3.1 Are There Mutual Interests?

The profound preparation of a negotiation in business transactions, in politics or in other conflicts is important for a successful negotiation outcome and represents the foundation of every negotiation. The time required for this can correspond to the planned duration of the negotiation, in some cases the preparation phase even takes more time. Only if the negotiator is informed about every detail of the negotiation and the other party and has derived a suitable approach and strategy from this, can the desired result of the negotiation be achieved. Sufficient knowledge and analysis of the negotiating partners, the positioning of one's own side, the anticipation of the motives of the other side and the possible arguments of the other side are decisive elements in the preparation phase, as explained in detail in the A-6 negotiation concept developed by Dr. Marc Helmold. The aim of the preparation is to strengthen one's own security in the subsequent negotiation. The repartee and the ability to react to the negotiating partner should be ensured. If not already done, the information about the negotiating partner should also be checked again here. Important points in business negotiations are e.g. market position, conditions, pricing policy as well as the analysis of the strengths and weaknesses of the negotiating partners. Of course, you have to contrast this with a critical analysis of your own company's position. Here, professional manuscripts and standardized meeting points are essential to ensure optimal preparation. The preparation can also include a dress rehearsal in which the participants go through all the options with potential negotiating partners, similar to the rehearsal of an orchestra before a big concert. Preparations also need to explore what other categories can be negotiated as additional elements besides price or terms.

Lanz describes in a good example that the "negotiation pie" is usually bigger by adding value-added elements (Lanz 2018). "A freelancer who wants to rent a room. The landlord demands 13 EUR rent per square meter, the potential tenant counters and offers 7 EUR. After much haggling, they agree at 10 EUR." Is this a good negotiation result, the negotiation expert wonders? Here, Obrien recommends looking for factors in the negotiation mix that add value (Obrien 2016). Added value can be increased by adding complementary, i.e. additional or supplementary, elements to the negotiation mass (Fig. 3.1). In price negotiations, cents are very often haggled over, but additional elements such as payment terms, maintenance agreements, response times in the event of incidents, future price reductions or the assumption of installation costs can be included in the negotiations, which increase the added value in the negotiation mass (Dathe and Helmold 2018).

Is everything now optimally negotiated? You might think so, but a true win-win solution may well be even more advantageous. From the very beginning, the two haggled exclusively over the price instead of agreeing on their mutual interests (e.g. possible move-in soon, minimisation of renovation costs, but also caretaker arrangements, garden design, property management, upgrading of the rental property. . .). In doing so, they have missed the chance to increase the "cake" via the third and fourth principles of the Harvard negotiation method. These two principles offer the chance to include other "profitable" possibilities and ideas in the joint contractual partnership:

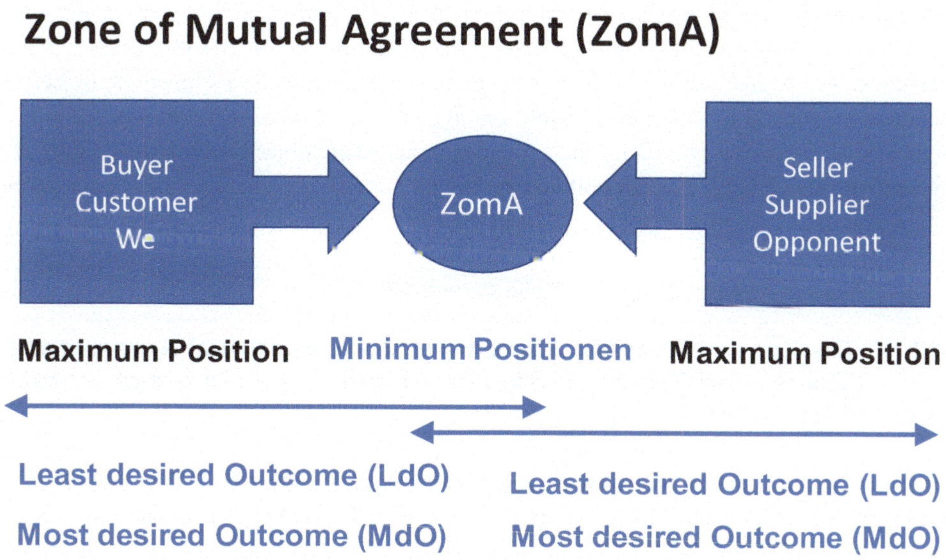

Fig. 3.1 Creating added value in negotiations. (Source: Own representation based on Obrien (2016))

- Identify alternative courses of action with different variations
- Develop choices by working out several decision options together, if possible
- Insist on objective assessment criteria for the final decision
- Evaluate the options according to the objective evaluation criteria
- Select the two to three best alternatives

The third Harvard principle embodies the opening of the solution horizon for further alternatives that have not been thought of before. Creativity should be used to think outside the box and, together with the negotiating partner, to look for and think up as many options for action as possible that can be reconciled with the mutual and common interests.

The fourth Harvard principle then follows with the decision-making process. Now it is important to jointly include neutral and as objective as possible criteria for the decision-making process in order to make the decision-making process comprehensible for all sides—and thus fair. These can be market comparisons and other benchmarks, legal standards or expert opinions, or even ethical standards. They do not all have to coincide with the needs of the negotiating partner either; what is important is that they are mutually accepted.

So brainstorming before tenant and landlord finally agree on a compromise for rent via a handshake could benefit both even more. They could discuss other interests and possibilities. For example, they could include the tenant's willingness to do the renovation work themselves and explore other creative arrangements based on their mutual interests: The landlord may be willing to waive some of the rent in exchange for services provided by the freelancer, such as maintaining the garden, taking on some of the janitorial duties, or even designing and maintaining the landlord's website. In addition, negotiators could discuss the rent based on factual criteria, such as the municipality's rent index, thus including an objective criterion as a benchmark (Godeck 2017). If soft factors beyond positions, i.e. needs and interests of the parties, are creatively included in objective negotiations, the "pie" enlarges by itself and agreements become real win-win solutions. If the decision-making criteria for the agreement reached are objective and accepted by all, agreements are perceived as fair and no negotiating partner feels that they have been taken advantage of.

3.2 The Zone of Possible Agreement: Zone of Mutual Agreement (ZomA) and Successful Tips for Identifying a Margin of Mutual Agreement

Once you are clear about your own goals and their respective relevance, the next step is to explore the possible room for negotiation (Table 3.1). The scope for negotiation in each category ranges from the minimum to the maximum goal, whereby no element in negotiations should be completely static (Schranner 2018). Identification of negotiation leeway should be done before the actual negotiation. If one has employees and colleagues, they can gauge the other party's reaction to certain negotiation points in advance (Helmold and Terry 2017; Wilkes 2016). In addition to maximum and minimum demands, the point of abandonment should also be identified to show the negotiating counterparty that the negotiating leeway has been exhausted. Potential added values are also part of exploring the negotiating space. In international negotiations, for example, a supplier's price may be a minor issue, as he intends to use the order to enter the German market or perhaps wants to show from a marketing point of view that he has a renowned German customer (BME 2018). Motive can also be to establish a functioning logistics network to Europe or Germany in order to penetrate the market here. All authors recommend this important step in the early phase of the negotiation initiation (Helmold and Terry 2017; Schranner 2015; Polwin-Plass 2016) (Fig. 3.2).

Table 3.1 Recommendations for the successful conduct of negotiations

Concentration on target corridors with minimum and maximum targets
Generation of added value in negotiations
Analysis of possible interests and motives of the other side
Identification of (cultural) constraints on the other side
Concentration on the common zone of a consensual solution
Exploring different alternatives for action
Objective evaluation of all claims and alternatives

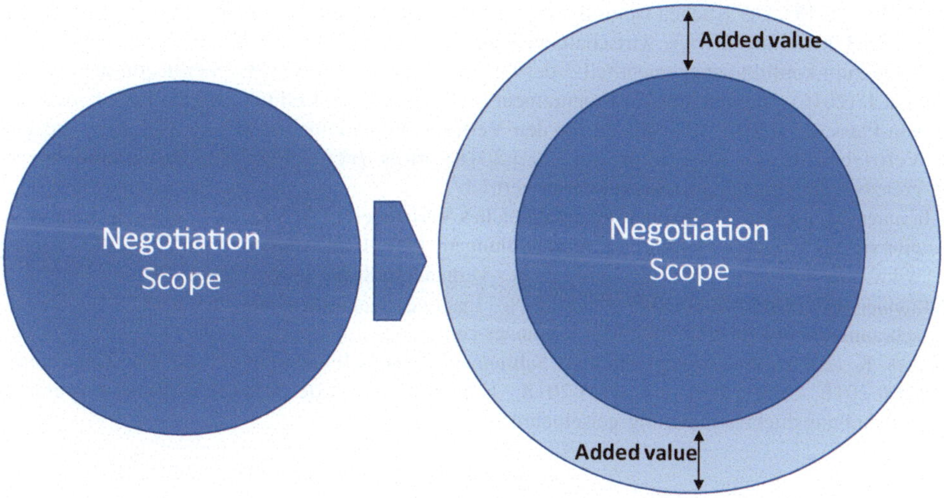

Fig. 3.2 Zone of mutual agreement. (Source: Own representation based on Obrien (2016))

The following aspects are of central importance for the identification of the scope:

- Identification of the potential maximum and minimum goals of the negotiating opponent (What does the other side intend?)
- Are there added values that are attractive to the negotiating counterparty?
- Analysis of possible motives of the participants of the other side (different departments often have different goals)
- Who could be used as an influencer? (Are there possible influencers?)
- Identify possible incentives of the other side (Which offers are attractive for the other side?)
- What are my chances in each category to be negotiated? (Interests of the other side)
- Are there constraints from the other side?

References

BME (2018). Bundesverband Materialwirtschaft, Einkauf und Logistik. Mittelstandspreis geht an Jokey. 10.11.2017. Abgerufen am 18.5.2018. https://www.bme.de/jokey-group-gewinnt-den-bme-innovationspreis-2017-2330/.

Dathe, T. & Helmold (2018). Erfolg im Chinageschäft. Handlungsempfehlungen für kleine und mittlere Unternehmen (KMU). Springer Wiesbaden.

Godeck, M. (2017). Die 10 wichtigsten Kennzahlen im Einkauf. In Technik und Einkauf. Abgerufen am 1.5.2018. https://www.technik-einkauf.de/ratgeber/die-wichtigsten-kennzahlen-im-einkauf/.

Helmold, M. & Terry, B. (2017). Global Sourcing und Lieferantenmanagement in China. DeGruyter Berlin.

Lanz, H.P. (2018). Der Kuchen ist größer als du denkst. Wirtschaftsmediation. Frankfurt. Abgerufen am 25.3.2018. https://www.wirtschaftsmediatoren-ihk.de/f%C3%BCr-hilfesuchende/beitr%C3%A4ge-zum-konfliktmanagement/teil-3-der-kuchen-ist-gr%C3%B6%C3%9Fer-als-du-denkst/.

Obrien, J. (2016). Negotiations for Procurement Professionals. 2nd Edition. Kogan Page Croyden.

Polwin-Plass, L. (2016). Checklisten für den Vertrieb. Verhandlungsstrategie. 22.9.2016. In: Die Vertriebszeitung. Abgerufen am 20.3.2018. https://vertriebszeitung.de/verhandeln-im-grenzbereich-strategien-und-taktiken-im-vertrieb/.

Schranner, M. (2015). 7 Prinzipien für erfolgreiches Verhandeln. BME-Keynote Matthias Schranner gibt sieben Tipps für zielführende Verhandlungen. 15.1.2015. Abgerufen am 20.3.2018. https://www.bme.de/7-prinzipien-fuer-erfolgreiches-verhandeln-888/.

Schranner, M. (2018). Schranner Negotiations Institute. Abgerufen am 19.5.2018. https://www.schranner.com/de/institute/matthias-schranner-ceo .

Wilkes, K. (2016). Was bewegt Matthias Schranner? Zehn Millionen mehr, bitte! Die Zeit Online. 22.6.2016. Abgerufen am 17.5.2018. https://www.zeit.de/2016/22/matthias-schranner-verhandlungsfuehrer-regierung-geiselnahme.

Six Steps to Negotiation Success: The A-6 Model for Negotiations

4

It is not enough to want, one must also do.
—Johann Wolfgang von Goethe (1749–1832)

Contents

M. Helmold et al., *Successful Negotiations*,
https://doi.org/10.1007/978-3-658-35701-6_4

Summary

Negotiations must be analytical, systematically conceptualized, well-structured and result-oriented. One model that has been applied in practice and is successful is the A-6 concept by Prof. Dr. Marc Helmold (M.B.A.). Target groups are not only small and medium-sized enterprises (SME), but also multinational corporations. In particular, companies that enter into business relationships in an intercultural context benefit from the A-6 model. Numerous negotiation successes in the automotive and railway industries have demonstrated its practical relevance. The concept was developed due to the fact that usually not all employees of a department can experience the same external training for budget reasons. For this reason, Dr. Helmold, as a manager with various trainings in the field, developed his own model, which is now successfully applied in teaching or within his consulting work [Helmold. Erfolgreiche Verhandlungen und Best-in-Class Empfehlungen für den Verhandlungsdurchbruch. Manuskript und Workshopunterlagen im Master- und MBA-Studium (2018)].

4.1 Six Steps to Successful Negotiation

Negotiations must be analytical, systematically conceptualized, well-structured and result-oriented. One model that has been applied in practice and is successful is the A-6 concept by Prof. Dr. Marc Helmold (M.B.A.). Target groups are not only small and medium-sized enterprises (SME), but also multinational corporations. In particular, companies that enter into business relationships in the intercultural field derive benefits from the 6-A model (Helmold 2018). Numerous negotiation successes in the automotive and railway industries have illustrated its practical relevance. The concept emerged due to the fact that usually not all employees of a department can experience the same external training due to budget constraints. For this reason, Dr. Helmold developed his own model as a manager with various trainings in the field, which is now successfully applied in teaching, industry and within his consulting work (Helmold 2018).

Step 1 of every negotiation involves an analysis and description of the initial situation. This situation analysis has a significant impact on negotiation success, as numerous authors state (Helmold 2018; Obrien 2016; Schranner 2018). The analysis within the A-6 concept should cover four crucial areas: 1. the negotiating partners, 2. the motives, 3. the scope of the negotiation, and 4. the minimum and maximum goals with priorities and weightings of the respective parties. As described earlier, for the transparent presentation of the analysis, the script/manuscript helps as a suitable preparation form Fig. 2.3. Step 2 focuses on the selection of appropriate strategies and tactics, followed by appropriate argumentation and sequencing of each argument in the negotiation in Step 3. Step 4 involves the actual conduct of the negotiation. Finally, steps 5 and 6 follow with the successful defence against counter-arguments and the drafting of the contract.

In summary, the six steps of the A-6 negotiation model (Helmold 2018) are as follows:

- A-1: Analysis of the negotiating partners and determination of the starting position
- A-2: Selection of appropriate strategies and tactics
- A-3: Structure and argumentation of the negotiations
- A-4: Conducting the negotiations (negotiation management)
- A-5: Defending against counter-arguments and fighting resistance
- A-6: Shaping the results of negotiations and respecting agreements

4.2 Step 1 (A-1): Analysis of the Negotiating Partners and Determination of the Starting Position

4.2.1 Assessment of the Initial Situation

The first step in any negotiation involves a careful assessment and description of the initial situation and must include four significant elements, as Fig. 4.1 shows. In addition to the analysis of the output situation and the typification of the negotiating partners into decision-makers and influencers, the motives and interests must be assessed. Furthermore, the scope of the negotiation and the target corridors of the respective parties must be defined.

The analysis raises different W questions to help guide and must be answered as part of Step A-1, such as:

- Who is my negotiating partner?
- Who is the decision maker?
- What is the intercultural background of my negotiating partner?
- Who influences the decision maker?
- Who can help me on the other side?
- What do I want to negotiate?
- What are the international peculiarities?
- What are my goals?
- What is my target corridor?
- What are the goals of my negotiating partner?
- What strategies does my negotiating partner use?
- When must a negotiated result or partial result exist?
- Where do I negotiate?
- Where does my negotiating partner want to negotiate?
- What are the intercultural pitfalls or idiosyncrasies?

Fig. 4.1 Elements of analysis as the first step of negotiations. (Source: Marc Helmold's own representation)

4.2.2 Analysis of the Negotiating Partners

The first element of the situation analysis involves defining the individual roles and responsibilities of the negotiating partners (Helmold 2018). Negotiations in international business transactions are generally conducted with several people from a wide range of functions (Helmold 2018). Consultants, translators, other third parties or representatives from the public sectors may also be involved in the negotiations (Helmold 2018). In internationally operating companies, more than 15 people may be involved on one of the negotiating sides. For example, a project or sales manager mandates his employee to lead the negotiations and involves other stakeholders (Helmold 2018). In addition to the sales department, other departments are technically involved in the negotiations in this way: Engineering, Quality, Marketing, Finance, Methods, Production and Logistics. In addition, the end customer requires a specific upstream product from a supplier, so purchasing and the upstream supplier are also involved (Helmold 2018). Last, the contract and each draft must be reviewed by the legal department. This example shows that there are different groups in a negotiation. Groups are complex entities and more than just a collection of personalities. Rank dynamics, role allocation and responsibilities are elementary aspects in a negotiation and require transparent evaluation and analysis (Helmold 2018). Chapter 10 goes into detail on the topic and specifics of interdisciplinary project negotiations Chap. 10. Looking at rank dynamics in psychology, according to Hofert, several questions arise (Hofert 2015): why does one person take the lead in each group? What formal or informal elements make the leader the leader? Why are there almost always critics or detractors in groups? For what reason do the masses like to follow one opinion?

The Austrian psychotherapist Raoul Schindler developed his rank dynamics model through observation in the 1950s (Hofert 2015). The added value of the rank concept lies in clarifying processes in groups for everyone. Those who recognize these dynamics can reflect on them as well as understand destructive tendencies such as marginalizing people and make others aware of them. The rank dynamics model is a positional model according to which the distribution of power in groups arises through dynamic processes. According to this model, there are five positions in each group, which do not always have to be occupied—but the larger the group, the more likely it is that all positions will be occupied (Hofert 2015).

4.2.2.1 Type: Alpha

The alpha is the leader and the decision maker in the group and in the negotiations. He or she has power through formal or informal influences such as rank, hierarchy, experience or his or her reputation within the group (Helmold 2018; Schranner 2009; Hofert 2015). The other members of the group have to follow him. Externally, he represents dominance and authority (Helmold 2018; Schranner 2009; Hofert 2015). Supervisors or experienced employees in leadership positions are often alphas because of their formal power. The alphas need the betas as supporters and foundation of their power. Betas therefore have a significant influence on decision makers. Alphas are usually clearly identifiable in a Westernized society through behavior, gestures, or seating arrangements. In other regions such as Asia (China, Japan or South Korea), this is not always immediately apparent (Helmold 2018).

4.2.2.2 Type: Beta

The beta is an expert or subject matter expert and influences the decision maker through his expertise. He or she supports the leader of the group (alpha) and helps him or her stay in his or her position (Helmold 2018; Schranner 2009; Hofert 2015). Buyers or sellers are often betas, as they usually do not have the final mandate to close the negotiations. Predominantly, they also do not have final budget responsibility or decision-making power, so betas use their influence with the alpha (Helmold 2018; Schranner 2009; Hofert 2015). The beta is a significant influencer of the decision maker. In any negotiation, there are multiple influencers that need to be evaluated within the analysis in terms of influencing factors (rank, relationship, and position with the alpha) and expertise (what expertise does the beta possess?). In the international context, betas often have a special relationship with the decision maker, based on elements such as family or group affiliation (descent from the same country, affiliation with a university).

4.2.2.3 Type: Gamma

Gamma people are part of the group but do not have much influence. They are clerks or administrative staff members who are expected to assist in negotiations, often by taking minutes or providing information (Helmold 2018; Schranner 2009; Hofert 2015). The group member likes to be guided by the alpha or beta. There can be multiple gammas. Gammas are usually the "low-level" clerks or assistants who work for the beta and alpha (Helmold 2018).

4.2.2.4 Type: Omega

The omega person of a group is the counterpart who wants to become alpha or maybe even was or is intentionally kept in his position by the alpha because he is a possible competitor (Helmold 2018; Schranner 2009; Hofert 2015). Sometimes the omega also becomes a scapegoat or even a pawn when he is pushed out of the team (Hofert 2015). He can play an important role in one's own negotiation, as he has information that can be of interest for one's own negotiation analysis (Helmold 2018).

The term **"alpha"** or **"alpha human" is** used in negotiation psychology as an animal metaphor for assertive, **dominant, and authoritarian people** in leadership situations to characterize position and habitus within a group or movement (Hofert 2015). Alpha people are formal (through rank and hierarchy) or informal (through recognition in the group) leaders. In this book, alpha is referred to "masculine" (the alpha), as are the other three types beta, gamma, and omega.

The alpha needs the beta as a supporter, so the alpha as decision maker usually treats the beta as an ally positively. The alpha is functionally usually the manager or department head. It might take power itself if the good of the group or the achievement of the goal is in danger. In negotiations, the alphas and betas must be identified within the analysis phase (Helmold 2018). Argumentation Sect. 4.4 and negotiation Sect. 4.5 need to be designed with these two groups in mind to achieve the final negotiation success (Helmold 2018). In addition to decision makers (alpha) and influencers (beta), gamma people are involved as part of the negotiation group. This group has no power, formal or informal, nor can they significantly influence the decision maker. Therefore, it is advisable to treat gammas with respect but not to pay special attention to them (Helmold 2018). Often, the boundaries of assignment to betas and gammas are fluid, so a clear identification must take place within the situational analysis of person typologies. (Helmold 2018). In the international context, friends, spouses as well as family members can play a more important role due to the personal proximity to the decision maker, so caution is required here (Helmold 2018). The omega, on the other hand, is a perceived adversary or competitor and usually appears as an internal critic, nagger or lateral thinker. He has experience, often recognizes early on where difficulties may arise, and can serve as a source of information (Helmold 2018). From his experience, Schranner recommends the establishment and permanent maintenance of a

Role in negotiation			How to approach…
Decision maker	Alpha	α	Decision maker and/or budget owner
Influencer	Beta	β	Influencer
Co-Worker	Gamma	γ	Clerk or adminstrative staff
Informants V-Mann	Kappa	K	Informant, who provides information
Critic	Omega	Ω	Wants be alpha, Scape goat

Fig. 4.2 Distinction and typology of personalities in negotiations. (Source: Own representation Marc Helmold and Helmold 2018)

network of so-called double agents who provide one's own negotiating side with valuable information that is useful for the negotiations (Schranner 2009). Since the omega has and represents his own point of view, he can also become or even aims to become an alpha (Hofert 2015). Far-sighted alphas integrate him and grant him a special role (Hofert 2015) (Fig. 4.2).

4.2.3 Special Features of Alpha Types

Alpha people have the formal power to concede or make concessions to demands in negotiations, so the focus in negotiation must be on this type (Helmold 2018). In negotiations, there are few decision makers, usually only one, so one's strategies and tactics must be geared towards the alpha (Helmold 2018). In identifying and determining the negotiation responsibilities and types of the other party, the following elements according to Hofert are helpful (Hofert 2015).

Alpha people are usually very self-confident, extroverted and show this to their environment. Self-confidence or extroversion is predominantly underlined by an appropriate appearance (behaviour, clothing, articulation). They are convinced that they are ready and capable for extraordinary achievements. This is also articulated in their body language, for example their upright posture and firm handshake. And in the way they look their conversation partners confidently in the eye. Their spoken language corresponds to this. It is not insecure, but confident (Hofert 2015). Alpha people speak a clear language and are extremely performance- and result-oriented. They often prefer short and concise sentences with a clear message ("We will …"; "We should …"; "I am of the opinion that …").

Alpha people can motivate themselves and want to make a difference. Due to their function as decision-makers, alpha people usually have little time to prepare for

Table 4.1 Special features of alpha people

Alpha people are empowered to make decisions and have power
Alpha people are usually very self-confident and extroverted
Alpha people want to make a difference
Alpha people take responsibility
Alpha humans mark their territory
Alpha people use (body) language as an instrument
Alpha people take a stand

negotiations and therefore use information from influencers, i.e. beta people (Helmold 2018). This can be a connecting factor for their own argumentation and thus their own negotiation success Sect. 4.3. Alpha people want to make a difference and achieve goals that they want to realize. Accordingly, they have a lot of energy and radiate it in negotiations (Hofert 2015).

Alpha people take a position on the basis of their position of power, so that comments and statements must be carefully analysed in order to respond to the respective statements with targeted reactions (Helmold 2018). They take responsibility and are people of action. They are not afraid to take responsibility even when a decision or task is risky (Helmold 2018). Alpha people use (body) language as an instrument and mark their territory (Hofert 2015).

Table 4.1 summarises the characteristics of alpha people. In the context of Sect. 4.3, suitable recommendations for action are given on how to take the characteristics of alpha people into account appropriately and wisely in one's own negotiation management in order to achieve the ultimate negotiation success (Helmold 2018).

4.2.4 Type: Kappa—Establishment and Use of Informants

Informants (German: V-Mann) in negotiations are persons who pass on special knowledge or information to us as part of our preparations for negotiations. Information in this context means legal aspects such as state of mind, strategies or negotiating positions. Not meant are trade secrets or strictly confidential data protected by property rights (Helmold 2018). As a German synonym, the term "V-Mann" is used in this negotiator. Informants or V-men have to be specifically built up and promoted, mostly they remain in the background. Informants in negotiations are not used to reveal secrets, but to reveal insider information, moods, opinions, goals and negotiation strategies of the other side. The term V-Mann (double agent, whistleblower) has a rather negative connotation in politics, but in negotiations of business partners it is a legitimate and suitable tool, as Helmold or Schranner recommend (Helmold 2018; Schranner 2009). Suitable informants are omega or beta people Sect. 4.2.2 who have detailed knowledge on the other side (Helmold 2018). Both sides are suitable, with omega people usually having more detailed knowledge and beta people often having more influence on the decision maker (Helmold 2018). Of course, the other side will also try to build an informant network on their own negotiating side (Helmold 2018). In this case, it is worthwhile to let the other side believe that there are informants in one's own ranks, providing the other side with selected information that is helpful for one's own success (Helmold 2018). Figure 4.3 shows the graphical representation of V-men on the opposing side of the negotiation who provide us with useful information (Helmold 2018).

Informants are very popular in Asian countries such as China, Taiwan, Japan or South Korea (Helmold 2018). The informant can be the secretary, the buyer, the salesperson or the clerk. It is important when building up informants that they stand in front of the decision makers as winners and are regularly mentioned in a positive way (Helmold 2018). The "positive recall effect" will cause the decision maker (alpha) to be sympathetic to the informant (usually beta or gamma) and show it. There is even the possibility that a gamma informant will grow into a beta informant by gaining the trust of the alpha (Helmold 2018).

4.2.5 Determine Negotiation Leeway with Minimum and Maximum Targets: QKLT Plus Alpha Methodology

4.2.5.1 QKLT Plus Alpha Methodology

In addition to the typification of the persons on the negotiating counterparty, an assessment of the negotiating scope and objectives in phase A-1 is of central importance (Helmold 2018). A suitable model is the systematic identification of the negotiation scope and the transparent determination of demands according to the QKLT plus alpha concept (quality, costs, logistics, technology and all other aspects). Targets must always include a corridor, i.e. lie within a minimum demand and a maximum demand (Helmold 2018). Almost all known negotiation concepts suggest target corridors instead of static targets (Helmold 2010, 2018; Schranner 2009).

The authors Helmold, Dathe and Hummel recommend listing and prioritizing the possible elements with the minimum and maximum requirements in the respective relevant categories (least desired outcome = minimium objective; most desired outcome = maximum objective). These should be made transparent within the script/manuscript Fig. 2.3. Finally, all objectives should be quantified monetarily in terms of income or expenditure in order to take into account all the advantages and disadvantages of options for action using the total cost of ownership method (Helmold 2010). Numerous companies make the mistake of focusing only on unit price and any one-time costs in negotiations. Better quality performance can also result in significant savings in process costs due to fewer complaints or warranty processing (Helmold 2010).

Figure 4.4 shows the QKLT plus alpha categories as a starting point for identifying bargaining positions (Helmold 2010, 2018).

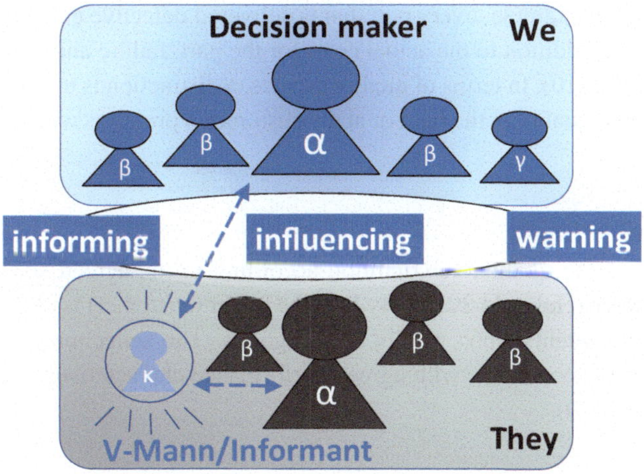

Fig. 4.3 Structure and use of informants (V-Mann). (Source: Marc Helmold's own representation)

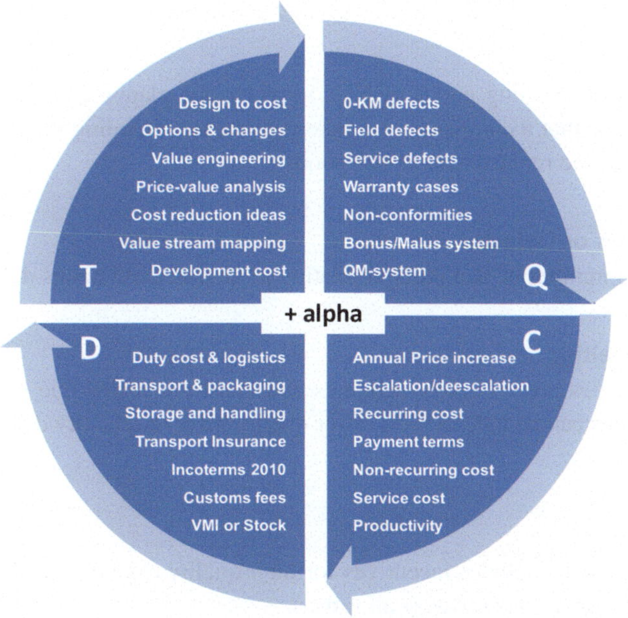

Fig. 4.4 Negotiation scope QKLT plus alpha. (Source: Marc Helmold's own representation)

4.2.5.2 Quality Objectives (Q)

Quality objectives are often neglected in negotiations in terms of monetary valuation. These can be quantified relatively easily and must be clearly regulated in contracts

(Helmold 2010). For example, every part that is delivered defective entails a monetary cost for the customer. In addition to the actual costs for the part, failure and complaint costs are incurred (Helmold 2010). In terms of quality aspects, a distinction is usually made between delivery quality and quality in the field or at the customer's premises within the scope of the warranty.

Delivery Quality
Delivery quality is the qualitative condition according to the agreed specification of the goods upon delivery (Helmold 2010). By law, the buyer (customer) is obliged to randomly check the delivery quality upon receipt of the goods. The seller must manufacture and deliver the goods in accordance with agreed performance characteristics, unless otherwise agreed (Helmold 2010).

Field Failures
Field quality is the level of quality in the field, i.e. in operation at the customer's site. Companies usually measure this on the basis of agreed performance characteristics or legal warranty claims (Helmold 2010).

Complaints
Complaints (non-conforming goods or NCG) involve the planning, execution and monitoring of all actions that a company must take and initiate regarding missing performance characteristics and the replacement of the goods.

Non-conformities or Defects
They include the number of bad parts in relation to all parts and goods delivered.

Contractual Penalties
Contractual penalties are monetary penalties and can be incurred due to late deliveries. Similarly, penalties can be agreed for a lower quality level or quantity delivered (Helmold and Terry 2016).

Bonus or Malus
A bonus (Latin: good) includes incentives for high-quality execution and delivery, while malus includes negative incentives (Latin: bad).

Quality Management Systems
A quality management system includes external certification by authorized certifiers (e.g. Technical Inspection Agency, TÜV). Many new customers insist on this certification (e.g. DIN EN ISO 9001:2015) for their suppliers, which can cause costs in the higher six-figure range.

4.2.5.3 Cost Objectives (K)

Cost targets include all expenses that are necessary for the procurement of goods and services (Helmold and Terry 2016). In addition to direct procurement costs (unit price), there are indirect expenses (qualification, construction of a machine) that are closely linked to procurement.

Price Increases

Price increases or escalations are periodic (often annual) cost increases by the manufacturer. Most often, these are justified by inflation and higher operating costs over the life of the project. Price increases can be dismissed by the customer with the manufacturer's and supplier's commitment to productivity improvements as part of a continuous improvement process (Helmold 2010).

Unit Costs

Unit costs are the costs per component (recurring cost or piece price). Unit costs are recurring per delivered part. The number of ordered parts multiplied by the piece price results in the procurement volume (material spend).

One-Off Costs

Non-recurring costs are costs and expenses for development, machines or innovations that are incurred only once and basically at the beginning of the project and represent investments that entail capitalization of fixed assets (Helmold 2010).

Service Costs

Costs for operation or within the agreed warranty period are service costs. In complex projects, this share can account for up to 50 % of the total project costs (Helmold 2010).

Productivity

Productivity includes improvements in cost structures through a continuous improvement process and the implementation of lean practices. Productivity improvements can account for a monetary improvement of more than 30 % to 40 % in three years, as studies show (Helmold 2010).

Terms of Payment

A payment target as a contractual condition is the agreed time of payment for the delivery of goods and services. The payment term has a direct impact on the liquidity (cash flow) of the company. Very good companies have very short payment terms with their customers (payment on delivery) and longer terms with suppliers, e.g. 60 days (Helmold and Terry 2016).

4.2.5.4 Logistics Objectives (L)

Logistics components can account for more than 40 % of the unit price of goods deliveries, especially in international trade (Helmold and Terry 2016). Germany has been the world's export champion for several years and reported a significant trade surplus in 2017 (Statistisches Bundesamt 2018). Transport, packaging and customs clearance must therefore be taken into account in negotiations. In addition, logistics concepts exist to ensure delivery performance, e.g. vendor managed inventory (VMI), where suppliers are responsible for inventory management (Helmold and Terry 2016).

Packing

This includes the costs for the packaging of the goods. Packaging primarily serves to protect the goods from damage, but also has other functions.

Transport and Logistics Costs

These include the costs of packaging, transport, storage and customs clearance.

Logistics Concepts

Customers expect high delivery reliability and usually have delivery concepts such as just-in-time (JIT). This delivery flexibility will also have an impact on the cost structure (Helmold 2010).

4.2.5.5 Technical Objectives (T)

Much of the negotiating mass is negotiated at a very early stage. At this stage, it is important to take into account technical elements that have a direct impact on the budget and costs.

Development Services

This includes the commissioning of external companies for the complete or partial development of products with the customer's performance features.

Technical Changes

In most cases, engineering changes entail cost increases that have to be negotiated. Usually, the discussions take place between the engineer or technician and an experienced sales manager. In this context, it is advisable to also train technicians and engineers through sustainable training.

Design-to-Cost

Design-to-cost is the complete or partial commissioning of external companies for the development of a component within the framework of a set budget and target price.

Table 4.2 Recommendations for step A-1: analysis phase

Detailed analysis of the negotiating counterparty and one's own position through W-questions
Determining the motives and interests of the other side
Identification of decision makers and influencers (alpha and beta)
Determination of the scope for negotiation according to QKLT plus alpha
Monetary quantification of all negotiating positions
Establishment of an informal and formal informant system
Determination of maximum and minimum targets
Consideration of intercultural aspects

Source: own representation Marc Helmold (2018)

Ideas for Cost Reduction or Improvement

During negotiations it is advisable to include future ideas for product improvement or cost reduction (Helmold 2010).

4.2.5.6 Alpha Targets (α)

Alpha goals are all goals that are not included in the first four categories. Alpha goals can include ethical, innovation or human resources goals. As part of this category, sustainability goals in the area of environment, human rights, working conditions or similar should be mandatorily included.

In summary, in phase A-1 a detailed analysis of the other party and one's own position must be carried out by means of W-questions. In addition, decision-makers and influencers (alpha and beta) of the opposing side must be determined, as these types represent decisive persons for the negotiation breakthrough. Finally, the individual negotiation objectives and sub-objectives are determined, ideally with the establishment of an informant system on the other side (Helmold 2018) (Table 4.2).

4.3 Step 2 (A-2): Selection of Appropriate Strategies and Tactics

4.3.1 Situational and Agile Use of Appropriate Strategies and Tactics

After the analysis and determination of the starting position, strategies and tactics in phase A-2 are the most important means to achieve one's own negotiation goals. The analysis (A-1 Sect. 4.2) and strategies and tactics (A-2) form the basis for building the argument Sect. 4.4 and negotiation Sect. 4.5 in steps A-3 and A-4 (Helmold 2018). In the context of negotiations, strategic and tactical behaviour means concentrating and focusing one's own potential in such a way that one is superior to the negotiating partner in certain respects and thus achieves success in the negotiation. The appropriate negotiation strategies are selected in advance and include an assessment of one's own negotiation motives and goals (Helmold 2018). Strategy selection is then followed by tactical implementation. In addition to the right strategy, tactics are key in negotiation. Tactics are the activities and means of deployment, often including psychological means, used in negotiations to achieve strategic goals (Helmold 2018). Strategic tactics are based on the ignorance of the other party and leads to a concentration of appropriate means for ultimate negotiation success (Helmold 2018). A negotiation strategy is the basis for the step of conducting negotiations and must never be revealed. A strategy always has a longer term focus on how to achieve one's negotiation success (Helmold 2018). Negotiations are conducted by people and hence are always dynamic. Therefore, negotiation patterns and strategies cannot be used statically, but must be used situationally and flexibly depending on the context and frame of reference of the negotiations (Helmold 2018). Contrary to the recommendation of Helmold (Helmold 2018) or Schranner (Schranner 2009) not to disclose strategies, Fisher and Ury propagate disclosure in the Harvard concept in order to be on the same issue level with the negotiation opponent (Fisher and Ury 1981) Sect. 2.2. From a practical point of view, however, strategies and tactics must not be made transparent so as not to give the negotiating partner an advantage in the negotiations and thus not to diminish the negotiation outcome in the long term (Helmold 2018).

According to various authors, negotiation strategies are divided into five categories: Compromise, Pressure, Collaborate, Evade, or Concede (Helmold 2018; Obrien 2016; Schranner 2009). Each strategy has an impact on negotiations, so strategies must be used in a systematic and planned way. Strategies must also be applied in an agile, flexible and dynamic manner (Helmold 2018; Obrien 2016). Figure 4.5 shows strategy recommendations in terms of value and speed of the negotiation outcome, as well as the value of the relationship and the long-term nature of the relationship.

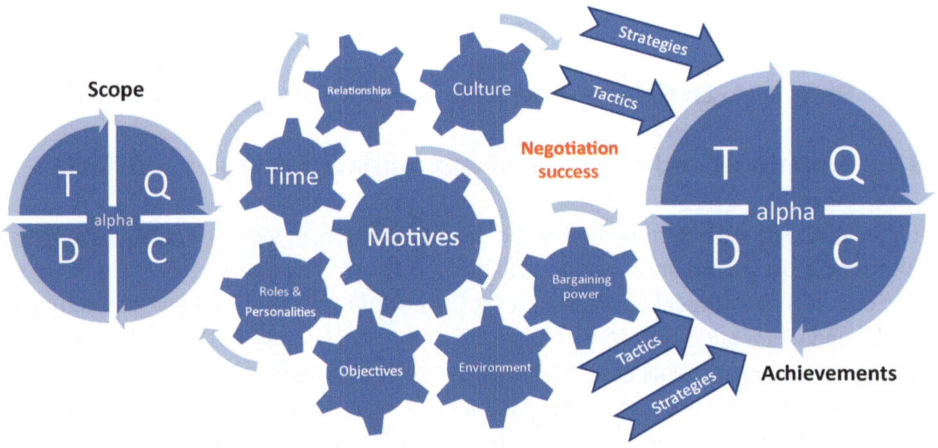

Fig. 4.5 Negotiation strategies in negotiations and the influence on relationship and outcome. (Source: Marc Helmold's own representation)

4.3.2 Strategies in Negotiations

4.3.2.1 Exerting Pressure

Exerting pressure (competitive negotiation; English: pressurize) can lead to the goal in negotiations if it is visible that the negotiating partner only has a limited amount of time or limited alternative actions available for his negotiation outcome (Helmold 2018). One's own time limits (English: deadline) can also lead to a strategy that is competitive. Alpha people in particular prefer a strategy in which they like to show their power. This power is often shown by exerting pressure. So-called warnings or deadlines are most often used as part of this strategy. Pressure usually involves counter-pressure and should only be used selectively in negotiations (Helmold 2018). Moreover, pressure can only be used effectively when negotiating from an appropriate position of power (Helmold 2018). In a cross-cultural context, there should be a thorough assessment of the extent to which competitive negotiation can be used (Helmold 2018). Especially in Asian countries such as the People's Republic of China or Japan, too much pressure can lead to a loss of face on the part of the other side and thus to the immediate termination of negotiations (Helmold 2018). Pressure should therefore always be used in good doses and with foresight in terms of strategic orientation (Helmold 2018). Chapter 7 describes country examples in which it must be assumed that negotiations tend to be competitive, and other examples in which overly competitive negotiations lead to failure Chap. 7.

Phrases for exerting pressure include:

- "Your offer does not fit my expectations, we expect an immediate correction!"
- "Your price is not justified, so I expect a ten percent reduction!"
- "I'll give you until eight o'clock tomorrow, otherwise I'll take the job elsewhere!"
- "Either we agree on Proposal A or Proposal B, otherwise I'm afraid we won't come to an agreement."

4.3.2.2 Collaboration

Collaboration means working together and cooperating on the basis of trust. Collaboration as a negotiation strategy is recommended for long-term negotiating partners who are trusted (Helmold 2018). A negotiation outcome based on trust of both parties should of course always be strived for, but from the author's point of view it requires a relationship that has been established beforehand. In business initiation, an overly personal and collaborative approach should be taken with caution (Helmold 2018). In practice, collaboration can be implemented with a framework or long-term agreement in which the cooperation elements are clearly regulated (see Sect. 4.7.1).

Examples of phrases for collaborative strategies are:

- "To further strengthen our relationship, I make the following proposal XXX."
- "Why don't we cooperate as follows?"
- "In the long run, both partners will benefit if we cooperate in this aspect."
- "Collaboration has the following benefits for both parties."

4.3.2.3 Evasion

Evasion can be a useful variant within negotiation strategies if one is not fully prepared in the respective sub-area or cannot make a decision, as decision-makers from one's own ranks may still have to be consulted (Helmold 2018). Evasion as a strategy can also be used to put the negotiating partner under time pressure and play for time. Especially in multinational corporations, buyers and sellers are usually under time pressure to achieve a negotiated outcome, which means that dodging and playing for time can be an appropriate strategy when it is clear on the other side that the negotiating parties want to make a deal with each other. In an international context, evasion may also involve actions to move the negotiating partner away from the negotiating table, for example by inviting them to dinner or other occasions. Even with competitive negotiating adversaries, it is advisable to evade and avoid the negotiating partner using these tactics and supposed agreement (Helmold 2018). Time pressure, a flight to catch or other important appointments are usually signals of evasion.

Figures of speech can look like this:

- "Shall we discuss the subject at the next hearing?"
- "Why don't we discuss this next time?"
- "I have other important appointments."
- "We can't discuss that topic because I'm pressed for time."
- "I would like to negotiate this at another time as I don't want to miss my plane/train."

4.3.2.4 Yielding

Giving in needs to be practiced. People, especially those with formal or informal power, tend not to want to give in, as Helmold describes from his experience in industry (Helmold 2018). Giving in and making concessions, that is, giving negotiating power and negotiating elements to the negotiating partner, must be practiced in advance. In particular, as part of the script/manuscript in the negotiation strategy, it must be clearly defined which elements can be given up to the negotiating partner in order to achieve a better result for oneself. Especially in international negotiations, a key strategy for success is to make concessions at the point where the negotiating counterparty's greatest interests lie (Helmold 2018). A concession should include a quid pro quo, which could look like this:

- "I understand your reasoning and agree with you."
- "I would be happy to agree to your request, but would expect XXX in return."
- "Your suggestion sounds good, against that I would like to make the following suggestion."
- "I am very happy to accommodate you, but I expect equally concessions on XXX."

4.3.2.5 Making Compromises

A compromise will only be successfully negotiated if both negotiating partners know each other and behave fairly (Helmold 2018). With long-standing negotiating partners, this strategy is effective. In contrast, with new negotiating partners, one should closely observe the strategies of the other side and negotiate situationally (Helmold 2018). With longstanding partnerships, both sides will work towards an amicable solution to preserve the relationship.

In compromise, the law of reciprocity, reciprocity, is central, for example with the following statements:

- "For further cooperation, I propose the following compromise!"
- "Here's what the negotiated outcome has in common for us!"
- "To further cement our relationship, I make the following proposal: XXX."

4.3.3 Tactics in Negotiations

4.3.3.1 Useful Tactics for Practice

Those who want to achieve their goals in negotiations should not rely solely on their experience and arguments (Helmold 2018). In addition to having the right strategy, tactics are key in negotiation (Helmold 2018). Tactics are the means, often psychological, used to achieve the strategic objectives. They involve operational measures to successfully implement the previously selected negotiation strategies (Helmold 2018). Useful tactics from a practical perspective are presented in Table 4.3.

4.3.3.2 Bad Cop, Good Cop

The tactic "bad cop, good cop" originates from police interrogation in the United States of America (Schranner 2009). The tactic originating from the FBI (Federal Bureau of Investigation) has one or more good and one or more bad cops approaching the negotiating partner. The "bad cop" is designed to intimidate or alienate the negotiating partner with demands that are usually too high, overt as well as intended direct attacks and demands. In

Table 4.3 Suitable tactics from a practical point of view

No.	Tactics	Brief description in the context of business negotiations
1.	Bad cop, good cop	The good and the bad buyer or seller
2.	Fixing of a time limit	Setting a "Deadline"
3.	Mirroring the negotiating partner	Show empathy
4.	Appeal to a higher authority	My boss says that ...
5.	Determination of the seating arrangement	Irritating the opposition
6.	Pointing out visions	Appeal to the relationship and long-term
7.	Hugs and flattery	Gifts and compliments
8.	Play for time	Tactics of small steps

Own representation based on Helmold (2018)

some cases, the "bad cop" also issues threats or warnings. The goal of the "bad cop" is to put the negotiating partner under stress. This is the starting point for the "good cop" who now approaches the negotiating partner in an understanding, supportive and cooperative manner in order to build an emotional connection. By offering supposed concessions, which have been previously agreed upon with the "bad cop", the good cop now tries to convince the negotiating partner of a negotiation result which corresponds to his own target corridor. In informal meetings, the negotiating partner is often shown understanding and concessions are made that are not actually concessions (Helmold 2018).

By alternating between provocation, pressure, understanding and empathy, the negotiating partner is to be made to respond to certain negotiating positions and to make concessions himself. The "bad cop" puts the negotiating partner in an emotionally agitated state, the "good cop" offers him the concessions as a way out of a threatening situation. The technique can be quickly detected by trained individuals, so this tactic should be used with caution. On the other hand, this technique can be used from a negotiating position that emphasizes power. For example, a purchasing manager can be the "bad cop" who puts the supplier under stress by making very high or excessive demands. In parallel, he suggests to the supplier that there are several alternative courses of action (competitors and rivals) (Helmold 2018). The buyer who is in regular contact with the supplier and shows understanding for the supplier's concerns and needs within the framework of his relationship is now suitable as a "good policeman". This usually results in a concession from the seller that lies within the target corridor (agreed in advance between the "bad cop", the superior purchasing manager, and the "good cop", the buyer) (Helmold 2018).

4.3.3.3 Setting a Time Limit

Managers who negotiate under time pressure are usually exposed to stress and will make concessions. In a real case in China, the vice president of the purchasing department of a multinational corporation met his Chinese negotiating partner in Beijing (Helmold 2018). It was clear that the purchasing manager would leave after three days, pushing for a quick outcome to the negotiations. However, the Chinese supplier was not impressed. On arrival, the supplier had invited the vice president to dinner as a customer in keeping with his status, and then showed him local sights. The next day and the day after were also packed with activities such as company tours, karaoke events, dinner together or theatre events, so that the actual negotiations were concentrated on the day of departure and put the purchasing manager under time pressure. In this case, the supplier knew the customer's time constraints and was able to extract concessions that way. Time provisions and deadlines can be successful tactics in negotiations because they usually put the negotiator under stress and pressure. Deadlines need to be communicated convincingly, briefly and directly so that the negotiating partner responds. Time limits should not be used too often, otherwise they lose their effect. Deadlines in negotiations are often linked to direct success or failure if an ultimatum is associated with them (English: take it or leave it) (Helmold 2018).

4.3.3.4 Mirroring the Negotiating Partner

Mirroring is an easy but effective technique in negotiations and conflicts. Mirroring is closely related to active listening and is a special negotiation technique. Mirroring can be done by active and analytical listening not only to the language but also to the body language of the negotiating partner. Mirroring means imitating and following the speech or facial expressions of the negotiating partner. Mirroring must not be carried out with emotionally or aggressively acting negotiating partners, as conflicts would escalate here. In negotiations, body language and content can be mirrored (Gramm 2015; Helmold 2018). Body language mirroring is the use of the same or similar gestures and behavior patterns (Helmold 2018). If the opposing negotiator crosses their arms, the other side does the same; if the opposing side opens their arms, this posture is also mirrored and imitated. It is also possible to mirror someone through language, through the speed and pitch of the voice, but also through the content, by first repeating the sentences of the negotiating partner and then responding to his or her demands (Gramm 2015; Helmold 2018). Mirroring makes the negotiator feel comfortable in the conversation and sees him/herself in tune with the other side. What is suggested when mirroring is "we are on the same wavelength". The other side is open to compromise and concession in this situation. You can also mirror someone linguistically by adjusting the level of language. In a company, you will find very different levels of language and communication styles, depending on whether you are in an executive meeting, in the lounge, in the marketing department or with the workers on the shop floor. Former Porsche CEO Wiedeking was a master at moving between worlds. After a board meeting, he would take off his jacket and tie, roll up his shirtsleeves, and head to the production floor, where he would talk to the men there in a casual, down-to-earth way. The workers felt they were on equal footing with their boss and thought to themselves, "You can talk to him." Wiedeking managed to communicate at the highest level of business while keeping in touch with the grassroots (Gramm 2015).

4.3.3.5 Appeal to a Higher Instance

The tactic "appeal to a higher authority" is characterised by the fact that one appeals to a higher authority in negotiations, for example to the management or the superior. In this tactic, maximum demands are made in the direction of the negotiating opponent under the assumption that these are demanded by the higher authority. In most cases, the negotiating opponent will agree to the demands because they do not want to negotiate directly with the supervisor or management. Furthermore, the opposing party will not question the corporate goals demanded by management.

4.3.3.6 Determination of the Seating Arrangement

The seating arrangement of the negotiating participants has an important influence on the climate and course of the negotiation. The possibilities of symmetrical, asymmetrical or chaotic seating arrangements are described in detail in Sect. 4.5.2 and include suitable tactics that are not yet used in Western cultures as they are in Asia or Arab countries, for example (Helmold 2018). Negotiators in Japan or the People's Republic of China often spend ten percent of the preparation time determining the appropriate seating arrangement and environment (Helmold 2018). The seating arrangement is often subject to certain stereotypes in the Central European or Western-influenced cultural area. Mostly, this is oriented towards two basic patterns: Both sides sit frontally opposite each other and the decision-makers position themselves in the middle in each case Sect. 4.5.2. This positioning is generally conveyed as the optimum in negotiation schools. When both sides sit opposite each other, this emphasises the respective fronts and the key players sit to the right or left of the negotiator. One recommendation, particularly applied in Asia, is to break up the system, have the decision maker sit on the outside if necessary, and do so temporarily and dynamically (Helmold 2018). In this way, the decision-maker can take stock of the situation in peace and quiet, as if from a grandstand, and receive feedback from the team. Furthermore, it allows him to assess moods of the opposing side and to break down resistance in a targeted manner (Helmold 2018). If it is recognized that the decision maker has taken the seating arrangement contrary to the stereotypical structure, this can also lead to irritation and stress on the opposite side of the negotiation. This circumstance can be used to gain concessions (Helmold 2018). It is also conceivable to specifically leave a place free for the key decision-makers so that they can be consulted in the event of escalations (Helmold 2018).

4.3.3.7 Identifying Visions

Shared visions also form an elementary tactic in negotiations (Helmold 2018). From a practical point of view, a long-term relationship and partnership makes sense in the most common business relationships, as projects usually extend over a longer period of time and can be linked to follow-up orders (Helmold 2018). In particular, where substitution of suppliers or customers is lengthy and involves high costs, negotiations should aim at a long-term commitment and partnership (Helmold 2018). Letters of intent or longer-term framework agreements can be used as an ideal tool here, even without an indefinite commitment and complete dependence of the negotiating partner.

4.3.3.8 Hugs and Flattery

In order to make the other party to the negotiation appear more sympathetic, a tactic known as "hugs and cajoling" is used (N.N. 2014). This tactic is used to make the other party appear sympathetic. Hugs and flattery can be done in verbal and physical ways. If we as negotiators are praised as "competent, professional and experienced", this is referred to as verbal hugging, whereas physical hugs are associated with gifts or favours.

4.3.3.9 Playing for Time

A tactic often used in Asian and Arab countries is negotiation in small steps and rapprochement (Helmold 2018). In practice, this can go so far that several years can pass between the initiation and the conclusion of the deal. This tactic can be used deliberately when negotiating large negotiation packages and working through them sequentially through partial outcomes. In addition, this strategy is recommended, for example, to use

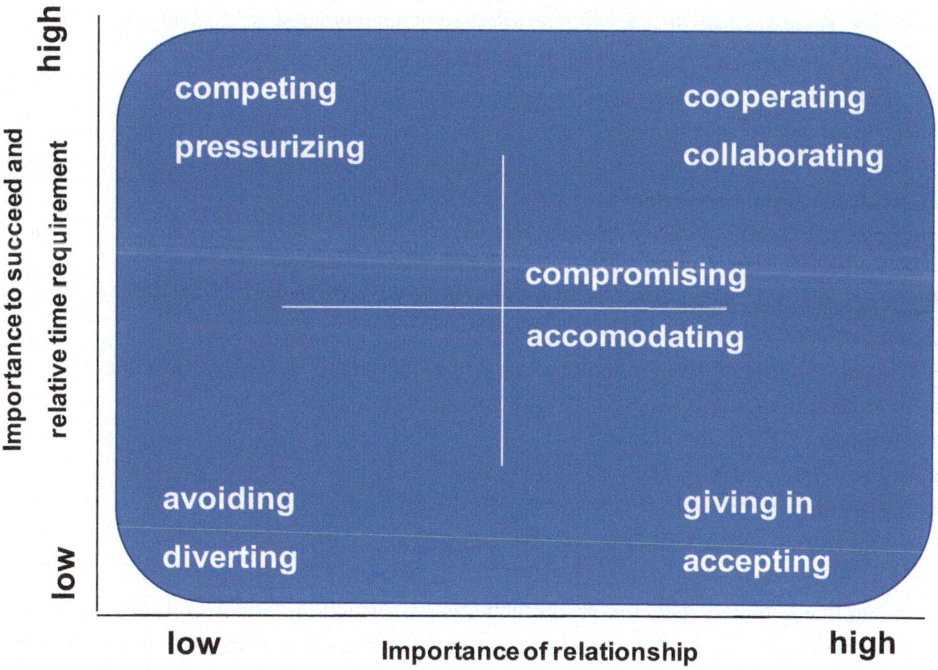

Fig. 4.6 Strategies and the influence on relationship level and time. (Source: Marc Helmold's own representation)

competitors from Asian countries of existing suppliers as so-called benchmarks and in this way to include a new competitor in the list of strategic suppliers through small order packages. Even if the business partners threaten to break off negotiations, they can continue to negotiate with small concessions (Helmold 2018).

Figure 4.6 shows the use of the previously described tactics in relation to the time success and the relationship level. Pointing out shared visions is a very suitable tool for the relationship, but this tactic takes a lot of time. Temporal provisions or exaggerations therefore lead more quickly to negotiation success (Helmold 2018).

4.3.3.10 Beware of Unfair Tactics by the Other Side

Other tactics that the other side can use in negotiations are often described as "dirty tricks" (Abdel-Latif 2015). In particular, tactics such as flattery or even exaggeration are used in the international context (Helmold 2018). False information (fake news) is also on everyone's lips these days and is sometimes spread in order to eliminate competitors (Helmold 2018). According to the author Abdel-Latif, the following tactics are experiencing a renaissance here, so it is important to recognize them:

1. Hugs and flattery—"I like your competence and professionalism."
2. Precedent—"This is what we did last time."

Table 4.4 Recommendations for step A-2: selection of appropriate strategies and tactics

Strategies must be used in an agile and situational manner
The analysis must include appropriate strategies and tactics
Strategies include pressuring, collaborating, evading, and giving in addition to compromising.
Strategies and tactics must be used with consideration of intercultural aspects
Mirroring the negotiating partner is one of several suitable strategies
Strategies and tactics influence the relationship level, strategies/tactics for a quicker negotiation success (exerting pressure) are suitable if the relationship does not play too big a role
Beware of the use of unfair tactics by the other side

3. Untruths and white lies—"The product will be delivered as soon as possible."
4. Exaggerations—"The problem will be solved within a day."
5. Promises—"We'll figure it out."
6. Meet in the middle—"Then we'll meet here."
7. Use of misinformation—"Competitor XXX has quality problems."
8. Intimidation—"This will cost you the contract."

As a summary in step A-2, the recommendations for action shown in Table 4.4 can be derived. Strategies and tactics must be planned in detail as part of the negotiation preparation, as they are of central importance for the success of the negotiation. International specificities have a significant impact on this selection (Helmold 2018). In addition to adequate means, the so-called "dirty tricks" must be identified.

4.4 Step 3 (A-3): Structure and Argumentation of the Negotiations

4.4.1 Shaping Arguments on the Basis of Motives and Interests

The structure of the negotiation argumentation and the definition of an argumentation strategy represent step 3 (A-3) of the negotiation model (Helmold 2018). Important arguments for conducting the negotiation and asserting one's own goals should be proactively identified and defined. The script/manuscript helps to determine and note the most important arguments and counter-arguments of the negotiating opponent for this purpose Fig. 2.3. Table 4.5 shows the most important basic rules for building and shaping powerful arguments (Helmold 2018). The recommendation here is to visualize and act out motives, interests, behaviors, statements, arguments, and counterarguments with priorities or valences (Helmold 2018). Playing through supports the construction of one's own argumentation in a special way (Helmold 2018). With the identification and prioritization, the analysis of the negotiation and arguments takes place from the perspective of the negotiation partner, so that one can recognize the strengths and weaknesses of one's own argumentation in this context (Helmold 2013, 2018; Helmold et al. 2017). A professional

Table 4.5 Argument structure and design

1.	Take an opposing perspective and look at arguments from the opponent's point of view
2.	Identify counterarguments and causal relationships
3.	Use of qualitative and quantitative facts and data
4.	Concise formulation of arguments and prioritization
5.	Preparations by visualizing important facts in international negotiations

Own representation based on Helmold (2018)

negotiation also includes the presentation of causal relationships with all advantages and disadvantages, i.e. cause, effect and benefit (Helmold 2018).

Fact-based backgrounds (Helmold 2018) are helpful for building one's own argumentation (in contrast to non-fact-based false statements, Sect. 4.3.3.9). These can be (as quantitative data) revenue figures, sales figures, operating costs, logistics costs, forecast values or other key performance indicators (KPI) (Helmold 2018). In addition, forecasting trends, articles, predictions, interviews or opinion polls can be used as qualitative tools in a targeted and effective manner (Helmold 2018).

Arguments must always be formulated concisely; in this context, it is advisable to specifically prepare the conciseness and value of statements in the national language with translators or native speakers in international negotiations (Helmold 2018). It is also helpful to preventively visualise important facts, data or arguments in an international context, e.g. on presentation slides, as posters, in tables or on the flipchart (Helmold 2018).

When prioritising arguments, it is important to ensure that the negotiation partner's perspective is made transparent in addition to one's own position (Helmold 2018). Figure 4.7 shows a complementary tool to the manuscript Fig. 2.3, through which it is possible to visually represent arguments, strengths and weaknesses (Helmold 2018).

4.4.2 Focus on Motives and Interests, Not Positions

When designing a suitable negotiation structure, the motives of the negotiating partner are of central importance (Helmold 2018). It is crucial here not to focus on positions, but to focus on motives and interests (Obrien 2016). Motives in this context are defined as "the motive and driving force for a particular behaviour or argumentation in negotiations" (Helmold 2018). Motives describe how important individual negotiation goals are (Helmold 2018) and are divided into primary and secondary motives. Primary motives are innate and vital needs such as hunger, thirst, security or safety. Secondary motives are learned needs and include the need for recognition, achievement, success, power, or wealth (Helmold 2018). Often, in international business initiations, the motives lie in the fact that a supplier from the Far East, for example, aims to enter the German market with the help of the customer, so that his motives lie in the support of quality requirements, in the logistics network and in the creation of further distribution channels. The customer's motives, on the

No.	Negotiation categories Q-C-D-T plus alpha	Priority VERY HIGH	Priority HIGH	Priority MEDIUM	Priority LOW
1.					
2.					
3.					
4.					
5.					
6.					

Fig. 4.7 Priority matrix for negotiations. (Source: Marc Helmold's own representation)

other hand, lie in favouring a low price and generating savings (Sect. 1.7.1) Sect. 1.4 (Dathe and Helmold 2018). In this context, it is of central importance to understand the motivations of both sides and to identify common goals (Helmold 2018).

According to the rule "Talk is silver, silence is gold", you should let the negotiation partner talk first and listen carefully Sect. 4.5.2 (Helmold and Terry 2017a). Once the negotiator has revealed his interests and motives, one can ideally highlight one's own points of view and the benefits for the negotiator. Figure 4.8 shows the elements to focus on to identify motives of the negotiating counterpart. To identify the motives of the negotiation opponent, one should therefore take time and consciously pay attention to statements, arguments, interests and behaviour (Helmold 2018).

Summarizing in step A-3, the significant recommendations for the structure of the negotiation shown in Table 4.6 can be derived. As an elementary step, the construction of the negotiation argumentation is a fundamental element before the actual conduct of the negotiation in step A-4, Sect. 4.5 (Helmold 2018). In addition to identifying the motives of the other party, statements, behavior, or interests must be considered when defining arguments and counterarguments (Helmold 2018). Qualitative and quantitative data are the framework of a fact-based negotiation argument. Finally, all content should be considered from the perspective of the other side in order to identify weaknesses (Helmold 2018).

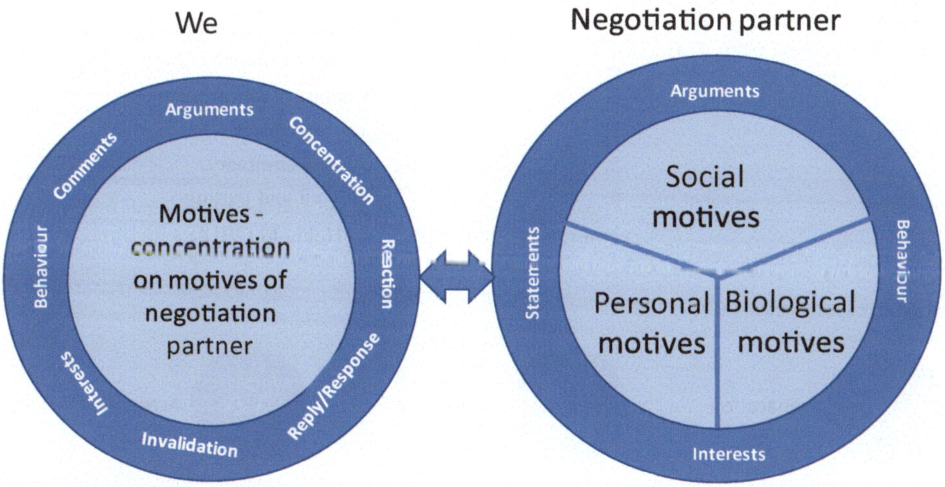

Fig. 4.8 Focusing on motives of the negotiating opponent. (Source: Marc Helmold's own representation)

Table 4.6 Recommendations for step A-3: structure of the argumentation

Identification of motives and interests of the opposing sides
Presentation of the arguments and counter-arguments
Prioritization of arguments and counterarguments
Consideration of the behaviour of the negotiating partner
Use of quantitative and qualitative data
Playing through arguments and counter-arguments
Formulate arguments concisely and clearly
Consideration of the correct and target-oriented formulation of arguments in international negotiations through the involvement of a native speaker and expert
Consideration of one's own arguments from the perspective of the negotiating partner
Weak point analysis of the own argumentation

4.5 Step 4 (A-4): Conducting the Negotiations (Negotiation Management)

4.5.1 Partial Phases of the Negotiation Process

Negotiations need to be systematically planned and executed with a well-prepared agenda (Obrien 2016). A negotiation basically takes place in six sub-phases, as Table 4.7 shows (Helmold 2018).

Table 4.7 Subphases of the negotiation process (step A-4)

1.	Negotiation preparation
2.	Room layout and seating arrangements
3.	Welcome and introduction
4.	Core negotiation
5.	End and summary
6.	Farewell and parting

Own representation based on Helmold (2018)

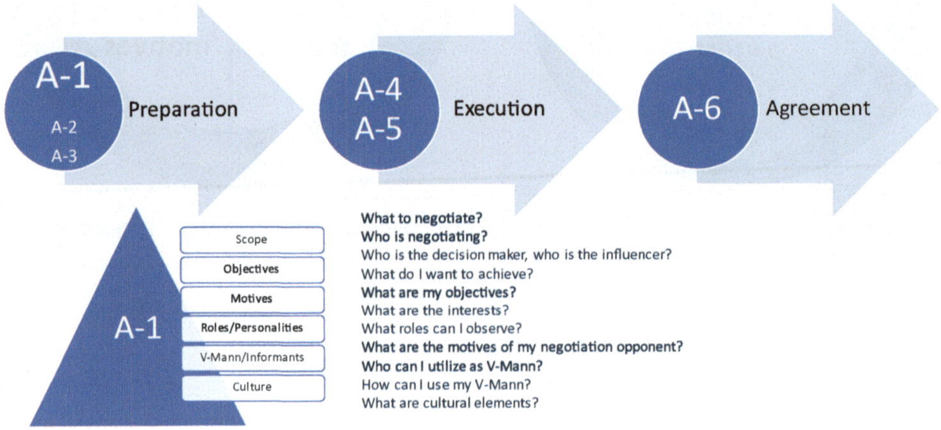

Fig. 4.9 Negotiation process and sub-phases within negotiation management (A-4). (Source: Marc Helmold's own representation)

Figure 4.9 shows the most important aspects in the individual sub-phases. In phase 1, negotiation preparation, the agenda, problem description, background, data, info, precedents, legal situation, statistics, pre-negotiation, information about negotiating partners, taboo topics, positive previous experiences, animosities and one's own interests, goals and motives must be coordinated internally (Obrien 2016; Helmold 2018). The goal of this phase is thorough preparation, coordination with all departments and interest groups (stakeholders), and harmonization of goals and demands within one's own negotiating side (Obrien 2016). For this purpose, the negotiation script Fig. 2.3 and supplementary tools can be ideally used, which are described in detail in Chap. 5. Similarly, the respective objectives and sub-objectives need to be categorised and weighted in a priority matrix Fig. 4.7. Scenarios can also be presented in case it may not be possible to agree on sub-objectives (Obrien 2016). In addition to negotiation points, roles need to be allocated, e.g. negotiator, facilitator, use of external advisors, observer and minute taker. It is also advisable to talk about tactics and strategies, for example assigning roles such as 'good cop, bad cop' (Obrien 2016, Helmold 2018).

Phase 2 comprises the determination of the negotiation room as well as the seating arrangement. In Western countries, less attention is paid to the selection of the meeting room and the location than in Asian or Arab countries (Obrien 2016; Helmold 2018). Section 4.5.3 describes key elements in this phase. In addition to one's own seating arrangement, one can also tactically influence the seating arrangement of the other side by trying to place influencers on the other side (Obrien 2016; Helmold 2018).

Phase 3 focuses on the greeting. Especially in an international environment, this phase can take several minutes. All participants should have business cards within reach to introduce themselves. Especially in highly hierarchical countries, attention to position and status is an important element in introductions (Helmold 2018) Sect. 1.6.1.1.

In phase 4, the actual core negotiation takes place. This part should be clearly structured by an agenda and proceed systematically (Helmold 2018).

After the discussion of all negotiation points, the results and agreements should be summarized. The minutes should be signed by both parties and also highlight differences of opinion and dissent (Helmold 2018).

As the last and 6th phase, the farewell is important. In Asian countries, for example, the negotiating counterparty may remain standing outside the building, waving goodbye, until one is out of sight (Helmold 2018).

4.5.2 General Rules for Successful Negotiations

For the actual negotiation, there are numerous references to negotiation rules by various authors (Obrien 2016; Helmold 2018; Schranner 2009, 2018). The A-6 concept recommends the following rules of conduct for the negotiation, which have proven themselves in practice (Helmold 2018):

- Focus your argument on a target corridor rather than a static target
- Show respect for the other party in the negotiation
- Pay attention to intercultural aspects in all phases of negotiations
- Show attention to the negotiating counterparty
- Listen actively and identify the motives of the negotiating partner
- Speak your arguments convincingly
- Convince with easily emotional language
- Let the negotiating partner speak first, only then reply
- If you have nothing to say, don't talk.
- Do not immediately respond to statements made by the negotiating opponent
- State your strongest argument first
- Try to understand and speak the language of your negotiating partner
- Prioritize your arguments
- Consider the arguments also from the point of view of the other side
- Emphasize the importance of your arguments, not the correctness of them
- Refute the arguments of the other side
- Focus on weak points in the argumentation of the negotiating side

- Focus on the weakest argument of the negotiating partner
- Make concessions only where it is of benefit
- Demand consideration for concessions

4.5.3 Power of the Place of Negotiation

The room layout and seating arrangement have an important influence on the climate of negotiations. The room layout as well as the external conditions such as seating arrangements, arrangement of chairs, lighting conditions, climatic conditions, drinks or not, hospitality or not can have a lasting negative or positive influence on negotiations (Obrien 2016; Helmold 2018). Through appropriate room size, climatic conditions, lighting conditions, drinks or snacks, one can create a positive basic attitude and show the negotiating partner that one values good relations and a harmonious atmosphere. Conversely, so-called "dirty tricks" such as a room that is too small, too cool or too hot can create an uncomfortable negotiation climate (Helmold 2018). The negotiating partner feels uncomfortable and wants nothing more than to leave the negotiating venue. This makes him make ill-considered concessions (Helmold 2018).

As a golden rule, the negotiator should always sit near the door as Figs. 4.10, 4.11 and 4.12 show. This leads to a comfortable feeling as he can theoretically leave the room at any time (Helmold 2018). In the symmetrical seating arrangement, decision makers sit opposite each other (Fig. 4.10), whereas in the asymmetrical seating arrangement, decision makers do not sit opposite each other (Fig. 4.11). If the seating arrangement is intentionally designed in such a way that own employees sit in the rows of the negotiation opponent, this is called chaotic seating arrangement. This can be used to influence the other side (Fig. 4.12).

4.5.4 Question Forms and Techniques

4.5.4.1 Use and Application of Questioning Techniques

Experts in negotiation, in addition to having strong rhetorical skills, can listen actively and analytically to the negotiating partner with empathy Sect. 1.2 (Helmold 2018). Negotiations must always be built on empathy and be analytical. Empathy is the ability and willingness to recognize and understand sensations, thought processes, opinions, motives, personality traits, character traits or cross-cultural characteristics of the negotiation opponent and to direct his or her activities accordingly (Helmold 2018). The questioning techniques presented in Table 4.8 support empathic behaviour (Helmold 2018).

In the national and international context, questions and the questioning techniques described in Table 4.8 serve to identify motives and intentions (Helmold 2018). Furthermore, questions can also be used to defend against attacks, to invalidate arguments or as a

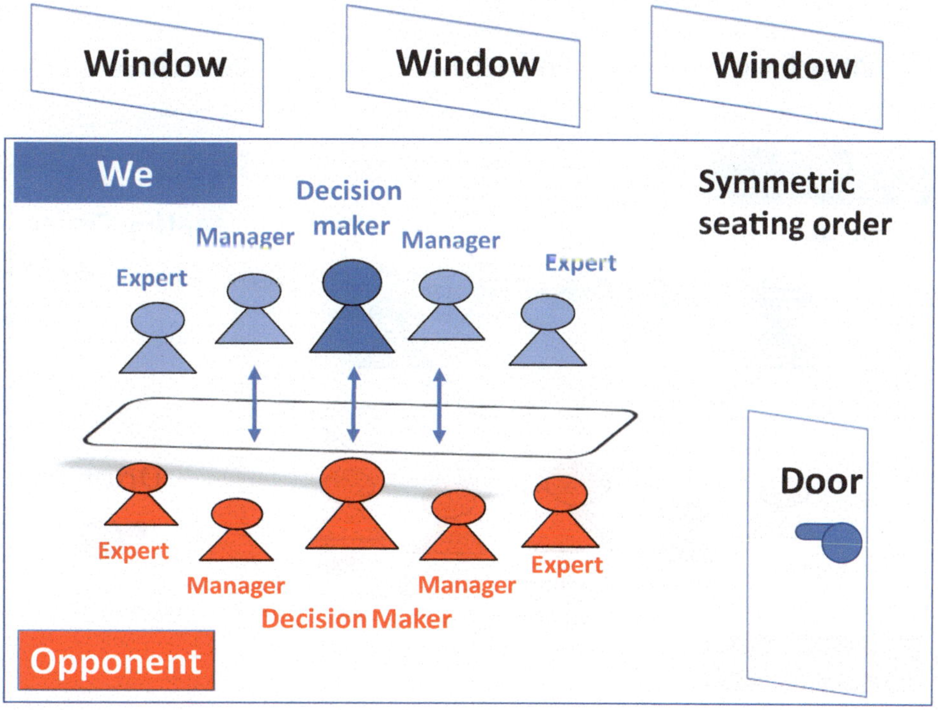

Fig. 4.10 Symmetrical seating arrangement. (Source: Marc Helmold's own representation)

deceptive manoeuvre (Helmold 2018). Lastly, in business negotiations, one can also escape conversation traps and detect the interest of sellers or buyers (Obrien 2016). Using the following examples, negotiators can succeed in making sales and purchasing conversations more effective and targeted. Possible questions can be defined in this context within the preparation (Obrien 2016).

4.5.4.2 Open Questions

Open questions can basically be answered by your counterpart in numerous ways. These questions have a conversation-opening effect and serve to obtain important information from the other party in the negotiation (Obrien 2016). Open-ended questions are designed to draw out the negotiating partner. Examples of open-ended questions in negotiations are described in Table 4.9. They are usually used at the beginning of negotiations (Obrien 2016).

4.5.4.3 Closed Questions

Closed questions are characterised by the fact that there are only two possible answers: the affirmative answer (yes) or the negative answer (no). Closed questions usually have a manipulative effect on the negotiating partner and can be used in such a way that the

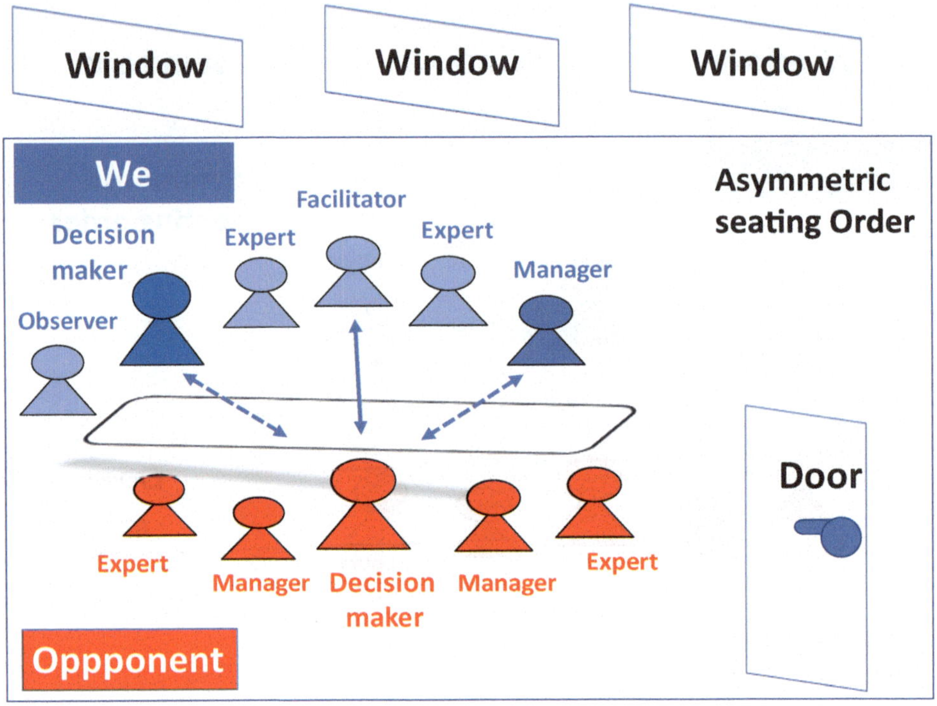

Fig. 4.11 Asymmetrical seating arrangement. (Source: Marc Helmold's own representation)

negotiating partner has to answer the question with a "yes" or "no", as Table 4.10 shows. This questioning technique can also be used to obtain specific information (Obrien 2016).

4.5.4.4 Alternative Questions

With alternative questions, there are two different possibilities, as Table 4.11 shows with examples. This questioning technique is also used for manipulation and can distract the negotiating partner, e.g.: "Do you want to purchase product A or product B?" Alternative questions are used to focus the opposing negotiating side specifically on two alternatives we want, so that other options are excluded (Obrien 2016).

4.5.4.5 Suggestive Questions

Suggestive questions are characterised by the fact that the negotiating partner only has to agree to a certain proposal, as shown in Table 4.12 with examples. With suggestive questions, negotiation experts succeed in subtly steering and manipulating the other party in their own direction (Obrien 2016). It is crucial that this questioning technique is only used in doses so that the other party does not feel too manipulated.

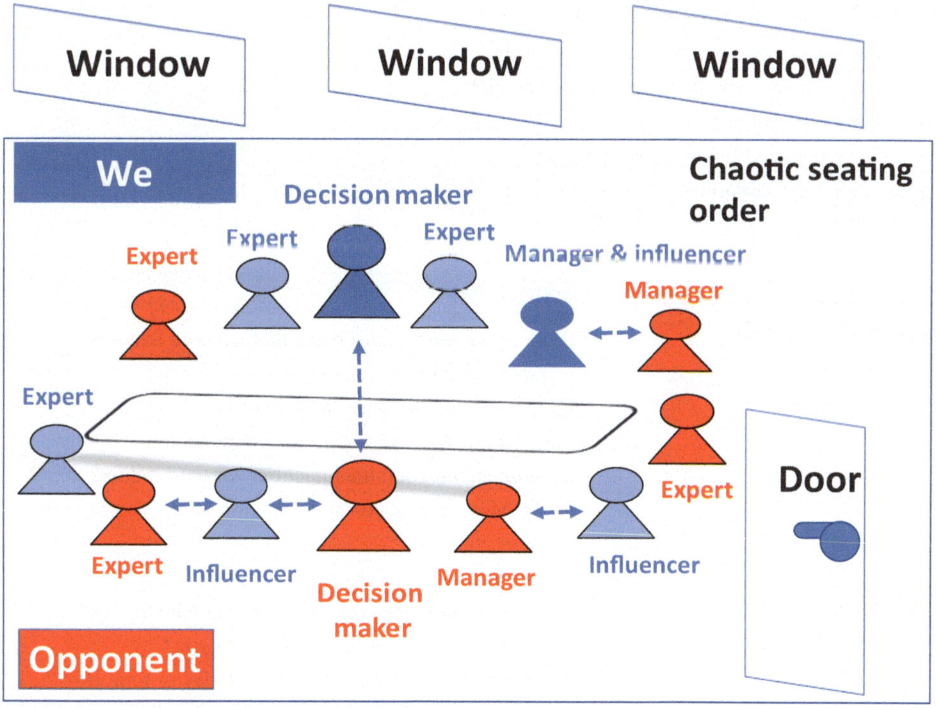

Fig. 4.12 Chaotic seating arrangement. (Source: Marc Helmold's own representation)

Table 4.8 Forms and techniques of questioning in negotiations

Question forms	Question approach	Question behaviour	Question effect
Closed questions	Do you agree that . . .?	Dominant	Constricting
Trick questions	Wasn't it just your opinion that . . .?	Suspicious	Disrupting the negotiating climate
Leading questions	It is your opinion that . . .?	Sync and corrected by dr.jackson for	Controlling from the outside
Open questions	What do you say . . .?	Partnership	Liberating
Reflective questions	If I understand correctly, you mean that . . .?	Trusting	Improving the negotiating climate
Directing questions	So you're saying that. . .?	Self-determination initiating	Controlling from the inside

Own representation based on Helmold (2018)

Table 4.9 Examples of open questions

What important criteria do you envision for the business?
What are your asking prices to get us to closing?
What other competitors are there that are in the bidding process?
When do you intend to award the contract?
What criteria are important to you in the manufacture of the product so that we can meet your requirements?

Table 4.10 Examples of closed questions

Would you like to have these performance features?
Is quality important to you?
Would you like to place the order today?
Are you the decision maker for the project?
Do you need a good manufacturer for the product?
Is Mr. Meier the responsible decision maker for the order?

Table 4.11 Examples of alternative questions

Do you want this or that performance feature?
Is quality or price more important to you?
Would you like to place the order today or tomorrow?
Are you or Mr. Meier the decision maker for the project?
Do you want to buy the red or blue car?

Table 4.12 Examples of suggestive questions

Surely quality is more important to you than just price?
Do you also want a long-term partnership?
Are you sure you want this feature?
It must also be important to you that we can significantly increase your potential with this service?
Surely you want to say goodbye to the business with the best result?

Table 4.13 Examples of stimulation and motivation questions

Are you in charge of this great organization?
Did you ensure the immediate and first-class implementation of the negotiation result?
Have you taken care of the professional web appearance?
Did you provide for the great exhibition?
Did you pick out that great restaurant?

Table 4.14 Examples of rhetoric questions

Can you imagine how we can continue to successfully expand our long-term partnership?
Do you have any idea how satisfied your customers are when they use our product?
Can you imagine how efficiently your business processes run when you use our product?

Table 4.15 Examples of confirmation questions

Am I correct in assuming that your purchase decision is based on the TCO principle and includes all costs?
Do I understand you correctly that you want to purchase the best quality product?
If I understand you correctly, you want a car with low fuel consumption so that the follow-up costs for you are as low as possible and calculable?
If I understand you correctly, the goods should be available the very next day, because after all your customers expect you to be able to pick up products within 24 h?

4.5.4.6 Stimulation and Motivation Issues

Stimulus and motivational questions are used to create a positive mood. Stimulus questions are often used in an international context in the form of flattery Sect. 4.3.3.8. Examples are: "How do you know our country so well?" or "Why do you know our local customs and language so well?". Stimulus questions should be asked using subliminal and subtle praise to put the negotiator in a positive mood. Particularly with egocentrics and alpha people, it is recommended Sect. 4.2.2.1 to include stimulus questions at intervals to appeal to their ego (Obrien 2016). Table 4.13 shows examples of stimulation and motivation questions.

4.5.4.7 Rhetorical Questions

Rhetorical questions, as shown in Table 4.14, target the emotional needs of the negotiating partners and stimulate them to reflect and think along. The other side is encouraged to identify arguments themselves and to see proposals as positive. The addition of figurative or metaphorical examples also significantly increases the credibility of the proposal (Obrien 2016). Thus, this questioning technique represents a key to get to the emotional needs of negotiators and thus generate motivation to a great extent. According to studies, 80% of our purchasing decisions are made at the emotional level (Obrien 2016).

4.5.4.8 Confirmation Questions

Confirmation questions signal connection and emotional closeness to the negotiating partner (Obrien 2016). These show the negotiating counterparty that their fears, concerns and needs are understood through active listening. Confirmation questions are also called mirroring questions and can be used effectively to create a personal bond with the negotiator Sect. 4.3.3.4 (Obrien 2016). Confirmation questions will be answered by the other party with a clear affirmation ("Yes, that's true!"). Table 4.15 shows examples of confirmation questions.

Table 4.16 Examples of indirect questions

Intended information	Indirect question
Prospects of winning the contract	I assume that there are two competitors who can win the bid?
Degree of internationalization of the supplier and experience with foreign customers	I think you already have many international clients?
Target price corridor and value of the total budget for the current project	In the last big project you had a budget of EUR 1 million?

Own representation based on Helmold (2018)

4.5.4.9 Indirect Questions

The use of indirect questions is recommended when direct questions are inappropriate (Obrien 2016). In order to obtain relevant and useful information, the question is ostensibly asked about another topic. However, this question is phrased in such a way that the answer provides information about the actual question. Table 4.16 shows examples of indirect questions.

4.5.5 Discussion Types

In addition to the use of questioning techniques, it is purposeful to respond to personality types in a meaningful and effective way. Table 4.17 shows different discussion types and the recommended behaviour. A mixture or combination of discussion types is often found in practice.

In summary, it can be stated that negotiation management (step A-4) is the core of every negotiation and of the A-6 negotiation concept. An essential part in this context is the use of the described tools such as the script/manuscript or the priority matrix. The environment and the selection of the negotiation venue are an important part of the negotiation concept. On the basis of steps A-1 to A-3, questioning techniques can be used in a targeted and meaningful way and recommendations for action can be applied successfully for certain types of discussion (Table 4.18). Finally, the most important recommendations for action are summarised in Table 4.19 (Table 4.18).

Table 4.17 Discussion types and typologies in negotiations

Typology	Description for the conduct of negotiations	Recommended behaviour
The experienced	Experienced and experienced	Respond and appeal to experience
The Clever Man	Arrogant and dominant	Appeal to the ego with stimulation questions
The Litigious Man	Destructive criticism	Remain objective and calm; encourage constructive behaviour
The Exalted	Waiting to trick someone	Give few direct answers; let opponents speak
The All-Knowing	Knows everything better	Ask closed questions
The loquacious man	Talking for the sake of talking	Interrupt tactfully; agree on speaking times
The Sluggard	Uninterested and bored	Asking directly for opinions; enabling a sense of achievement
The Blocker	Sabotaging and crippling	Remain objective; direct address; break off negotiation; exclude from negotiation
The reticent one	Silent and withdrawn	Engage and ask easy and closed questions

Own representation based on Helmold (2018) and PMH (2018)

Table 4.18 Recommendations for step A-4: conduct negotiations

Focusing the argumentation on a target corridor
Respectful interaction with each other
Attention and active listening
Selection of the appropriate place of negotiation
Concise formulation of arguments
Prioritization of arguments
Negotiating partner speaks first, reply only if useful
Consideration of one's own arguments from the opponent's point of view
Concentration on weak points in the argumentation of the other side
Concessions only with quid pro quo
Consideration of questioning techniques and discussion types

Table 4.19 Recommendations for breaking resistance

Recognizing and understanding resistance
Breaking down resistance with fact-based arguments
Resistance can also be broken by warnings
Giving in and making concessions where my priorities don't lie
Change the place of negotiations in case of resistance
Distractions can be helpful in the face of resistance

4.6 Step 5 (A-5): Defending Counter-Arguments and Fighting Resistance

4.6.1 Open and Hidden Resistance

4.6.1.1 Definition of Terms

Resistance in negotiations is defined as the rejection, oppositional action or opposition with regard to certain negotiation points by the negotiation opponents (following Helmold and Terry 2016; Hilsenbeck 2004) Resistance usually arises from opposing opinions, positions and motives (Schranner 2015). It is characterized in negotiations by being exercised consciously or unconsciously by negotiation opponents (Hilsenbeck 2004; PMH 2018). Resistance is encountered in negotiations in a wide variety of verbal or non-verbal forms, which in most cases the acting persons are not aware of. In negotiations, resistance is expressed through speech (verbal) or through gestures or facial expressions (nonverbal, i.e. behaviour or facial expression) Chap. 6. Crucial in this context is the recognition of rejections or contrary positions by the negotiation opponent and the identification of motives to invalidate or break the resistance (Helmold and Terry 2016; Hilsenbeck 2004; Schranner 2015). There are multiple reasons for resistance, as described by psychologist Werner Berner, for example (adapted from Berner 2016; Hilsenbeck 2004):

- Fears on the part of the negotiating party if proposals are seen as threatening
- Lack of mandates or restrictions in individual negotiating positions
- Resistance from interest groups on the other side of the negotiations
- vested interests of the negotiating party
- Tactical considerations of the other side, if other negotiation points are to be won thereby
- Revenge or retaliation when negotiators try to thwart plans
- Outstanding invoices due to previous negotiations
- Previous experience or experience from other negotiations

4.6.1.2 Open Resistance

Open resistance is characterised by the fact that it is consciously exercised by the opponents in the negotiation and that they also associate an objective with it. Open resistance is relatively easy to recognise, as manifestations and behaviours are openly revealed:

- Open contradiction (examples: "I disagree . . .")
- Open rejection (example: "I cannot agree with your proposal . . .")
- Open intervention (example: "I do not like your proposal. I therefore suggest that . . .")
- Rejection by obvious shaking of the head
- Rejection through gestures with the arms or with the index finger

Normally, open resistance has a rational cause that can be discussed with those affected and that all parties have an interest in overcoming (Hilsenbeck 2004). This form of resistance is usually constructive, so that dealing with open resistance is possible. Breaking down resistance or invalidating and mitigating it through fact-based argumentation can be an appropriate strategy here (Helmold and Terry 2016; Hilsenbeck 2004; Schranner 2015). In this way, the energy that the resisters have invested in their resistance can be channelled to achieve the negotiation goal.

4.6.1.3 Covert Resistance

Dealing with covert or latent resistance is much more difficult. In this form of resistance, the persons exercising resistance usually have no interest in being recognised (Hilsenbeck 2004) Sect. 6.3.5. For personal or tactical reasons, they act from hiding or from the 2nd row. Their interests are usually of a destructive nature, i.e. they want to prevent something from happening without being recognised as the perpetrators. In many cases, paradoxically, the resisters are not even aware that they are resisting. This makes dealing with this form of resistance even more difficult (Volk 2018). If covert resistance is not recognized in time, the entire outcome of the negotiation may possibly be at stake. Covert resistance in negotiations can manifest itself in the following ways:

- Comments and statements with qualifications (example: "I understand your point of view, but . . .").
- The absence of important decision-makers (alpha types) or influential persons (beta types)
- Appearing too late in negotiations of important decision makers (alpha types) or influencing persons (beta types)
- The permanent postponement of negotiations due to alleged scheduling difficulties
- Non-verbal signals of resistance such as mental absence or disinterest Sect. 6.3.2
- The demand for perfect solutions
- The requirement that the negotiating opponent move first
- The extensive and lengthy consideration and discussion of relatively unimportant special cases

- Agreement in principle with simultaneous registration of reservations to be clarified at a later date

4.6.1.4 Dealing with Resistance

Resistance must be recognized in negotiations, and it is also essential to question the motives of the resistance. In the case of open and rational resistance, counter-arguments and the reformulation of one's own goals can lead to invalidating the resistance and achieving a negotiation result. For issues that do not play a key role in the negotiation, resistance can also be ignored and the demands of the negotiating adversary addressed or addressed at a later time. If the resistance cannot be resolved, and it is on key issues in the negotiations, there is unlikely to be a successful negotiation. Unconscious or hidden resistance is more difficult to detect, as the examples in Sect. 4.6.1.3 show:

- Recognize resistance
- Evaluate resistance
- rebut resistance
- break resistance

It is advisable to listen to the other side and understand the motives as soon as you recognize resistance (Volk 2018). A change of location or discussion at lunch or in the evening over a shared meal can lead to the other side opening up and articulating the motives and reasons for resistance directly or indirectly. Table 4.19 shows how resistance can be successfully broken through warnings and fact-based arguments.

4.6.2 Defence Against Counter-Arguments

Counter-arguments of the negotiating partners can be refuted by facts. If their demands do not correspond to one's own priorities, one can make concessions here in order to be able to demand concessions from the other side in significant aspects. In addition, when defending and invalidating counter-arguments, one's own arguments can be made even clearer by using certain conjunctions or linguistic formulations and connecting them through the counter-arguments as well as one's own arguments, for example:

- You are right on some points, but on reflection ...
- I understand your reasoning, yet ...
- I understand your point, however ...
- Even if you are of the opinion that ..., I am still of the opinion ...
- Of course it is true that ..., but ...
- Certainly it's true ..., yet I mean ...
- I admit that, ... but in my opinion ...
- It is true that ..., however ...

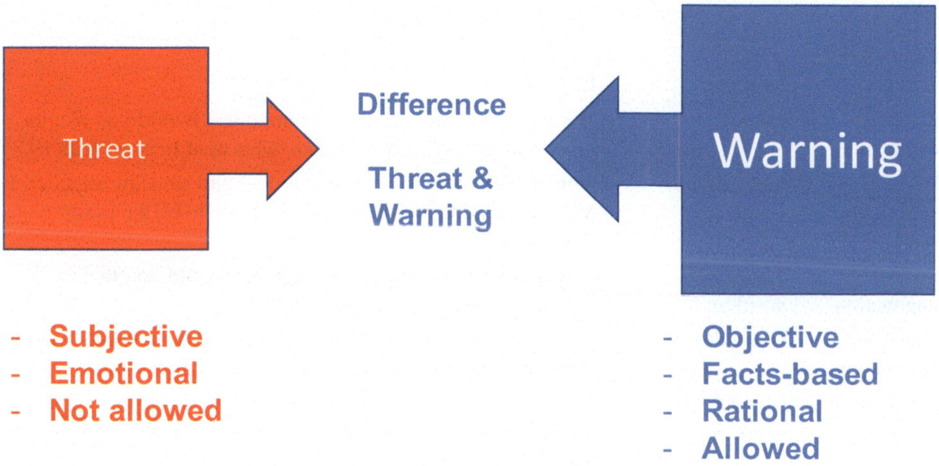

Fig. 4.13 Warnings and threats. (Source: Marc Helmold 2018, based on Schranner 2009)

In addition to defending counterarguments by identifying weaknesses in the argumentation, a warning can be a useful tool for defending counterarguments (Fig. 4.13). Warnings are fact-based and rational signals and arguments for a rejection of mostly exaggerated or unacceptable positions of the negotiating counterparty, instead of issuing threats (Schranner 2015).

According to Schranner, warnings take place in the mind of the negotiating opponent and make him understand what the consequences of failure on individual points or the overall negotiation may mean (Schranner 2015). If an agreement is not reached, the other side can imagine what will happen as a horror scenario, for example by asking: "What will happen if we don't reach an agreement?" If it is felt that the negotiator is not aware of the strength of his own position, he can be asked, "What do you think I will do if we cannot reach agreement now?" In doing so, the questions must be "open-ended." The more openly the question is phrased, the more the negotiating partner will deviate from his position. However, it is important to emphasize the desire for a joint solution at the same time. Another variant in such a situation is the question: "What should I do according to your advice?" Here, the negotiating partner is additionally acknowledged in his position because he is asked for advice and it is signalled that his expertise and knowledge are trusted. At the same time, it's the ideal introduction to a fluid conversation because his mind is "racing" again. But what to do if the warning is ignored? Because the other person may not believe the warning. Therefore, the credibility of a warning should always be demonstrated to him pictorially. In this way, it is demonstrated what one intends to do without actually doing it (Schranner 2015).

If after a warning the negotiating partner still refuses to relent, then it becomes important to act and put the warning into practice. The counterpart must understand in no uncertain terms that he cannot win unilaterally and that it is indeed in his interest to return to the

Table 4.20 Positive and negative conduct of negotiations

Type of negotiation	Subject	Example
Positive negotiation	Growth opportunities	We have many new projects coming up. Would you like to grow with us? We need partners who want to grow with us.
Positive negotiation	Innovations	You are our most innovative supplier and strategic supplier. I am convinced that you want to continue to be the most innovative supplier in your field.
Positive negotiation	The pole position	You are our preferred No. 1 supplier. Would you like to continue to occupy the pole position?
Negative negotiation	Difficult times	We are in difficult times. The financial situation is bad. Market share is shrinking. The competition is getting stronger.
Negative negotiation	Changing the landscape	The competitive situation and market landscape have changed fundamentally. Are you aware of this fact? What are you doing to continue to survive in the market?
Negative negotiation	Significant market changes	We are confronted with a new competitive situation. Supply and demand have changed. Numerous new suppliers want to enter the market. What are you doing to remain competitive?

Own representation based on Helmold (2018)

negotiating table. The goal, then, is to return to a satisfactory agreement. Such means should be used only until one's goal is achieved—not to win. For every action leads to a reaction. The more aggressive one's methods are, the more bitterly the negotiating partner reacts. The result is that the very resistance that was supposed to be overcome hardens. In this situation, too, the following applies: The negotiating partner should not be cornered. A cornered opponent is dangerous. He will act rashly and irrationally. He should always be left with a way out, a bridge to cross. It shows professionalism to build him a "golden bridge". And if the negotiating partner does not cross the offered bridge? Then it's time to make good on the warning and follow through with all the announced actions. Whoever backs out now will lose face and make himself ridiculous and untrustworthy (Schranner 2015).

4.6.3 Positive and Negative Negotiation to Ward Off Resistance

The type of negotiation leadership must be applied situationally and flexibly within Dr. Marc Helmold's concept of negotiation (Helmold 2018). Negotiation leadership can be consciously implemented in a positive or negative way (Helmold 2018). Table 4.20 shows examples of positive and negative types of negotiation leadership that are key within Step A-5 (Helmold 2018). The topics help the reader to practically apply them in the respective negotiation situations (Helmold 2018).

4.6.4 Showing Power Through Competence

Formal and informal power are important elements in negotiations (Helmold and Terry 2016; Schranner 2009). **Formally** given positional **power** is mainly based on hierarchical structures and hierarchical levels, which are usually represented in an organizational chart (abbreviation: organigram), while **informal power is** not necessarily based on this (Grochowiak 2015). The formal organizational structure is the result of a structured and systematic hierarchy that the management considers appropriate. Basic elements of the organizational structure are jobs, which are grouped into groups and departments as subsystems, and reporting lines. The cooperation between the subsystems is defined by the process organization, which regulates the workflows. The organizational chart is a graphical representation of the organizational structure that shows communication paths and processes. In addition to formal power, there are also power structures that are not immediately visible, which are based on informal circumstances. Often, individuals are granted special authority by the members of a group because of their personal characteristics (e.g. high level of professional competence, many years of collaboration, extensive experience). An informal leader can have an integrating and stabilizing effect. However, conflicts with the superior (the formal leader) can also arise (Grochowiak 2015).

4.6.5 Informal Power and Organisational Structures

In corporate and negotiation practice, however, it often turns out that the officially defined structure is usually not identical to the actual structure (Grochowiak 2015). In addition to the formal company organization, informal or informal phenomena arise as a result of unplanned human behavior. This is caused by individual needs and perceptions of employees (Helmold 2018). They manifest themselves as follows:

- In informal interest groups
- In informal communication
- In informal processes
- In informal organisational structures
- In informal norms and
- In informal leaders

Finally, Sect. 4.6 (step A-5) offers the following recommendations for breaking down resistance. If the formal and informal power structure is understood, it forms the starting point for recognising and overriding resistance. Formal power structures are made up of organizational and operational structures. Informal power structures are more likely to arise from charismatic leaders and their experience, knowledge or affiliation with a group. Informal leaders can be identified by the V-man and used to achieve their own goals (Helmold 2018). If the organizational structure and procedures are known, positive or

Table 4.21 Recommendations for step A-5: overriding resistors

Understanding formal and informal power structures
Formal power structures: Recognizing the organizational structure and reporting lines by understanding the organizational structure and process organization (organizational charts, process descriptions)
Informal power structures: use of the liaison person (V-Mann) to understand power relations (formal and informal)
Identify formal leaders and their influencers
Understanding informal leaders, norms and procedures
Identify and possibly use potential critics and their arguments for own purposes
Warn, do not threaten—put warning into action if negotiator does not give up resistance
Apply techniques of positive and negative negotiation

negative negotiation guidance can be used to achieve negotiation success (Helmold 2018). If warnings are not taken seriously by the other party, the warning should always be put into action (Helmold 2018). Table 4.21 shows the final recommendations for step A-5 in Dr. Marc Helmold's negotiation concept (Helmold 2018).

4.7 Step 6 (A-6): Shaping the Results of Negotiations and Respecting Agreements

4.7.1 Recording and Ratification of Agreements

Step A-6 is the last element in Dr. Marc Helmold's negotiation concept and is of central importance with the drafting of the contract (Helmold 2018). Once an agreement has been reached, both sides in the negotiation should record all important points in writing in a protocol and have these signed by their interlocutor. It is also advisable to draw up an action plan with responsibilities and deadlines, which both negotiating sides can use to see whether the agreed activities are being adhered to. The concretization of the negotiation results is a fundamental step to avoid intentional or unintentional misinterpretations (Helmold 2018). It is advisable here to verbally summarize a summary of all results and agreements at the end of the negotiations (Schranner 2009; Helmold 2018).

After negotiations, the draft contract should ideally already be completed, which contains key points and milestones. Likewise, a mutual pre-ratification can be carried out, which is then confirmed by the legal department (Helmold 2010).

When formulating agreements, care should be taken to ensure that no or few advance payments have to be made (Schranner 2009).

Furthermore, in the case of international negotiations, it is appropriate to hold a ceremony to officially ratify the treaties. With customers, employees and other stakeholders present, this can be ideally used for marketing purposes and as a motivator within one's own company (Helmold 2018). Asian companies also very often use these occasions to issue press releases (Helmold and Terry 2017a). In addition to the celebrations, negotiators should thank the negotiating team, thereby acknowledging them.

4.7.2 Design of Agreements in the International Context

4.7.2.1 Central Elements in International Legal Transactions

Due to the increasing internationality of commercial transactions through sales or procurement, international legal transactions are also gaining in importance (Helmold 2018). International legal transactions contain some special features which have to be considered when ratifying contracts (Helmold 2018). The following points should be considered in international negotiations and agreements (Helmold 2018):

- Choice of Law, UN Sales Law
- Place of performance, Incoterms 2010
- Warranty, guarantees
- Interest, interest on arrears
- Payment transactions, currency and choice of bank
- Place of jurisdiction

4.7.2.2 UN Sales Law

In the case of international sales contracts, the question of the applicability of the UN Convention on Contracts for the International Sale of Goods, also known as the Vienna Sales Convention, which is based on the United Nations Convention on Contracts for the International Sale of Goods of April 11, 1980 (CISG), always arises in commercial sales (IHK Berlin 2018).

According to Art. 1 CISG, the territorial scope of application of the UN Convention on Contracts for the International Sale of Goods is opened if a contract of sale is concluded between contracting parties who have their establishments in different states which are each contracting states of the CISG or whose private international law declares the CISG to be applicable. The nationality of the contracting parties, the question of merchant status or whether the contract is of a commercial or private law nature are irrelevant. In addition, the contracting parties may contractually agree on the applicability of the CISG (Helmold 2018).

In factual terms, the UN Convention on Contracts for the International Sale of Goods shall apply if the subject matter of the contract is the purchase of goods. Goods within the meaning of the UN Sales Convention are only movable objects. Contracts for the sale of real property and rights are therefore not covered by the UN Sales Convention. Furthermore, according to Art. 2 CISG, the UN Sales Convention does not apply to contracts for the sale of securities and means of payment, watercraft and aircraft, as well as to auctions, execution and other judicial measures. Furthermore, the UN Sales Convention does not apply to cross-border contracts for the purchase of goods for personal use. Finally, the UN

Sales Convention does not apply to contracts which do not involve the transfer of possession or ownership of an object for consideration, but rather the performance of work or other services. An example of this is the preparation of an expert opinion, which may be handed over in writing at the end, but in which the focus is actually on the intellectual performance (IHK Berlin 2018).

The UN Sales Convention does not comprehensively regulate the legal aspects of a sales contract. For example, it does not contain any provisions on the limitation of claims and on producer liability. In these areas, therefore, the applicable domestic law remains decisive (IHK Berlin 2018).

4.7.2.3 Place of Performance, Incoterms 2010

Since 1936, the International Chamber of Commerce (ICC) in Paris has published "International Rules for the Interpretation of Customary Commercial Terms", known as Incoterms (International Commercial Terms). Since that time, the Incoterms have been repeatedly adapted to changing trade practices, most recently in the fall of 2010 (Helmold 2010). Incoterms are globally recognized, uniform contractual and delivery terms that enable the parties to a sales contract to standardize processing in international, as well as national, commercial transactions. The Incoterms define the distribution of costs, the distribution of risks and the duties of care between the contracting parties. The importance of the Incoterms rules lies in the clarity of the mutual obligations gained through their use (IHK Berlin 2018). With the help of Incoterms, misunderstandings and cost-intensive disputes can be prevented, thus reducing the risk of legal complications for both contracting parties. Legal problems such as the conclusion of the contract, the transfer of ownership, the handling of payments or the legal consequences of breaches of contract, on the other hand, are not regulated. The relevant provisions are those of the purchase contract or the law on which the contract is based (IHK Berlin 2018). Table 4.22 provides a brief overview of the most important Incoterms (Helmold 2018). Ex works means that the buyer

Table 4.22 International commercial terms 2010 (Incoterms)

EXW	Ex works
FCA	Free carrier
FAS	Free alongside ship/free longside ship
FOB	Free on board/free on board
CFR	Cost and freight
CIF	Cost, insurance and freight/cost, insurance and freight
CPT	Carriage paid to/freight paid
CIP	Carriage, insurance paid to/freight insured
DAP	Delivered at place/delivered named place
DAT	Delivered at terminal/delivered terminal
DDP	Delivered duty paid/delivered duty paid

Incoterms 2010 (IHK Region Stuttgart 2018)

has to take over transport, insurance and customs clearance ex works (IHK Berlin 2018). In the case of duty paid on delivery, transport, insurance and customs clearance are the responsibility of the manufacturer and supplier (IHK Berlin 2018). Transport and customs clearance, for example from China or India to Europe, can account for more than 20% of the actual purchase price, so Incoterms must be an essential part of the negotiations (IHK Berlin 2018).

4.7.2.4 Guarantee and Warranty

Internationally, there may be different warranty periods that differ from German warranty law (Helmold 2018). Warranty claims and warranty periods should therefore be discussed and agreed as part of the negotiations. In particular, replacement times, replacement deliveries, touch-ups or repairs should be taken into account here (Helmold 2018). If one wishes to adhere to legal claims, clauses in international contracts can indicate which country's law applies (AHK 2018).

4.7.2.5 Interest on Arrears and Late Payments

Due date and default interest rates for potential monetary claims should be defined in terms of amount for certainty, to account for damages and time delays in potentially lengthy litigation (Helmold 2018).

4.7.2.6 Currency and Payments

Determining the currency and securing incoming payments are key issues in international trade in goods (AHK 2018). With the United States alone, Germany turned over more than EUR 160 billion in 2017 (AHK 2018). In addition, other countries such as China, the United Kingdom or Switzerland can be found among the strongest trading partners in the foreign trade balance (AHK 2018). Even with the much smaller Switzerland, foreign trade turnover (imports and exports) amounted to more than 94 billion EUR. Around a quarter of all receivables and liabilities of German companies vis-à-vis foreign business partners are accordingly denominated in a foreign currency, the balance of payments statistics of the Deutsche Bundesbank show (Deutsche Bank 2018). Internationally, different rules apply to payment transactions, especially for transactions outside the euro area. Thanks to the Single Euro Payments Area, known as SEPA, money transfers between different European countries are now uncomplicated and inexpensive. However, as soon as orders or invoices are placed in a different currency, companies have to protect themselves against the corresponding exchange rate risks. On the other hand, different payment practices (such as ERU or USD payments in regulated markets to Asia and Latin America), non-transparent fees, strict reporting requirements or legal restrictions on foreign exchange transactions can significantly hamper foreign business. There is a risk of lost sales, disgruntled customers or even contractual penalties if a delivery of goods is delayed due to payment problems. Conversely, it can also lead to liquidity disadvantages, unforeseen additional costs or lost sales opportunities if foreign customers have no way of paying for goods and services quickly, securely and cost-effectively (Deutsche Bank 2018).

4.7.2.7 Jurisdiction and Arbitration Courts

In most cases, one of the two countries involved is agreed as the place of jurisdiction in international legal transactions (Helmold and Terry 2017b).

An arbitration clause in contracts is particularly recommended for contracts with a larger scope of delivery and correspondingly higher contract sums. If an arbitration court is agreed, a national court which is called upon by a contracting party despite the arbitration clause would declare itself incompetent (IHK Schleswig-Holstein 2018).

Arbitral awards are often easier to enforce, arbitral tribunals are usually faster as there is no move through the instances. Arbitral tribunals are often more relevant as the arbitrators tend to be professionals. Arbitration proceedings are not open to the public (this is essential when dealing with matters that require secrecy). However, arbitration proceedings are sometimes more expensive than a state court instance, but there is only one instance, whereas state courts usually have two or even three instances. One may save translation costs, as a German judge may, for example, require all English documents to be translated into German (IHK Schleswig-Holstein 2018). Regarding enforceability, there are international conventions to which the vast majority of our sales countries are party, most notably the "UN Convention on the Recognition and Enforcement of Foreign Arbitral Awards", to which 137 countries were party by December 31, 2005. A list of these countries can be found at http://www.uncitral.org (IHK Schleswig-Holstein 2018). Below are the most well-known "institutional arbitration tribunals". These are organizations that conduct arbitration proceedings on a permanent basis. These arbitration organizations have arbitration rules that regulate the conduct of arbitration proceedings (similar to the Code of Civil Procedure (ZPO), which regulates proceedings before state courts. However, the arbitration rules are nowhere near as formally strict as the ZPO) (IHK Schleswig-Holstein 2018):

- Probably the best known international arbitral tribunal is the Court of Arbitration at the International Chamber of Commerce (ICC) in Paris.
- The International Court of Arbitration at the Zurich Chamber of Commerce
- The Arbitration Court of the Austrian Federal Economic Chamber in Vienna, which gained importance especially in East-West disputes
- The German Institute of Arbitration in Cologne (Deutsche Institut für Schiedsgerichtsbarkeit e. V. in Köln—DIS) is also of international importance.
- The Arbitration Institute of the Stockholm Chamber of Commerce

In international legal transactions, the arbitration court in London (London Court of International Arbitration) or the arbitration court of the United States (American Arbitration Association, AAA) can be selected in the Anglo-Saxon legal sphere (IHK Schleswig-Holstein 2018). Table 4.23 shows recommendations for the drafting of contracts.

Table 4.23 Recommendations for step A-6: drafting the contract

Recording and signing of the results of the negotiations
Use of both languages of origin or agreement on one language, e.g. English
Consideration of aspects such as:
Place of performance
Incoterms
Interest on arrears
Jurisprudence
Warranty claims
Currency and payments
Rapid and immediate drafting and ratification of contracts
Observance and compliance with all negotiated points
Ceremonial setting at the conclusion of international negotiations
Successive monitoring and confirmation with the other party that the contract is being observed and complied with by both parties.

4.8 Recommendations for the Effective Implementation of the A-6 Negotiation Model

In summary, the A-6 negotiation concept is an ideal framework for international negotiations. The systematic, structured and transparent approach in six sequential steps enables users to conduct negotiations successfully and achieve a negotiation breakthrough. It integrates both intercultural recommendations and practical tips for negotiations and is unique in this form in the field of negotiation models (Helmold 2018).

The valuable recommendations for action specifically link practical and conceptual aspects with cultural and theoretical components based on proven negotiation success and successfully implemented projects by Dr. Marc Helmold. The A-6 concept is a mature and systematic negotiation model with numerous proven and complementary tools in practice (English: Tools), which requires a holistic application (Helmold 2018). Training of all employees directly or indirectly involved in negotiations is mandatory prior to negotiations. For employees who are at the beginning of their career, it is advisable to provide internal negotiation experts as advisors. Detailed preparation for negotiations, including analysis of the negotiation scope, determination of responsibilities and identification of motives and motivations of the other party, are essential for a breakthrough in negotiations. In conducting negotiations, motives rather than positions should be questioned in order to understand the motives and behaviour of the negotiating opponent and to act on them. There are strategies and tactics for conducting negotiations that can be used while taking intercultural peculiarities into account. It is crucial to focus one's own argumentation on the decision-makers and influencers using professional questioning techniques and concise formulations. Non-verbal signals and their patterns reveal whether

Table 4.24 Summary recommendation for the A-6 negotiation model

Holistic application of the A-6 negotiation model
Training of all negotiating staff to acquire competencies
Coaching and mentoring of "beginners" by negotiation experts
Detailed negotiation preparation as the key to negotiation success
Application of appropriate tools such as the analysis of strengths and weaknesses
Consideration of intercultural elements in negotiations
Concentration on the motives and interests of the negotiating party
Analysis of personalities and responsibilities
Assessment of negotiating leeway
Use of quantitative and qualitative data
Prioritization of negotiation goals with minimum and maximum targets
Use of appropriate strategies and tactics
Focus on decision makers and influencers
Respectful approach and avoidance of loss of face
Use of the right questioning techniques and concise formulations
Consideration of non-verbal signals and communication
Logging of all agreements and disagreements
Integration of important elements such as jurisdiction, legal system or Incoterms in international contracts
Observance of the agreement and rapid ratification of the treaty
Ceremonial adoption of the agreements at international negotiations

negotiations are successful or not. At the end of a negotiation, according to protocol, the contract and agreements should be solemnly adopted (Helmold 2018). Table 4.24 shows the most important and summary recommendations (Helmold 2018).

Literature

Abdel-Latif, A. (2015). Nicht verblüffen lassen. Schützen Sie sich vor den zehn dreckigsten Verhandlungsfallen. Abgerufen am 1.4.2018. https://www.focus.de/finanzen/experten/adel_abdel-latif/nicht-bluffen-lassen-schuetzen-sie-sich-vor-den-zehn-dreckigsten-verhandlungsfallen_id_4772172.html.

AHK (2018). Außenhandelskammern. Offizielle Seite der deutschen Außenhandelskammern. Abgerufen am 3.6.2018. https://www.ahk.de/.

Berner, W. (2016). Widerstände. Die Psychologie der Veränderung. Widerstände: Vom Umgang mit Ängsten, Trotz und Interessenpolitik. Abgerufen am 30.5.2018. https://www.umsetzungsberatung.de/psychologie/widerstaende.php.

Dathe, T. & Helmold, M. (2018). Erfolg im Chinageschäft. Handlungsempfehlungen für kleine und mittlere Unternehmen (KMU). Springer Gabler Wiesbaden.

Deutsche Bank (2018). Internationalen Zahlungsverkehr erfolgreich steuern. Seite der Deutsche Bank. https://www.deutsche-bank.de/pfb/content/geschaeftskunden/zahlungsverkehr_dokumentaerer-zahlungsverkehr.html.

Fisher, R. & Ury, W. (1981). Getting to Yes. Penguin Group London.

Gramm, F. (2015). Körpersprache in Verhandlungen bewußt einsetzen. Abgerufen am 1.4.2018. https://friedergamm.de/koerpersprache-in-verhandlungen/.

Grochowiak, K. (2015). Hierarchie, Kompetenz und Macht. Wie mächtig bist Du? In. Unternehmerwissen. Veröffentlicht am 26.11.2015. https://www.unternehmer.de/management-people-skills/180271-hierarchie-kompetenz-kommunikation-wie-maechtig-bist-du.

Helmold, M. (2010). Best-in-Class Lieferantenmanagement in der Automobilindustrie. Shaker Aachen.

Helmold, M. (2013). Claim-Management in der Praxis. Was tun bei Leistungsstörungen in der Lieferkette. In: FM-Logistik. Ausgabe 1–2/2013. S. 76–77.

Helmold, M. & Terry, B. (2016). Lieferantenmanagement 2030. Springer Gabler Wiesbaden.

Helmold, M. & Terry, B. (2017a). Global Sourcing und Lieferantenmanagement in China. DeGruyter Berlin.

Helmold, M. & Terry, B. (2017b). Global Sourcing and Supply Management Excellence in China. Springer Singapur.

Helmold, M., Dathe, T. & Büsch, M. (2017). Praxisbericht aus der Bahnindustrie—Bombardier Transportation. Veränderte Anforderungen durch Global Sourcing. In: Beschaffung aktuell. 4.5.2017. Abgerufen am 17.5.2018. https://beschaffung-aktuell.industrie.de/einkauf/veraenderte-anforderungen-durch-global-sourcing/.

Helmold, M. (2018). Erfolgreiche Verhandlungen und Best-in-Class Empfehlungen für den Verhandlungsdurchbruch. Manuskript und Workshopunterlagen im Master- und MBA-Studium.

Hilsenbeck, T. (2004). Verhandeln. Handbuch von Dr. Thomas Hilsenbeck. Abgerufen am 30.5.2018. http://www.thomas-hilsenbeck.de/wp-content/uploads/Dr-Th-Hilsenbeck-Handbuch-Verhandeln-Vers-5_0.pdf.

Hofert, S. (2015). Rangdynamik. Warum Alphas Betas brauchen und Omegas eigentlich nützlich sind. 20.11.2015. Abgerufen am 25.3.2018. https://teamworks-gmbh.de/rangdynamik-warum-alphas-betas-brauchen-und-omegas-eigentlich-nuetzlich-sind/.

IHK Berlin (2018). Internationales Vertragsrecht und UN-Kaufrecht. Abgerufen am 3.6.2018. https://www.ihk-berlin.de/blob/bihk24/Service-und-Beratung/international/downloads/2252700/074b1ae0b731ef9780be39c15db30776/UN_Kaufrecht-data.pdf.

IHK Region Stuttgart (2018). Internationale Lieferbedingungen. Incoterms 2010. Abgerufen am 3.6.2018. https://www.stuttgart.ihk24.de/Fuer-Unternehmen/international/Internationales_Wirtschaftsrecht/Internationale_Liefergeschaefte/Incoterms/Incoterms_2010/684806.

IHK Schleswig-Holstein (2018). Ratschläge zur Gestaltung internationaler Verträge. Abgerufen am 3.6.2018. https://www.ihk-schleswig-holstein.de/blob/swhihk24/international/downloads/export/1372586/dc4f9c7d776e25fb8f8ad9c4cc3065fd/Ratschlaege_zur_Gestaltung_Internationaler_Vertraege_Januar_2006_Gerstner-data.pdf.

N.N. (2014). Management. Die fünf häufigsten Verhandlungstricks – wie Sie die Gegenseite auskontern. 10.06.2014. Manager-Magazin. Abgerufen am 1.4.2018. http://www.manager-magazin.de/lifestyle/artikel/a-974305-3.html.

Obrien, J. (2016). Negotiations for Procurement Professionals. 2nd Edition. Kogan Page Croyden.

PMH (2018). Projektmanagementhandbuch. Umgang mit Widerstand im Projektmanagement. Abgerufen am 28.5.2018. https://www.projektmanagementhandbuch.de/soft-skills/umgang-mit-widerstand-im-projektmanagement/.

Schranner, M. (2009). Verhandeln im Grenzbereich. Strategien und Taktiken für schwierige Fälle. 8. Auflage. Econ München.

Schranner, M. (2015). 7 Prinzipien für erfolgreiches Verhandeln. BME-Keynote Matthias Schranner gibt sieben Tipps für zielführende Verhandlungen. 15.1.2015. Abgerufen am 20.3.2018. https://www.bme.de/7-prinzipien-fuer-erfolgreiches-verhandeln-888/.

Schranner, M. (2018). Schranner Negotiations Institute. Abgerufen am 19.5.2018. https://www.schranner.com/de/institute/matthias-schranner-ceo.

Statistisches Bundesamt (2018). Pressemitteilung Nr. 039 vom 08.02.2018: Deutsche Exporte im Jahr 2017: +6,3% zum Jahr 2016. Exporte und Importe erreichen neue Rekordwerte. Abgerufen am 15.3.2018. https://www.destatis.de/DE/PresseService/Presse/Pressemitteilungen/2018/02/PD18_039_51.html;jsessionid=86A76343A81D3E6B58E2A4A4716DC45E.InternetLive2.

Volk, H. (2018). Emotionale Dynamik eines Gespräches verstehen. Was den alltäglichen Wortwechsel entgleiten lässt. In: Beschaffung aktuell. 06.2018. S. 70–71.

Appropriate Tools for Negotiation Success 5

One waits for time to change, the other seizes it vigorously and acts. *Dante Alighieri (1265–1321).*

Contents

Summary

The industry structure analysis according to the Five Forces Model is a strategic management tool developed by Michael E. Porter. As the name suggests, the model is used to analyze the competitiveness, positioning and attractiveness of a sector or industry. Usually, the analysis of the industry is followed by a detailed strengths and weaknesses (SWOT) analysis. Porter's industry analysis is used to determine the attractiveness of an industry and one's negotiating position in conjunction with the strengths and weaknesses analysis. In addition to the industry structure and SWOT

M. Helmold et al., *Successful Negotiations*,
https://doi.org/10.1007/978-3-658-35701-6_5

analysis, tools such as the risk and opportunity analysis (ROP) or the margin enhancement plan are ideal supplements in negotiations.

5.1 The Five Forces Analysis (Porter's Five Forces)

5.1.1 Benefits of the Model

A suitable instrument for the consideration of industry-specific factors is the five forces or industry analysis according to Porter (Johnson and Scholes 1997). This is also called industry structure analysis and is a strategic management tool developed by Michael E. Porter (Porter 1985). As the name suggests, the model is used to analyse the competitiveness, positioning and attractiveness of an industry or sector (Porter 1985). Usually, the analysis of the industry is followed by a detailed strengths and weaknesses analysis. Porter's industry analysis is used to determine the attractiveness of an industry and one's negotiating position in conjunction with the strengths and weaknesses analysis (Porter 1985). For this purpose, the five components of the industry structure (English: Five Forces) are analysed and evaluated: bargaining power of suppliers, bargaining power of customers, threat of new competitors, threat of substitute products and rivalry among competitors in the industry. Figure 5.1 shows the five forces of the industry structure analysis.

The industry structure model offers an analysis grid with which the structure of an industry and the competitive situation can be systematically examined. From the development of the competitive situation in an industry, it can be derived whether this is attractive for the company, i.e. enables a long-term profitable development, with the help of

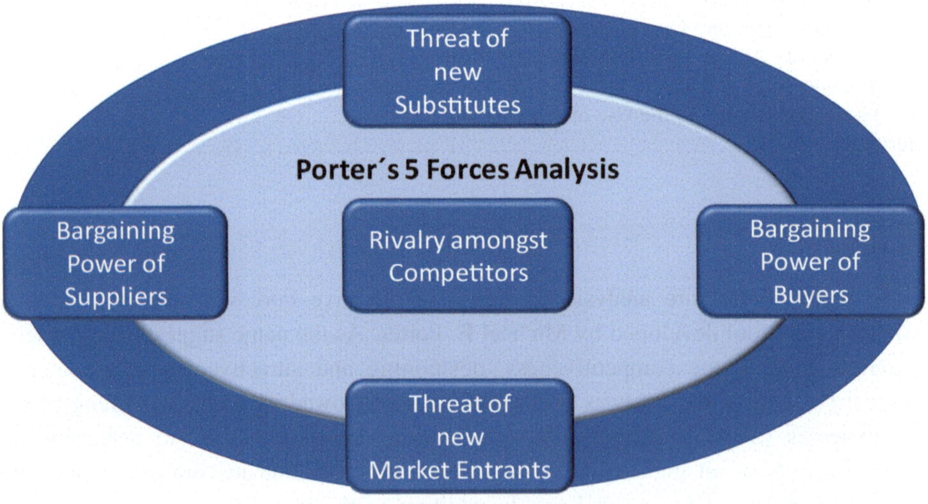

Fig. 5.1 Porter's 5-forces analysis. (Source: adapted from Johnson and Scholes 1997)

negotiations vis-à-vis other market participants such as suppliers, customers or competitors (Johnson and Scholes 1997).

Porter's model is based on the approach of industrial economics. It assumes that the attractiveness of an industry for a company operating in it is determined by the market structure, as this influences the behaviour of market participants (Johnson and Scholes 1997). To determine industry attractiveness, the following five components of industry structure, known as the "Five Forces", need to be examined (Stuzka 2018):

- Bargaining power of suppliers
- Negotiating power of customers
- Threat from new competitors
- Threat from substitute products (subsitutes)
- Intensity of competition in the sector

5.1.2 Bargaining Power of Suppliers

The bargaining power of suppliers determines how much they can enforce their interests in a business relationship with the company. High bargaining power of suppliers will usually lead to them either charging higher prices or being able to deliver poorer quality at the same price (Johnson and Scholes 1997). Since this has a negative impact on the company's profit potential, the lower the bargaining power of suppliers, the more attractive an industry will be (Johnson and Scholes 1997).

Indicators of high bargaining power of suppliers are:

- High level of differentiation in the supplier's products, e.g. if the supplier has a strong brand itself
- Low presence of substitutes
- High conversion costs for the customer in the event of a change of supplier
- Low importance of the respective purchasing for the supplier, i.e. the purchasing volume with a supplier only accounts for a small part of the supplier's total turnover.
- High cost importance of purchasing for the company: Either the costs have a high share in the total costs of the company's purchasing, or the input material has a high influence on the cost position or differentiation possibilities.
- High supplier concentration: An oligopolistic (or even monopolistic) market structure among suppliers leaves the company with few alternative suppliers and makes it easier for suppliers to impose high prices.
- Low risk of backward integration: the undertaking cannot credibly threaten to produce the relevant inputs itself (at least less credibly than the supplier can threaten forward integration)

5.1.3 Bargaining Power of Customers

As with suppliers, the bargaining power of customers determines the extent to which they can assert their interests in a business relationship with the company. A high degree of bargaining power on the part of customers will usually result in them either demanding lower prices or being able to obtain better quality at the same price. Such behaviour has a negative impact on the profit prospects of one's own company, which is why the less bargaining power customers have, the more attractive an industry is (Johnson and Scholes 1997).

Indicators of high bargaining power of customers are:

- Little differentiation in the company's products and those of its competitors, e.g. in the case of mass-produced goods
- Low changeover costs for the customer in the event of a change of supplier
- High availability of substitutes: Substitutes are available or customers have sufficient knowledge about alternative suppliers or input materials.
- High importance of the respective sale for the company, i.e. the purchase volume of a customer accounts for a high share of the company's total turnover
- Little influence of the product on the cost position or differentiation possibilities of customers
- High customer concentration: An oligopolistic (or even monopolistic) market structure among customers leaves the company few alternative sales opportunities and makes it easier for customers to impose low prices.
- High risk of backward integration: the customer can credibly threaten to manufacture the relevant products itself

5.1.4 Threat from New Competitors

The market entry of new competitors usually leads to an increase in price pressure. The ratio of supply to demand becomes less favourable. In order to utilise their capacity and attract customers, the new competitors will contribute to a decrease in prices, which lowers the attractiveness of the whole industry. The risk of new competitors entering the market depends on the level of barriers to entry. Higher barriers mean a more protected position for existing competitors and thus increase industry attractiveness (Johnson and Scholes 1997).

Typical barriers to entry are:

- Economies of scale: New competitors usually start with lower sales volumes than incumbents and are therefore at a cost disadvantage if economies of scale play a role in the industry.
- Absolute cost advantages: Learning curve based on proprietary products, proprietary low-cost design, proprietary access to necessary inputs (e.g., raw materials).

- Product differentiation often increases customer loyalty, making it more difficult for new competitors to win customers
- Capital requirements: A high investment requirement, e.g. for research and development, production facilities, infrastructure or even for marketing, only enables capital-rich companies to enter the market. In addition, high investment requirements increase the risk of market entry, making it less attractive.
- Changeover costs for customers when switching supplier reduce their willingness to switch
- Access to distribution channels: If important distribution channels are tied or occupied, a new competitor has poor sales opportunities.
- Expected reactions from established competitors
- State influence: State restrictions, requirements and regulations as well as subsidies can make market entry more difficult or lead to disadvantages for new competitors.

5.1.5 Threat of Substitutes

Substitute products are understood to be substitutes in a broader sense, i.e. products that fulfil similar customer needs but are currently perceived differently by customers, appeal to different customer groups or are sold in other regions. Such substitute products have a negative impact on the attractiveness of an industry, as customers might switch to these products if needed (Johnson and Scholes 1997).

Factors influencing the threat of substitute products are:

- Price-performance ratio of the substitute products compared to the own products
- switching costs for customers when switching to a supplier of a substitute product
- Customer attitudes towards the substitute products, e.g. whether customers perceive them as such at all

5.1.6 Rivalry Between Competitors

Finally, the fifth factor influencing the attractiveness of the industry is the rivalry among competitors and the intensity of competition in the industry (referred to by Porter as rivalry among competitors). A high intensity of competition manifests itself either as price competition (competitors undercut each other on prices) or as performance competition (competitors outbid each other on product quality and additional services, thereby increasing costs). Both forms of competition have a negative impact on profit prospects and thus on market attractiveness (Johnson and Scholes 1997).

Important factors influencing the degree of competitive intensity in the industry are:

- Number of competitors: A high number of competitors leads to high competitive pressure. According to macroeconomic theory, a high number of competitors leads to production at approximately marginal cost and low profits.
- Industry growth: In fast-growing industries, competition is often less than in slow-growing or even shrinking industries, as it is possible to expand one's own sales without having to take market share from competitors.
- Overcapacity/utilisation: If capacity substantially exceeds demand, suppliers will struggle to achieve high utilisation. This leads to price pressure and thus declining industry attractiveness
- Share of fixed costs in total costs: If the share of fixed costs is high, there is a strong incentive to achieve high capacity utilization in order to cover at least part of the fixed costs. Due to the high supply pressure, prices then often fall almost to the level of variable costs
- Exit barriers: In order to reduce overcapacity, it is often necessary for competitors to exit the market. However, this is made more difficult or delayed if high conversion or decommissioning costs arise, the business area is important for the competitors concerned for strategic reasons (e.g. synergy effects with other business areas) or past investments lead to an (irrational) commitment to the business area ("sunk costs").
- Product differentiation: If the competitors' offers differ considerably, the interchangeability of products/services decreases, which also reduces the price pressure.

5.2 The SWOT Analysis

The SWOT analysis (S-strengths, W-weaknesses, O-opportunities, T-threats) is an instrument of strategic management (Johnson and Scholes 1997; Fig. 5.2). It is used to derive suitable strategic solution alternatives for the achievement of the organisation's goals from the strengths and weaknesses of an organisation (internal view) and the opportunities and threats of the environment (external view) (Büsch 2013). The strengths and weaknesses analysis is an ideal tool for examining negotiation margins and determining the position in complex negotiations, but also for individual processes, products, teams or other objects of consideration and for developing alternative solutions (Büsch 2013). Within negotiations, it can be used during the analysis phase (A-1), strategy selection (A-2), argumentation building (A-3), and he actual negotiation (A-4) as a proactive tool to explore negotiation positions (Helmold 2018; Dathe and Helmold 2018; Helmold et al. 2017).

SWOT analysis refers to the internal capabilities and resources that a company has (Helmold and Terry 2016a):

- High quality standards
- Certified quality management systems
- High quality processes
- Excellent and competent employees

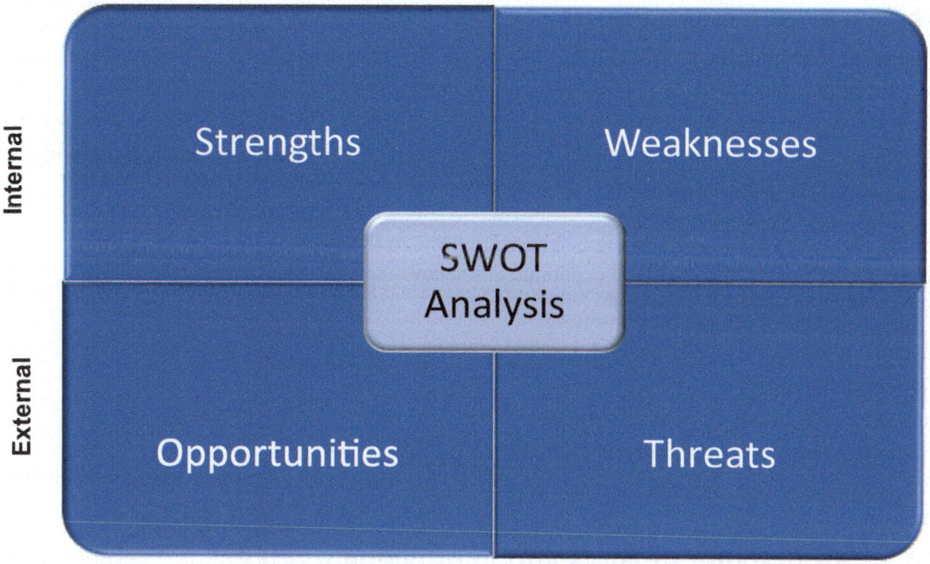

Fig. 5.2 Strengths and weaknesses analysis (SWOT analysis). (Source: adapted from Helmold and Terry 2016a)

- Lean production methods
- Innovative products
- Efficient logistics processes

5.3 Monetary Risks and Opportunities (ROP Analysis)

Projects often have a multi-year lifecycle from development to delivery to after-service (Helmold and Terry 2016a). Every project includes risks and opportunities (ROP) associated with project completion. A risk is a possible event with a negative impact. The event is in the future of the project's progress and threatens or weakens the successful achievement of the project's objectives (Helmold 2018). These risks reduce the profitability of the project in a monetary sense (Helmold 2018). The opportunities/opportunities, on the other hand, are events that have a positive impact on the project outcome. In practice, these risks and opportunities are related to probability factors and quantified in monetary terms (Helmold and Terry 2016a; Table 5.1).

Table 5.1 Risks—opportunities

Additional and unplanned resources to achieve project objectives	Reduced consumption of resources, e.g. personnel or material with savings
Higher material costs due to suppliers	External production and international procurement
Additional requirements by customers	Implementation of customer requirements with reduced effort

Table 5.2 Measures for improved economic efficiency

Faster development of project milestones
External production by international suppliers (global sourcing)
Lower quality effort
Increased sales prices through distribution
Additional orders from customers (options)

5.4 Profitability Analysis and Improvement (MEP)

Profitability analysis and project improvement (Margin Enhancement Plan—MEP) is the systematic and structured planning and execution of activities that have a positive impact on the economic situation of the project (Helmold and Terry 2016a). These measures ensure economic improvement along the entire project life cycle and all functions. MEP measures cover all functions from development and purchasing to marketing and sales (Helmold and Terry 2016a; Table 5.2).

5.5 5F-Concept

The 5F-concept describes the attributes for successful negotiations. Negotiations must be firm and decisive in argumentation (Helmold 2018). Arguments can be based on a detailed analysis of the negotiation's scope and opponents, and must be fact-based and objective. In addition to this attribute, negotiations must be focus-driven in order to achieve a negotiated outcome (Obrien 2016). This may include conceding on partial points. Nonetheless, arguments should be made forcefully and forcibly in negotiations. Last, negotiations should be friendly and truthful (Helmold 2018). Table 5.3 shows the German and English terms of the 5F-concept.

Table 5.3 The 5F concept for successful negotiations English and German translation of the terms

Firm	Firm and decisive
Factual	Fact-based and objective
Focused	Focusing and honest
Forceful	Research and forceful
Faithful	Friendly and truthful

Table 5.4 Recommendations for negotiation tools

Use of classical tools such as industry analysis (5 forces analysis)
Carrying out a strengths and weaknesses analysis (SWOT analysis)
Identification of realistic opportunities and possible risks (ROP analysis)
Monetary quantification of risks and opportunities
Proactive plan for profitability improvement of products or projects with a detailed target-performance comparison (MEP)
Use of the 5F-concept

5.6 Recommendations for the Use of Appropriate Tools

This chapter provides recommendations on how tools can be used in a targeted manner. These tools (negotiation tools) help to sound out an optimal starting position and thus to implement a result- and goal-oriented negotiation. Table 5.4 summarizes the tools (Helmold and Terry 2016b).

References

Büsch, M. (2013). Praxishandbuch Strategischer Einkauf: Methoden, Verfahren, Arbeitsblätter für professionelles Beschaffungsmanagement (German Edition). 3. Auflage. Springer Gabler Wiesbaden.

Dathe, T. & Helmold (2018). Erfolg im Chinageschäft. Handlungsempfehlungen für kleine und mittlere Unternehmen (KMU). Springer Gabler Wiesbaden.

Obrien, J. (2016). Negotiations for Procurement Professionals. 2nd Edition. Kogan Page Croyden.

Helmold, M. (2018). Erfolgreiche Verhandlungen und Best-in-Class Empfehlungen für den Verhandlungsdurchbruch. Manuskript und Workshopunterlagen im Master- und MBA-Studium.

Helmold, M. & Terry, B. (2016a). Lieferantenmanagement 2030. Springer Gabler Wiesbaden.

Helmold, M. & Terry, B. (2016b). Global Sourcing and Supply Management Excellence in China. Springer Singapur.

Helmold, M. & Dathe, T. & Büsch, M. (2017). Praxisbericht aus der Bahnindustrie – Bombardier Transportation. Veränderte Anforderungen durch Global Sourcing. In Beschaffung aktuell. 4.5.2017. Abgerufen am 17.5.2018. https://beschaffung-aktuell.industrie.de/einkauf/veraenderte-anforderungen-durch-global-sourcing/.

Johnson, G. & Scholes, K. (1997). Exploring Corporate Strategy. Text and Cases. 4th Edition. Prentice Hall London.

Porter, M.E. (1985). Competitive Advantage. Creating and sustaining superior Performance. Free Press New York.

Stuzka, A. (2018). Branchenstrukturanalyse. Porters Five Forces. Manager-Wiki. Abgerufen am 15.5.2018. http://www.manager-wiki.com/externe-analyse/22-branchenstrukturanalyse-qfive-forcesq-nach-porter.

Nonverbal Communication in Negotiations 6

Everyone has stupid thoughts, but the wise man keeps them quiet.
Wilhelm Busch (1832–1908).

Contents

M. Helmold et al., *Successful Negotiations*,
https://doi.org/10.1007/978-3-658-35701-6_6

Summary

Negotiations are primarily characterized by verbal communication, in that the negotiating parties communicate with each other through language and exchange their points of view (Obrien, Negotiations for Procurement Professionals, Kogan Page, Croyden, 2016). However, besides the spoken word, there are fundamental signals defined as nonverbal communication or body language (Obrien, Negotiations for Procurement Professionals, Kogan Page, Croyden, 2016). Non-verbal communication (Latin: communication without words) is the part of communication that is not guided by the conventionalized rules of a spoken language, expressed according to non-conventionalized rules of a language used, but through posture (Latin: habitus), movements (Latin: gestures) or facial expressions (Latin: facial expressions) (Purchasing Manager 2018). Habitus refers to the postures that are perceived in interpersonal communication. It is the totality of all body signals (Helmold, Erfolgreiche Verhandlungen und Best-in-Class Empfehlungen für den Verhandlungsdurchbruch. Manuskript und Workshopunterlagen im Master- und MBA-Studium, 2018). Gestures include the totality of gestures that serve as movements of interpersonal communication. In particular, movements of the arms or hands are signals that can provide information about feelings and position in negotiations. Facial expressions, also called expressions or facial expressions, are facial expressions or include signals from parts of the face such as blushing, sweating, frowning, or raising the eyebrows. Executives often try to avoid showing emotions in business negotiations as much as possible because they believe that emotions are not appropriate in business situations (Helmold, Erfolgreiche Verhandlungen und Best-in-Class Empfehlungen für den Verhandlungsdurchbruch. Manuskript und Workshopunterlagen im Master- und MBA-Studium, 2018). However, they do this unconsciously because behavior and body language are directly linked to emotions (Helmold, Erfolgreiche Verhandlungen und Best-in-Class Empfehlungen für den Verhandlungsdurchbruch. Manuskript und Workshopunterlagen im Master- und MBA-Studium, 2018).

6.1 Nonverbal Communication

Negotiations are primarily characterized by verbal communication, in that the negotiating partners communicate with each other through language and exchange their points of view (Obrien 2016). However, in addition to the spoken word, there are fundamental signals that are defined as nonverbal communication or body language (Obrien 2016). Non-verbal communication (communication without words) is the part of communication that is not guided by the conventionalized rules of a spoken language, which is expressed according to non-conventionalized rules of a language used, but through posture, movements or facial expressions (Einkaufsmanager 2018). Habitus refers to the postures that are perceived in interpersonal communication. It is the totality of all body signals (Helmold 2018). Gestures include the totality of gestures that serve as movements of interpersonal communication. In particular, movements of the arms or hands are signals that can provide information about feelings and position in negotiations. Facial expressions, also called expressions or facial expressions, are facial expressions or include signals from parts of the face such as blushing, sweating, frowning, or raising the eyebrows. Executives often try to avoid showing emotions in business negotiations as much as possible because they believe that emotions are not appropriate in business situations (Helmold 2018). However, they do this unconsciously because behavior and body language are directly related to emotions (Helmold 2018). The body does not know if it is in private or business and sends nonverbal signals. Negotiation experts such as Schranner and Dr. Helmold recommend the opposite: using emotions specifically and situationally (Schranner 2009; Helmold 2018). Emotions can also be deliberately used to deceive, evade, yield, or pressure the negotiating opponent (Helmold 2018). Elements of nonverbal communication refer to:

- Upright or casual sitting posture
- Closed or crossed legs
- Posture of the hands
- Firm hand or facial expression
- Comfortable or uncomfortable standing
- Spontaneous smile
- Drooping corners of the mouth
- Hectic movements
- Sweat and blush
- Touching body parts such as nose, arms or ears
- Tailoring the clothes like the tie or the suit
- Wiping dust from the suit

Figure 6.1 shows the elements of non-verbal communication with posture, facial expression and movements or gestures (Helmold 2018; Dathe and Helmold 2018). On the one hand, the posture of the body, facial expressions or even movements can provoke or entice the interlocutor, ensure a good atmosphere or, in the worst case, spoil the mood (Abdel-Latif 2015). On the other hand, non-verbal signals of the negotiating partner can be used sensibly and wisely for one's own interests (Mühlisch 2006).

Example

Examples here can be the greeting and the seating position. The following greeting indicates a harmonious and **equal relationship:** The interlocutors shake hands with a

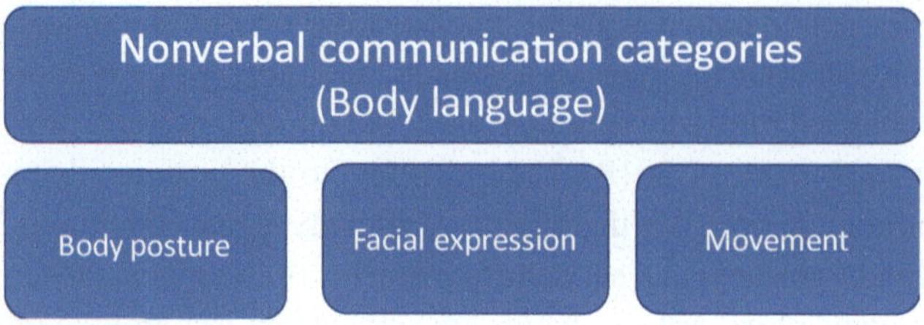

Fig. 6.1 Non-verbal communication and body language. (Source: own representation)

smile and keep half an arm's length apart. The hand position is parallel. The case is different if your conversation partner wants to dominate you. Then he not only touches your hand in greeting, but also grabs you by the lower or even upper arm. In this way, your counterpart nonverbally demonstrates his **claim to leadership.** This also applies if your partner turns his hand upwards while you shake hands. An **upright sitting position** signals "my mind is wide awake and I am listening". If your hands are clearly visible on the table, your partner appears to inspire confidence. He subconsciously symbolizes that he has nothing to hide and is putting his arguments openly on the table (Helmold and Terry 2016). However, when he puts his elbows on the table and clasps his fist with his hand, he builds a protective wall. Something doesn't sit well with your counterpart and he is probably bracing himself for a verbal exchange. However, a **position that** is too **relaxed and provocative** is also unfavourable. If, for example, the negotiating partner leans backwards in negotiations and **crosses his arms behind his head, as** if he were comfortably on the sofa in front of the television, then he wants to show his power and provoke the negotiating opponent. The interlocking of the hands is supposed to show composure and superiority. However, experts advise caution here: the negotiation opponent shows an open chest, but the elbows point like a weapon pointed at the other side (Obrien 2016). As a counter tactic, it is recommended to present a document to the negotiator who is too superior, so that he has to change his posture, bend over the table and use his arms (Obrien 2016). Another recommended tactic here is to change the location of the negotiation away from the table and towards a whiteboard or flipchart. When a whiteboard or flipchart is available and presents an issue, the superior and arrogant negotiator is forced to get off their "high horse" and listen to what is being said (Helmold 2018).

In order to be clear about the importance of non-verbal communication, it is important not only to determine the levels at which this takes place, but also to analyse the flow of information and the overall context in detail in order to relate signals in non-verbal communication to the negotiation or conversation. For example, an Asian business partner travelling to Germany for a one-hour meeting with his business partner may seem tired and bored because he was unable to sleep on the plane and the time difference may be noticeable through body signals such as yawning, tiredness and inattention (Helmold 2018). Statements must therefore be made about the nature and sensitivity of the information-receiving receptors in the overall context (Helmold 2018).

6.2 Positive and Negative Signals

6.2.1 Sending Positive Signals as a Recommendation

Negotiation experts and behavioural researchers generally recommend sending positive signals when initiating business (Helmold 2018). This fact also applies to negotiations. A friendly greeting in an upright posture with a positive facial expression and a firm handshake sends positive signals to the negotiating partner. Also, deliberate changes in posture, facial expressions or gestures at many stages of a conversation or negotiation can direct the focus to the future and a successful and amicable outcome. These signals can look like this, for example:

- Changing the distance to the interlocutor, e.g. moving closer to show sympathy or moving away to show respect.
- Relaxing your posture combined with a smile to defuse critical negotiation situations
- Call a break and leave the room to de-escalate blockades
- Stand up and go to the blackboard to visualize facts and get closer to each other

6.2.2 Conscious Use of Negative Signals

In addition to positive signals, however, negative signals can also be deliberately used on a case-by-case basis. These can be used situationally in negotiations if the demands of the negotiating opponent are exaggerated, not objective or unrealistic. In this case, signals can and must be sent out to show the negotiating opponent that there is no prospect of agreement. However, it is generally recommended to enter negotiations in a positive mood, as both parties are usually interested in finding a solution (Helmold 2018; Bauer-Jelinek 2007).

6.3 Signals of the Body Posture

6.3.1 Positive Signals and Signs of Approval

6.3.1.1 Slightly Bent Forward, Open Posture and Open Facial Expression

The negotiating partner shows attention and interest in what is happening and in the negotiation. He shows positive signals and follows the negotiation with concentration. The negotiator is open to different points and waits for the negotiator to start and make a request. The negotiation can begin and negotiation points should be addressed using a clear agenda and set objectives (Helmold 2018). Figure 6.2 shows the example of the opening of the negotiation (Table 6.1).

Fig. 6.2 Negotiation and conversation opening. (Source: own representation)

6.3.1.2 Slightly Bent Forward, Open Posture and Outstretched Hands and Open Facial Expression

The negotiating partner shows attention and interest, he stretches out his arms and opens his hands. This signal can be seen as an invitation. He shows positive signals and follows the negotiation in a concentrated way, the open hands suggest a willingness to talk. He is open to different points and will pay attention to my concerns (Helmold 2018). The willingness of the negotiating counterparty to start the negotiation can be used to identify negotiating positions, motives and goals by waiting and letting the negotiating partner talk (Helmold 2018) (Fig. 6.3; Table 6.2).

Table 6.1 Signal of consent: open and bent forward posture, hands interlaced

Suggested response:
Structured start of negotiations with agenda and objectives. Presentation of the negotiating positions in the individual negotiating dimensions. Friendly atmosphere should be maintained as the negotiating partner is ready to listen attentively and with concentration. He will follow my agenda and make comments

Fig. 6.3 Opening negotiations and conversations with open hands. (Source: own representation)

Table 6.2 Slightly bent forward, friendly and open posture. Hands outstretched and open facial expression

Suggested response:
Structured start of negotiations with agenda and objectives. Presentation of the negotiating positions in the individual negotiating dimensions. Friendly atmosphere should be maintained as the negotiating partner is ready to listen attentively and with concentration. He will follow my agenda and make comments. The chances of reaching an agreement are very high. My negotiating partner will pay attention to me and respond to my concerns or partial concerns

6.3.1.3 Slightly Bent Forward, Open Posture, Hands Open, Open Facial Expression, Notes

The negotiator shows attention and interest of the negotiator. He signals that he is very well prepared. He shows positive signals and will follow the negotiation in a concentrated and detailed way. He is open to different points, but has staked out his own positions and is waiting for the negotiating partner to start and make his point. In this situation, it is also advisable to let the negotiation partner talk in order to understand his concerns, motives and positions (Helmold 2018) (Fig. 6.4; Table 6.3).

Fig. 6.4 Slightly bent forward, open posture, hands open, open facial expression, notes. (Source: own representation)

Table 6.3 Slightly bent forward, open posture, hands open, open facial expression, notes

Suggested response:
Structured and systematic negotiations with agenda and goals. Agenda, duration and process should be agreed with the negotiating partner in advance or at the beginning of the negotiation. Presentation of the negotiating positions in the individual negotiating categories. Rationality and friendliness should be maintained as the negotiator is prepared to listen attentively and with concentration. He will follow my agenda and make comments, very likely formulate his agenda points. The chances of reaching an agreement are high

6.3.2 Rejection Signals

6.3.2.1 Leaning Back, Arms Folded behind the Head

Reactions with folded arms suggest rejection and doubt on the part of the negotiating partner. It may also just be a tactic of the negotiating partner to show his superiority. However, this signal shows disinterest and no signal for a negotiation conclusion. If the negotiating partner does not change his behaviour, the negotiation should be adjourned and his negotiating position redefined (Helmold 2018) (Fig. 6.5; Table 6.4).

Fig. 6.5 Signals of rejection: Leaning back, arms folded behind the head. (Source: Own representation)

Table 6.4 Leaning back, arms folded behind the head

Suggested response:
Temporary break or termination of the negotiations with further sounding out of the negotiating partner's negotiating positions. The recommendation here is to present a document to the negotiating partner or to explain a fact on the blackboard in order to lure the supposedly rejecting negotiating partner out of his blockade. It may be that this attitude is caused by fatigue or exhaustion. Accurate determination of whether the respective positions are so far apart or not. Possible redefinition of individual goals. If the goals are too far apart, break off the negotiation and start again.

6.3.2.2 Temporary Distraction by Mobile Phone Or Laptop and Disinterest

Playing with the Laptop and Temporary Distraction

Playing with the mobile phone or the laptop shows brief disinterest or temporary refusal. The negotiating partner is unfocused, not on the point and does not follow the negotiation completely. He or she does not take part in the proceedings because he or she may want to make a quick phone call or has seen a message. You yourself should not be distracted in negotiations and should be on the point. If the negotiator does not press for a short break, it is advisable in this case to interject less important points, which, however, might not be accepted immediately if the negotiator is fully concentrated. In the case of points that are not too essential, he will be more willing to make concessions in order to return to the supposedly more important topic (Helmold 2018).

Fig. 6.6 Signal of rejection or deliberate avoidance by distraction. (Source: Own representation)

Table 6.5 Temporary distraction by mobile phone or laptop and disinterest

Suggested response:
In this case, the interest in the negotiation should be retrieved. It is advisable to regain the interest of the negotiating partner with direct questions or with a document. When taking phone calls or answering short messages on the smartphone, short pauses can be quite rewarding

Lack of Interest Or Visible Arrogance by Resting Head on Hand Or Leaning Back
Disinterest and inattention are clear and direct signals of rejection. In this case, it is advisable to adjourn the negotiations unless the behaviour of the negotiating partner changes. Figure 6.6. shows examples of rejection by looking away, resting the head on the hand and disinterest (Helmold 2018) (Table 6.5).

6.3.3 Thinking and Waiting

In this situation, the negotiator waits and weighs the proposals of the other side. If there is a negotiating team with several members on the other side, there will be a desire for a vote. Therefore, one should give the other side time to think and weigh. One should already be prepared oneself for possible answers, arguments or counter-arguments. Although the index finger and the posture suggest doubt, the eyes are still wide open. These gestures and facial expressions show that the negotiation partner is still listening attentively and following the argumentation (Helmold 2018; Fig. 6.7). As long as the attention is given, the two to three strongest arguments should be mentioned para. 4.4. Possible counter-

Fig. 6.7 Signal of waiting or doubt by weighing alternatives. (Source: Own representation)

Table 6.6 Think and wait

Suggested response:
The negotiating partner thinks about and considers the offer made. In a friendly and cooperative atmosphere, he will now look for possibilities to reach a compromise or an agreement, either alone or in his negotiating team. Therefore, the negotiator should be given time to consider. If the negotiator is acting as part of a team, short breaks can also be suggested so that the other side's team can deliberate. You should evaluate concessions, counter-arguments and arguments for different options.

arguments should be specifically invalidated by defending and concentrating on the weakest argument Sect. 4.6 (Table 6.6).

6.3.4 Attacking the Other Side Through Targeted Attacks

The negotiating partner underlines his direct demands by attacking and sending a clear signal in the form of clenched fists or a raised index finger directed at the negotiating partner (Fig. 6.8). Attacks and advances reveal the negotiator's motives and interests. Comments and demands of the negotiating opponent should be followed rationally and

Fig. 6.8 Attack by counterpart through targeted attacks. (Source: Own representation)

Table 6.7 Attacking the other side with targeted attacks

Suggested response:
The negotiating partner attacks and makes an offer. One should respond to proposals in a wait-and-see and rational manner. A "no" should be avoided at all costs, even if the proposals are excessive. The negotiating opponent has put his cards and motives on the table, so I can build my further strategy and tactics on this basis. Nodding and smiling signal agreement to the negotiating partner, so that he continues to reveal his motives and arguments.

attentively. In this situation, listening is more important than talking; points should be noted carefully. Signals of agreement such as temporary smiles or nods can also be advantageous in order to give the other party signs of supposed agreement (Table 6.7).

6.3.5 Signals of Deception Or Untruthfulness

6.3.5.1 Signs of Untruths Or Exaggerations

In principle, neither side deliberately lies in negotiations or conflict talks, but rather tries to conceal or not address aspects in order to strengthen its own position (Helmold and Terry 2016). For example, a buyer will not want to disclose to a seller that he has no alternative courses of action, even if he can only and exclusively use products from that supplier. A seller, on the other hand, will not disclose that he will bid an order at cost, i.e., without making a profit (long-term price floor), in order to utilize existing capacity in his own factory, otherwise production areas would stand empty. Untruths, lies or white lies are protective gestures and generate stress, which manifests itself physically as follows:

- pull or scratch the earlobe
- wring one's hands
- lick one's lips

- wipe the sweat from one's brow or neck
- repeated plucking at the clothing
- unmotivated straightening of the hair
- play with one's fingernails

Tilted gaze, touching parts of the face or temporary deviation are signals of lying or exaggeration. Signals of untruths are difficult to detect, but can be uncovered through observation and by conducting negotiations in a more in-depth and analytical manner. In particular, exaggerations are common in intercultural settings and are often seen as lies by the recipient and negotiating partner (Helmold and Terry 2016).

6.3.5.2 Touching Parts of the Body, Blinking Or Looking Away

Touching the nose or earlobe, blinking or shying away may be signs of untruths or exaggerations (Figs. 6.9, 6.10 and 6.11). In this situation, detailed questions should be asked and analytical negotiation tools used to detect exaggerations or lies. As a matter of

Fig. 6.9 Touching the earlobe or other parts of the body. (Source: own representation)

Fig. 6.10 Touching the nose. (Source: own representation)

Fig. 6.11 Signal of deception: brief blinking, looking away or looking at the phone. (Source: own representation)

Table 6.8 Touching body parts such as nose or ears, blinking or looking away

Suggested response:
When uncovering lies or exaggerations through factual questioning and analytical negotiation, one should not make this observation known, but use it for one's own goals. No accusations or insinuations should be made to the negotiating opponent, but one should follow with the knowledge of one's own negotiating strategy and tactics. Leaving the negotiating opponent in the belief that his untruth has not been recognised has advantages for one's own conduct of the negotiation.

principle, one should not imply a lie, but rather reveal the lie with targeted counter-questions or make exaggerations recognizable and build one's own strategy on this (Helmold 2018) (Table 6.8).

6.3.6 Signals of Stress

6.3.6.1 Positive and Negative Stress

In negotiations, mistakes are very often caused by stress. Under stress, the emotional side of people comes out. Stress means tension, pressure and physical signals such as a faster heartbeat, the increased blood flow to the brain, the tension of the muscles or energy supply through blood sugar and fats. When stress occurs, the body is put under tension and stimuli are transmitted to the brain via the sensory organs eyes, ears or nose in dangerous situations (Eckert and Tarnowski 2017). Norepinephrine and epinephrine are released, which put the body in maximum readiness to perform. If the stress is successfully managed, the organism returns to normal and the adrenaline dissipates (Eckert and Tarnowski 2017). However, if the stress persists, then the brain sends a replenishment request of adrenaline. In that case, the second stress axis, the so-called wet stress axis, is activated and cortisol is released into the blood so that the organism remains adapted and at maximum performance level in the stressful situation (AOK 2018). The increased release of cortisol signals danger to our system and a chronic state of stress occurs. Over time, the adrenal glands can then become exhausted and no longer produce enough cortisol. I.e., cortisol levels drop below normal levels after becoming excessive and symptoms such as fatigue, lack of energy, etc. can occur (AOK 2018). In science, a distinction is made between positive stress (eustress) and negative stress (distress). Distress is also referred to as negative stress. “Dis” is a Latin prefix and stands for “bad”. With all its negative physical, mental and emotional consequences, it is so stressful for the person concerned over a longer period of time that it can eventually lead to burn-out. Eustress is derived from the Greek prefix “Eu” for “good”. This type of stress is usually not perceived as a burden. It usually involves activities that are particularly enjoyable and that one performs with great passion. Here, stress can have an invigorating effect and even promote performance (AOK 2018). For one’s own position, one should assess how long the eustress can be maintained and when symptoms of fatigue set in. When fatigue sets in, the negotiation should be interrupted or terminated. Distress, on the other hand, is detrimental to one’s position, so that negotiations should be adjourned in order to maintain a clear head. Distress on the part of the negotiating partner can temporarily lead to advantages for the negotiator, but here too consideration should be given to postponing the negotiations.

6.3.6.2 Signals of Stress

Figures 6.12 and 6.13 show symptoms of stress from short-term fingernail biting or tie straightening. Similarly, touching other parts of clothing or the body is a signal of stress, suggesting untruths or exaggerations. By asking specific questions and using appropriate questioning techniques, untruths or exaggerations can be identified and made visible Sect. 4.5.4. When identifying untruths, the negotiating partner should not be confronted by reproaches, but the knowledge should be used in a targeted manner in one’s own argumentation by rebutting the opponent’s arguments in order to sustainably assert one’s own demands (Helmold 2018) (Table 6.9).

Fig. 6.12 Chewing fingernails. (Source: Own representation)

Fig. 6.13 Straighten the tie. (Source: Own representation)

Table 6.9 Signals of stress

Suggested response:
Stress can have both positive and negative effects on negotiations. Every phase of stress is followed by a phase of exhaustion. Therefore, one should know how stress affects one's own performance. If stress has a positive effect on one's own performance, this advantage can be used. It is important to recognize the moment when the body shows signs of fatigue such as lack of concentration or tiredness. If stress is visible on the other side of the negotiation, this advantage can be used in a targeted manner by presenting one's own negotiating positions in a rational and calm manner.

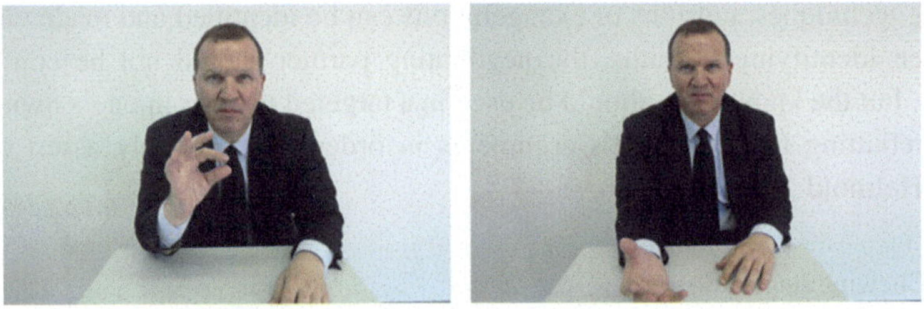

Fig. 6.14 Signal of agreement: Facing position. (Source: Own representation)

6.3.6.3 Signals of Possible Agreement

Figure 6.14 shows a position facing the negotiator with signals of agreement by opening the hand or indicating to meet the negotiator. In this situation there is a likelihood of finalising the negotiations and getting one's negotiating points accepted. It is possible here to enforce his demands by making smaller concessions to the negotiating partner. Smaller concessions give him the feeling of coming out of the negotiation as a winner. With the agreement, all negotiation points should be clearly recorded Sect. 4.7.1 (Helmold 2018) (Table 6.10).

Table 6.10 Signals of possible agreement

Suggested response:
Signals of possible rapprochement and agreement are a position turned towards the negotiating partner with gestures such as an open hand or an invitation to approach. In this situation, one should not deviate from one's core demands, but make small concessions in less important elements of the negotiations. At this point, negotiations may be interrupted or adjourned. This staying power will pay off

6.4 Facial Expressions: What Do Facial Expressions and Eyes Reveal?

Facial expressions are the visible movements of the facial surface, e.g. frowning, blinking, blushing, or rolling the eyes. In most cases, an overall impression is created from individual facial expressions, as the individual movements of the facial muscles take place in fractions of a second. Body language can only be controlled to a limited extent but is also difficult for the person opposite to recognize (Eckert and Tarnowski 2017). Especially in stressful situations, people resort to typical calming gestures, the so-called adaptors. A grip on the earlobe, scratching the chin or touching the palms of the hands are among them. Adaptors are usually performed in milliseconds and cannot always be recognized immediately, so patterns and symptoms of stress must be identified (Eckert and Tarnowski 2017).

Increases in adaptors usually indicate stress, discomfort, or increased concentration. Gestures that someone typically uses when speaking tend to decrease with cognitive effort. Finally, there are physical reactions that cannot be controlled at all, such as increased blood flow to the skin leading to visible blushing, or increased blinking frequency of the eyes, for example (Eckert and Tarnowski 2017).

Most often, adaptors occur in conjunction with other elements, such as the voice (Eckert and Tarnowski 2017). According to psychology, the voice can also betray symptoms of stress as described by Eckert & Tarnnowski (Eckert and Tarnowski 2017). Deviation from normal voice pitch is usually a good indication of emotional arousal in your conversation partner. A noticeably low voice pitch, but also sudden, louder or faster speech can be indications of sadness or guilt (Eckert and Tarnowski 2017).

It is not so easy to interpret the facial expressions of your fellow human beings correctly. Although emotions are relatively easy to recognize in facial expressions, they can quickly be misinterpreted. An emotion is usually expressed through the interaction of different facial expressions. Anger, for example, is expressed through contracted eyebrows, wide open eyes and compressed lips. Distinctive points for the facial expression are the forehead, the eye and the mouth area. These can sometimes be used in seemingly opposite ways. For example, one can smile and frown at the same time. (Eckert and Tarnowski 2017). The interpretation of facial expressions is always subjective. One often interprets large parts of the facial expressions of the counterpart instinctively correctly. However, one does not pay attention to many small facial expressions. By looking carefully, one can better grasp the true intention of the interlocutor (Eckert and Tarnowski 2017).

6.4.1 Positive Facial Expressions

A smile in combination with wide open eyes is usually a positive signal and signifies agreement and a friendly attitude towards the suggestions being made (Obrien 2016; Helmold 2018). Furthermore, a smooth forehead can be seen, signifying relaxation. Figure 6.15 shows dilated pupils and relaxed corners of the mouth, so a positive reaction from the negotiator is evident here. Other positive signals besides eye contact are a smile, a concentrated but not fixed gaze or relaxed corners of the mouth. Table 6.11 shows examples that can be used to derive positive signals.

Fig. 6.15 Positive signals in facial expressions. (Source: Own representation)

Table 6.11 Positive signals in facial expressions

Keep eye contact	Interest
Smile and open eyes	Open-mindedness, friendliness
Dilated pupils (large eyes)	Interest, friendliness, open-mindedness
Eyelid lift	Open-mindedness, calmness
Concentrated view	Interest
Relaxed corners of the mouth	Calm, relaxed
Closed, smiling mouth	Sympathy, open-mindedness
Upturned corners of the mouth	Friendliness, open-mindedness
Smooth forehead	Friendliness, open-mindedness

6.4.2 Negative Facial Expressions, Rejection and Deception

People also use their facial expressions consciously or unconsciously to express skepticism or rejection. Non-verbal and consciously used means for negative signals are for example the wrinkling of the nose (disgust, disgust), the pushing out of the lower lip (scepticism), staring (threat) or obvious yawning (boredom). In addition, there are also unconscious negative signals displayed by adaptors (Obrien 2016; Helmold 2018), as Fig. 6.16 shows. Table 6.12 describes negative signals and signs of rejection in facial expressions.

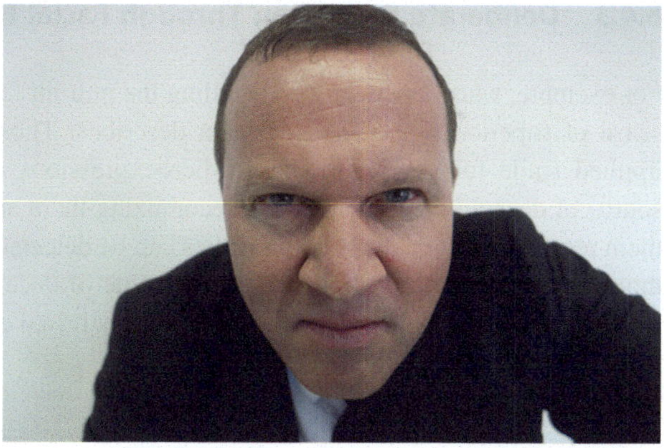

Fig. 6.16 Negative signals in facial expressions. (Source: Own representation)

Table 6.12 Negative signals in facial expressions

Sniff	Uncertainty
Frown	Thoughtfulness or disapproval
Constricted pupils	Tension, skepticism, doubt
Very frequent blinking	Uncertainty
Raised eyebrows	Astonishment or even scepticism
Open mouth	Astonishment
Pursed lips	Inner tension
Constantly looking the other way	Embarrassment or even disinterest
Slightly tighten the nostrils	Disgust
Push forward the lower lip	Disbelief or skepticism
Roll one's eyes	Incredulity, impatience or scepticism
Gape at an interlocutor	Conveying boredom or disinterest
Stare intently at people	Arrogance, arrogance
Petrified facial features	Rejection, increase of social distance
Elevation of an eyebrow	Disbelief
Narrow eyes	Doubt, incredulity

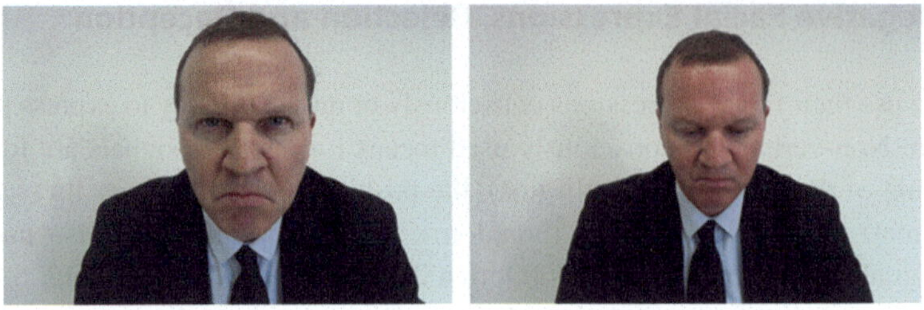

Fig. 6.17 Signals of deception in facial expressions. (Source: Own representation)

6.4.3 Deliberate Deception Through Facial Expressions

For example, when a person who is telling the untruth feels that you have bought his lie, a sense of superiority sets in, as Obrien describes. Those who are trained can detect an implied smile for a brief moment. Microexpressions are therefore the most important source of deception cues. However, recognizing them and being able to correctly classify them requires practice. Deceptions or lies can be detected by looking away briefly, smiling thoughtfully, or blinking frequently at the time of deception. Figure 6.17 shows looking away or closed eyes in conjunction with slightly raised corners of the mouth, suggesting a possible deception (Helmold 2018).

6.5 Recommendations: Analysis and Response to Non-verbal Communication

Analysis of nonverbal communication is difficult because people and behaviors are involved (Obrien 2016). Often microexpressions and expressions of nonverbal communication are shown in milliseconds (Helmold 2018). When analyzing nonverbal communication, attention should be paid to patterns of behavior and recurring cues. In this context, a zero line (baseline) can be established from which behavioural patterns (clusters) can be identified by testing signals and stimuli, as shown in Fig. 6.18. On this basis, recurring patterns in behaviour, facial expressions or gestures can be discovered, so that it is possible to identify which non-verbal signals have which meaning. These insights and aids can then be usefully applied in one's own negotiation strategy and tactics (Obrien 2016).

Table 6.13 summarizes the recommendations for analysis techniques within nonverbal expressions.

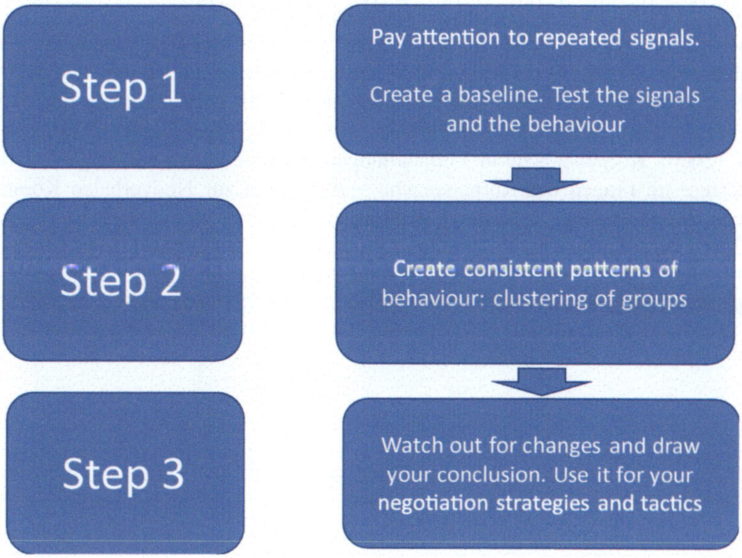

Fig. 6.18 Analysis of non-verbal communication. (Source: Own representation)

Table 6.13 Recommendations for non-verbal communication

Identification of signals in body language, gestures or facial expressions
Setting of a so-called zero line (baseline)
Analysis and identification of behavioural patterns through testing
Formation of "clusters" and categories
Use of key stimuli to "lure" the opponent
Targeted use of own behaviour and elements of non-verbal communication
Caution and attentiveness when interpreting body language, facial expressions or gestures

References

Abdel-Latif, A. (2015). Nicht verblüffen lassen. Schützen Sie sich vor den zehn dreckigsten Verhandlungsfallen. Abgerufen am 1.4.2018. https://www.focus.de/finanzen/experten/adel_abdel-latif/nicht-bluffen-lassen-schuetzen-sie-sich-vor-den-zehn-dreckigsten-verhandlungsfallen_id_4772172.html.

AOK (2018). Körperwissen. Wenn Stress krank macht. Unterschied zwischen Eustress und Stress. https://aok-erleben.de/wenn-stress-krank-macht-unterschied-zwischen-eustress-und-distress/.

Bauer-Jelinek, Ch. (2007). Die geheimen Spielregeln der Macht und die Illusionen der Gutmenschen. Ecowin Verlag Salzburg.

Dathe, T. & Helmold (2018). Erfolgreich im Chinageschäft. Strategien und Handlungsempfehlungen für kleine und mittlere Unternehmen (KMU). Springer Gabler Wiesbaden.

Eckert, M. & Tarnowski, T. (2017). Stress- und Emotionsregulation: Trainingsmanual zum Programm Stark im Stress. Mit E-Book inside und Arbeitsmaterial. Beltz Nordhausen.

Einkaufsmanager (2018). http://www.einkaufsmanager.de.
Helmold, M. (2018). Erfolgreiche Verhandlungen und Best-in-Class Empfehlungen für den Verhandlungsdurchbruch. Manuskript und Workshopunterlagen im Master- und MBA-Studium.
Helmold, M. & Terry, B. (2016). Lieferantenmanagement 2030. Wertschöpfung und Sicherung der Wettbewerbsfähigkeit in digitalen und globalen Märkten, Springer Gabler Wiesbaden.
Mühlisch, S. (2006). Körpersprache in Verhandlungen. Wie Sie nonverbale Signale richtig deuten und einsetzen. In: Fragen der Körpersprache – Antworten zur Nonverbalen Kommunikation. Junfermann Verlag. Auflage. 2 Verlag Paderborn.
Obrien, J. (2016). Negotiations for Procurement Professionals. 2nd Edition. Kogan Page Croyden.
Schranner, M. (2009). Verhandeln im Grenzbereich. Strategien und Taktiken für schwierige Fälle. 8. Auflage. Econ München.

Negotiations in Different Countries

7

He who is wise will, in conversation, think less of what he is talking about than of him to whom he is talking. As soon as he does this, he is sure not to say anything he regrets afterwards
—Arthur Schopenhauer (1788–1860)

Contents

M. Helmold et al., *Successful Negotiations*,
https://doi.org/10.1007/978-3-658-35701-6_7

Summary

Negotiations in different cultures have underlying peculiarities that companies must take into account, as numerous authors recommend. While salespeople or buyers of companies in international trade should not "bend", they should know and respect cultural and country-specific behavioural patterns in intercultural negotiations. It is not unusual to say a clear "no" in Germany, but in Asia this leads to a significant "loss of face" for the other side and thus to a negative negotiating position. Structured negotiation is the rule in Germany, whereas other countries such as India or Italy tend to negotiate in a situational and unstructured way (Sects. 7.7 and 7.11). In intercultural negotiations, therefore, strategies for success and failure as well as icebreakers and icebergs must be taken into account. Finally, special features in Arab countries are discussed, using Saudi Arabia as an example (Sect. 7.14).

7.1 Structure and Examples

Negotiations in different cultures have underlying characteristics that companies need to take into account, as numerous authors recommend (Obrien 2016; Helmold 2018; Dathe and Helmold 2018; Hall 1983; Hofstede 1980, 1991). While company salespeople or buyers in international trade should not 'bend', they should be aware of and respect cultural and country-specific patterns of behaviour in cross-cultural negotiations (Obrien 2016; Helmold 2018; Dathe and Helmold 2018). It is not uncommon to express a clear "no" in Germany, but in Asia this leads to a significant "loss of face" on the part of the other side and thus to a negative negotiating position (Helmold 2018, para. 7.6). Thus, a structured negotiation is the rule in Germany, whereas other countries such as India or Italy tend to negotiate in a situational and unstructured manner para. 7.7 and 7.11. In intercultural negotiations, therefore, strategies for success and failure as well as icebreakers and icebergs need to be taken into account. Table 7.1 shows the breakdown into success and failure strategies of several countries (Helmold 2018; Bügner 2017). In addition, door openers and barriers are presented. Figure 7.1 shows the structure and layout of the chapter with success and failure strategies in the most important industrial nations as well as some neighbouring countries of Germany (OECD 2018). Finally, special features in Arab countries are discussed using Saudi Arabia as an example Sect. 7.14 (Obrien 2016; Helmold 2018; Dathe and Helmold 2018). The classification of success strategies, failure strategies, icebreakers and icebergs provides support in intercultural negotiations, which can open doors but also close them (Helmold 2018; Helmold et al. 2017).

Recommendations for action are given at the end of each sub-chapter. The following countries are described according to the aforementioned criteria, as shown in Table 7.1. In selecting a total of 13 country examples, economic strength (gross domestic product), foreign trade balance and trade relations with Germany were taken into account (OECD 2018). Therefore, in addition to the ten strongest economies, neighbouring countries such as the Netherlands or Denmark are also listed. In addition, a country of the Arab region, Saudi Arabia, with particularities in Islam rounds off this cross-cultural chapter. Results and recommendations are based on a literature review combined with applied research findings and the authors' practical experiences in the mentioned countries (Helmold 2018).

Table 7.1 List of countries with special features in negotiations

7.2	Negotiating in Germany Sect. 7.2
7.3	Negotiating in France Sect. 7.3
7.4	Negotiating in the PRC Sect. 7.4
7.5	Negotiating in the U.S.A. Sect. 7.5
7.6	Negotiating in Japan Sect. 7.6
7.7	Negotiating in India Sect. 7.7
7.8	Negotiating in Russia Sect. 7.8
7.9	Negotiating in the UK Sect. 7.9
7.10	Negotiating in Denmark Sect. 7.10
7.11	Negotiating in Italy Sect. 7.11
7.12	Negotiating in the Netherlands Sect. 7.12
7.13	Negotiating in Brazil Sect. 7.13
7.14	Negotiating in Saudi Arabia and Arab countries Sect. 7.14

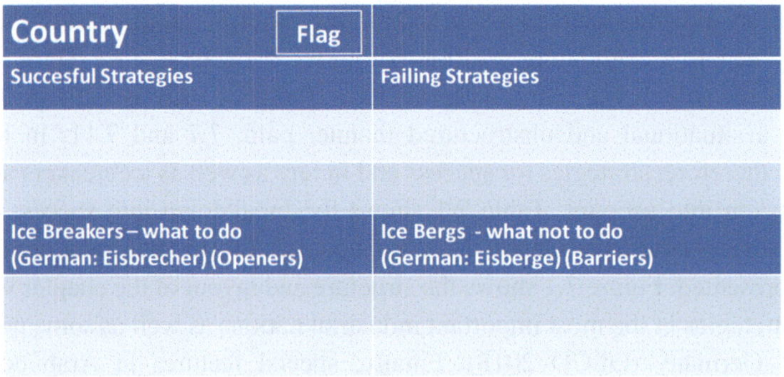

Fig. 7.1 Structure of the country examples. (Source: Marc Helmold's own representation)

7.2 Negotiations in Germany

7.2.1 General Rules

Negotiations in Germany are usually conducted with a clear structure and agenda (Schulz 2017). When Germans negotiate, it is quite possible that the negotiating partner will say, "That proposal is impossible. I cannot agree to it under any circumstances!" It is also not uncommon to say "No" or show open rejection towards the other party's proposal (Dathe and Helmold 2018). Due to the circumstances in the German market, Germans usually work under a high pressure of time, performance and competition. Competition takes place at all levels, not only within an industry between companies, but also within the companies themselves between individual departments and even within individual departments between colleagues. In order to achieve the best possible result for their own side, Germans therefore usually prepare themselves down to the smallest detail before a negotiation or a meeting. Negotiations must begin and end on time (Schulz 2017). In addition to the design of the formal external setting such as clothing, prestigious premises, written material and status symbols, elements such as transparent roles and responsibilities are of central importance in negotiations with German business partners. Formal rules such as addressing German business partners by last name and title are complementary important factors. German negotiators will tend to try to get the maximum out of the negotiation. Therefore, Germans usually enter the negotiation with maximum demands (or demands above the maximum) in order to still have room for negotiation, as Schulz states (Schulz 2017). Untruths, exaggerations or lies are a taboo subject in negotiations with Germans, as a loss of trust can immediately lead to the termination of negotiations or business relations (Sect. 4.3.3.10). Due to Germany's role as world export champion, managers and business partners are often experienced in the international environment, which usually makes negotiations easier (Helmold 2018). Sporting successes or mentioning Germany as the country of "poets and thinkers" can open doors, whereas sporting failures such as the early exit in the 2018 World Cup should not be brought up (Helmold 2018). Figure 7.2 describes

Germany	
Succesful Strategies	**Failing Strategies**
Punctuality and compliance with schedule	**Not being punctual at start, during negotiations and at the end**
Following agenda and structure	**Non-compliance with agenda or significant change of negotiation items**
Respecting and understanding roles and responsibilities	**Not respecting hierarchies**
Fact-based and detailed negotiations	**Personal contact or too close narrowing to negotiation partner**
Summarizing agreements, following agreements – no change during time	**Lies or not keeping promises**
Ice Breakers (German: Eisbrecher) (Openers)	**Ice Bergs (German: Eisberge) (Barriers)**
Positive attitude towards Germany as open society	Early mentioning of family and private background
Interests of German culture, history, industry, innovations etc.	Germany and the 2. World War
Sports, especially football (do not call it soccer)	Defeats in sports

Fig. 7.2 Negotiations in Germany. (Source: Marc Helmold's own representation)

the specifics with success and failure strategies in negotiations with German business partners. Furthermore, from the perspective of international business partners, openers and barriers in negotiations with German business partners are described (Helmold 2018).

7.2.2 Successful and Failed Strategies

See Fig. 7.2.

7.3 Negotiations in France

7.3.1 General Rules

The Germans love the French and the French way of life, but do not take them seriously, as Frank (Frank 2004a) states. The French, on the other hand, do not love the Germans, but admire them (Frank 2004a).

France is not only the land of gourmets and joie de vivre, but also one of the central countries in Europe. France is one of the founding countries and pillars of the European Union (EU) and an important trading partner. With 60 million inhabitants, France has a huge domestic market and is one of the most important international trading partners for Germany Figs. 1.4 and 1.5. Despite cultural convergence and similarities, there are significant differences in negotiation culture. According to Frank, misunderstandings between the French (Gauls) and Germans (Teutons) are bound to occur, so that contract negotiations or takeovers fail apart from key figures and balance sheets (Frank 2004a).

7.3.2 Successful and Failed Strategies

Figure 7.3 shows the successful and unsuccessful strategies for negotiating with French business partners. The first obstacle in negotiations is usually language. French people do not like to negotiate in another language (Frank 2004a). Even though English is one of the languages used at school and university, French people find it difficult to negotiate in English (Frank 2004b). In this context, the rule of success is to conduct negotiations partly or entirely in French. In most cases, an introduction in French is sufficient. Internal discussions are usually conducted in French by the other party, so that the negotiating partner should be allowed time to discuss things. It is also advantageous to have a translator at the table who can explain matters in the local language if necessary. It is also advisable to have a French-speaking lawyer present in the case of legally demanding issues (Frank 2004a). Frank describes that in the French negotiation culture subtleties, ambiguities and often hidden messages (French: sens cache) play an important role which are not immediately recognised (Frank 2004a). Thus, it is quite possible that misunderstandings may

France	
Succesful Strategies	**Failing Strategies**
Appraisal of the French innovations and system of liberty, brotherhood and equality	**Direct start into negotiations**
Numerics and numbers affinity. French like quantitative performance indicators	**Negotiations in English**
Formal compliance with hierarchies	**Competitive negotiations (Pressure)**
Understanding the networks and using French middlemen	**Refusal of lunch or dinner (up to two to three hours possible)**
Making sure that service in terms of meeting and eating is first class service	**Reviling the international role of France in the world**
Ice Breakers (German: Eisbrecher) (Openers)	**Ice Bergs (German: Eisberge) (Barriers)**
Interest in French culture, cusine and society	Economic inequalities with countries like Germany
Knowledge of academic background and using people with same backgroung (grande ecole)	Historical conflicts: France – United Kingdom
Discussion about success in sports	The role of France during the colonial times in Asia or Africa

Fig. 7.3 Negotiations in France. (Source: Marc Helmold's own representation)

occur. Furthermore, good manners, proper dress and polite phrases are important. In addition, good table manners and etiquette are essential, as negotiations often take place over a meal. When inviting French business partners, first-class service and very good food should be ensured. French people can spend up to more than four hours at dinner.

French people are proud of their past and the achievements of the French Revolution. Talking about these achievements is considered an ideal door opener or icebreaker to start a conversation with the negotiating partner. Sporting successes in a wide variety of areas, such as football, handball or judo, are also a guarantee for a positive conversational climate with French business partners.

Elegance and eloquence, coupled with enthusiasm, are characteristics of French negotiation. However, you should be able to justify your argumentation in detail using key performance indicators (KPIs), as the French are very fond of key figures and detail.

Competitive or too fast negotiations with a direct entry are considered to be failing strategies. In this context, one should not appear too technocratic and make one's arguments at the appropriate time. As described at the beginning of the chapter, the French have respect for Germany's economic success, but see comparisons as negative. Also, France's role as a colonial power or in the Algerian War should not be brought up in negotiations, but rather the leadership role of the great nation (French: La grande Nation) in the world should be addressed.

7.4 Negotiations in China

7.4.1 General Rules

Cultural differences are often a major challenge when negotiating with Chinese business partners. For a European, the ambiguity or the imprecise information that is communicated, the constant "beating around the bush" can be very nerve-wracking.

But the Chinese business partners also often have little understanding for the European "stubbornness in details" or "disregard for the principle of give and take". It is difficult for them to understand why some important information, although not explicitly stated but nevertheless obvious, remains hidden from the European partners.

To joint success helps only a lot of patience and keep a cool head. You should try to understand the meaning behind the words said, always show respect and interest and emphasize the common benefits.

Since Chinese business partners are usually good strategists, it is particularly important to understand Chinese negotiation strategy. In this context, the concepts 关系Guānxì and 面子Miànzi are introduced.

Many Chinese consider themselves good strategists. When negotiating, most Chinese business people follow their practiced negotiation strategies. Seeing through these strategies requires a good understanding of the principles 关系 Guānxì and 面子Miànzi.

面子Miànzi literally means "the face", in a broader sense the prestige corresponding to one's status. Applied to the negotiation scenes, it means that one first opens the discussion in a friendly manner and with innocuous topics. In the further course of the discussion, in addition to the factual arguments, one also brings up the topic of the reputation of the acting persons and subliminally suggests that this is connected with unspoken "special rights" existing in the organization or group or that the status would bring about the special success (Thomas 2011).

One can obtain 面子Miànzi in various ways, such as through formal powers, special qualifications, or if one can credibly show that one's actions can provide additional benefits.

In China, one is often asked to give others 面子Miànzi or not to let one's 面子Miànzi be lost. In negotiation practice, it is often expected that one should grant the best possible terms to the most important personalities. Usually the Chinese negotiating partner demands some kind of "quantity discount" for the contract package again shortly before the conclusion, so it is advisable to distribute the "sweets" accordingly over the course of the discussion.

In order to grant the negotiating partners 面子Miànzi, one should strive to always show respect and interest. Words of rejection should be avoided and the common benefits should be repeatedly emphasized. One should always try to understand the real meaning behind the words spoken.

关系Guānxì means knowing the right people in the right places well. Those who have a great 面子Miànzi in a useful network can often achieve things that others cannot. 关系Guānxì, or networks, play a paramount role in Chinese society, not least in business practice. People like to show面子Miànzi to trusted business partners and offer them favorable terms. In some critical situations, good relations with the authorities can be decisive for success.

To expand networks efficiently, Chinese people often mix their contacts from different walks of life. Those who make their influential 关系Guānxì available to others share their important resources. Such an act of true friendship deserves true recognition.

To initiate new 关系Guānxì, business dinners are often held in China. Overall, Chinese culinary culture is an important part of Chinese culture. The famous saying 民以食为天 mín yǐ shí wéi tiān, meaning "food is heaven for the people," makes clear the importance of culinary delights for the people. There are many popular television shows that introduce culinary specialties in China, such as the 舌尖上的中国shé jiān shàng de Zhōngguó ("China on the Tip of the Tongue") television series.

At a business dinner, of course, the primary purpose goes far beyond culinary pleasures. A sumptuous culinary spread gives the host 面子Miànzi, promotes 关系Guānxì building and thus business potential. Even the design of the meal, such as the location of the event, the number and quality of dishes, the group of participants, the seating arrangement, etc., and possibly even the clothing of the participants, gives an idea of the status the host attaches to the business partner.

Many Europeans find the Chinese restaurant very noisy, because for the Chinese, eating together is a joyful event, and this joy should be expressed loudly. Traditionally, during a sumptuous dinner, especially in the north of China, it is good manners to incessantly ask the guests to drink alcoholic beverages. Those who join in the drinking give the challenger 面子Miànzi. One toasts the friendship, cooperation or business deal, etc. As the consumption of alcohol increases, the mood usually rises. Those who refuse alcoholic drinks can explain this, for example, with health reasons. The fact that one has to sit behind the wheel afterwards is also accepted as a reason for not drinking. However, with the current anti-corruption campaign in China, alcohol consumption on official or business occasions is being drastically restricted.

It is important to observe the hierarchy of the participants even in such activities. No one touches the food until the most senior person at the table or the most important guest has started eating. When leaving, people stand up to shake hands as a courtesy. If one is especially respected, one is escorted out of the dining room to the elevator or even to the entrance of the restaurant. The highest form of respect on the part of the host is for the host to wave after the guest as they leave, until you have disappeared from view!

Although many contracts are made at the dinner table, in China you don't open the door, but usually start the conversation with "small talk". The conclusion of a contract may depend on how the mood of the conversation develops, which is why you should choose the topics of conversation carefully.

In principle, one should refrain from addressing topics that cast the country in an unfavorable light, especially if one is not sufficiently informed about the background. Due to a strong collectivism, any critical remarks on the part of an outsider towards the country or the country's culture can trigger a hostile reaction among the Chinese.

The Chinese are very proud of their long history and appreciate it very much when a foreigner deals with their culture. Those who are informed about the lore of the country, have some knowledge of Chinese history or are skilled with chopsticks can really shine.

There are also a number of "harmless" topics, e.g. culinary experiences, funny stories from family life or other Asia-related topics such as Fengshui, Kungfu etc.. The important thing is always to keep the mood positive.

7.4.2 Successful and Failed Strategies

See Fig. 7.4.

PR China	
Succesful Strategies	**Failing Strategies**
Get to know each other through middlemen and previous meetings and dinners	Refusal of business dinners and private invitations
Say positive words about the opposite side after greetings and introduction, e.g. through skillful use of metaphors	Falling into the house with the door and a too strong focus on technical issues
Negotiation in Chinese with the translation support of the local staff	Negotiation in English
Allow time for the translation while visualing the entire situation	Expectation of final decisions during the negotiation
Identification of the roles and responsibilities of the negotiation partner	Directly contradicting the decision makers, which inevitably leads to face losing
Ice Breakers (German: Eisbrecher) (Openers)	**Ice Bergs (German: Eisberge) (Barriers)**
China's rising role in the global economy, respect for historical achievements	Property infringements and pirated copies in china,
Exchange of culinary experiences, especially with Chinese cuisine	Mentioning human rights violations or mentioning air pollution and other ebvironmental issues
Showing pictures of the family and telling funny stories in private life	Rushing to press for the decision

Fig. 7.4 Competence requirements in negotiations. (Source: Marc Helmold's own representation)

7.5 Negotiations in the United States

7.5.1 General Rules

For German business people and negotiators, American negotiations often seem relaxed in tone but tough in substance (Helmold 2018). US Americans conduct negotiations differently than German business people. Often negotiations in America are very direct and very competitive. However, negotiations in America are also conducted with a lot of humour, which is mostly irritating for German business people in this combination (hard on the matter, humorous in tone) (Frank 2016). They see negotiations as a game in which bluffing, tactical leverage and tricks are standard and allowed (Frank 2016). You have to know these tactics so that you can show an appropriate counter-reaction (Helmold 2018). Americans, however, at the same time believe that a negotiation should ultimately aim at a conclusion or agreement (deal). This two-pronged style (exerting strong pressure and aiming to make a "deal" anyway) in negotiations often puts German negotiators in a disadvantageous position, as they often do not know or appreciate the different communication techniques in American negotiations (Frank 2016). It is not uncommon for negotiation outcomes to be negative or for negotiations to drag on for months (Frank 2016). The following elements should be considered when negotiating with Americans (Frank 2016)

- Punctuality for appointments
- Friendly tone with respect for etiquette
- Correctness of clothing
- First name salutation
- Charm, wit and empathy
- Concise and brief explanation of facts
- Action and result orientation

The precept that "time is money" probably influences business communication nowhere more than in the USA (Frank 2016). Punctuality is not just an expression of politeness here, but a sign of professionalism. American managers focus on quick, short-term, and easily enforced successes. If you want to sell yourself well, you must not overrun the usually tight time of your American counterpart. After a brief introduction of names and responsibilities, one should agree on the negotiation structure with a few key points with the negotiating counterpart (Helmold 2018). The rule here is that no more than ten negotiation points should be discussed (Helmold 2018). Frank recommends a tactic of "keeping it short and simple", which is goal-oriented and based on facts (Frank 2016). Effectiveness is the primary goal in negotiations in the US, so that despite disagreements, the negotiation structure or agenda must be worked through in the given time corridor (Helmold 2018). Politics, religion, skin color, or minorities are absolutely taboo topics. Political correctness in the business world is much more pronounced than in Germany. One should also be very careful when making jokes. The language of the Americans is direct to demanding, but never impolite. This is a trick that German managers should definitely adopt, as it is seen as a sign of strength here (Frank 2016). Also, German managers who have studied in the UK should not emphasize the English accent too much, because Americans do not like the comparison with the English and American language.

When it comes to concrete business negotiations, American managers place great value on efficiency: precise schedules and agendas have high priority here. For the German manager, US Americans often appear to be loud, direct and enthusiastic (Brooks 2016). This enthusiasm should be shared and backed up with attributes such as wonderful, great, perfect. Enthusiasm, perhaps exaggerated by German standards, for the merits of one's own negotiating offer does no harm. On the contrary, it shows your counterpart the extent of your commitment. Doing business must always be fun. Americans love not only neutral humor but also the ability to laugh at themselves. If you take these aspects into account, you will have both success and fun in the land of not always unlimited opportunities (Frank 2016).

7.5.2 Successful and Failed Strategies

Negotiations in the United States of America should proceed openly and directly on the basis of a structured agenda after a brief introduction. True to the motto "time is money", all points are worked through. The transparent and brief presentation of the negotiation points as well as advantages of milestones or budget targets should be justified with facts and figures. Addressing the negotiating side personally by name and with enthusiasm helps to create a good and harmonious atmosphere. Taboo topics are gender, nationality or skin colour, also one should be careful with physical touching or jokes. Political correctness is central to business life and behaviour in the USA (Fig. 7.5).

Despite their short history, Americans are proud of their country and the achievements such as liberality, freedom or democracy. Many Americans see the American way of life as the ideal state in the world (Helmold 2018). This is sometimes very difficult for many Europeans, Asians or Africans to understand, however, this should not be brought up too much in negotiations. Also, the role of the U.S. as a political or military force in the world should not be brought up or mentioned in negotiations (Helmold 2018). The recommendation here is to score points in negotiations with enthusiasm and a positive aura.

U.S.A.	
Succesful Strategies	**Failing Strategies**
Introduction and clear explanation of roles and responsibilities	**Forgetting explanation of roles and responsibilities**
Open and direct communication. Enthusiasm and positive reflection when describing proposals or positions	**Sarcasim and irony in negotiations**
Clarity in showing milestones and budget objectives	**Statements about sex, gender or background**
Personal approach. Using the first name	**Sports topics in other countries**
Interests and no open refusal to any proposals	**Stressing of young history of the U.S.A.**
Ice Breakers (German: Eisbrecher) (Openers)	**Ice Bergs (German: Eisberge) (Barriers)**
Knowledge about American sports like American football, baseball, basketball or ice hockey	Missing respect towards minorities
Enthusiam about the „American Way of Life"	Defeat in Vietnam war
Respect towards diversity and variety	Sexistic jokes

Fig. 7.5 Negotiations in the USA. (Source: Marc Helmold's own representation)

7.6 Negotiations in Japan

7.6.1 General Rules

Business dealings in Japan follow much stricter and more formal rules than in Germany. Western business travellers are not expected to behave like Japanese, but some basic rules should be observed. Some Western behaviors, such as expressing direct criticism, may offend the counterpart. By following some important rules, for example when handing out business cards, you show respect to your Japanese hosts and at the same time take away some shyness, especially if they have little experience with foreigners. It is not a matter of learning rules by heart and applying them schematically. Rather, you should respond to your counterpart (AHK Japan 2018). In general, the following applies: be friendly, polite and reserved, everything by a factor more than in Germany, and observe with open eyes and ears. If the Japanese business partners have been abroad more often and for a longer period of time or have a lot to do with foreign guests, it will be found that the conversation is more uncomplicated than previously assumed (Nitobe and Keller 2004). In Japan, great importance is attached to a well-groomed appearance. Especially in business life, a suit and tie for a man and a suit or trouser suit for a woman are indispensable. Only in summer, during the *"(Super) Cool Biz"* time, one can leave the tie in the suitcase.

Attention should also be paid to neat shoes and impeccable socks. Lace-up boots can often be a hindrance. In many companies, shoes are removed at the entrance and replaced with slippers (AHK Japan 2018). To eat at a traditional restaurant, shoes must be removed there before entering. This also applies when entering traditional hotels *(ryokan)*, doctors' offices and temples, even in front of changing rooms in department stores. In the toilet, special slippers are available, which must be exchanged for the normal slippers at the toilet entrance. A room laid out with tatami mats is entered without slippers, only on stockings. In addition to arriving on time, you should give the host a small gift. Gifts from Germany, which have a high reputation in Japan, are suitable for this purpose. In Japan, it is traditional to bow in greeting. For men, the hands should rest on the thighs and form a line with the upper body. For women, the hands are placed one over the other in front of the body. There are different levels of bowing: The more polite you want to be to your counterpart, the deeper you bow. For foreigners the rules are less strict, it is sufficient to indicate a bow with a clear nod. There are also Japanese who offer their hand in greeting, especially when dealing with foreigners, but this is not the rule. If you are unsure, you should wait and see how the other person behaves.

Choosing the right form of address is a science in itself in Japan. The standard form of address is -san appended to the surname. One step more polite, and used by default in emails, is the suffix -sama. It should be noted, however, that when speaking to outsiders about one's family or even one's company, polite salutations are not used for those in one's own group. The following points are mandatory to consider when greeting:

- Punctuality
- Presentation
- Exchange of business cards
- No physical proximity
- Native speakers as translators
- Small gift for guests

Japanese business practices and negotiations can be better understood by considering the Bushido code (Japanese: 武士道, meaning: the way of the warrior) (Winkels and Schlütermann 2013). Bushido is a code of conduct and ethics that still finds its application in business (Winkels and Schlütermann 2013). The roots of Bushido originate from the Japanese Middle Ages. Basic tenets come from Shintoism, Buddhism, and Confuciusism (Winkels and Schlütermann 2013). An essential component of Bushido are the seven most important rules of a samurai:

1. Gi: The right decision from the calmness of the mind
2. Yu: courage, bravery and heroism

3. Jin: The compassion, love and benevolence
4. Rei: The politeness and the right behavior
5. Makoto: The perfect sincerity
6. Meiyo: Glory and Honor
7. Chugi: sense of duty, loyalty and devotion

Numerous companies have therefore integrated these seven principles into their own corporate culture (Frank 2005). Panasonic has incorporated seven principles into its code of ethics, which must be adhered to by company employees worldwide (Panasonic 2018). In addition to the corporate code of ethics, consensus building through mutual approach is one of the key skills for negotiation in Japan. Often seen as inefficient by Europeans, German managers need staying power in negotiations (Winkels and Schlütermann 2013).

7.6.2 Successful and Failed Strategies

Promising success in negotiations is a punctual start as well as a greeting by introducing the participants in negotiations (Jansen 2000). Important in this context are business cards that show the title, function and name in two languages (Helmold 2010). Figure 7.6 shows the

Japan	
Succesful Strategies	**Failing Strategies**
Japanese Greeting (Japanese: Goshoukai or aisatsu) and introduction	**Competitive negotiations and face loss**
Undretanding of time, to give negotiator time to make decision	**Purely English negotiations**
Translation or execution of negotiations in Japanese	**Expectation of decisions in negotiation or pushing for a decision like YES or NO**
Time allowance to understand negotiation proposals and visualisation of difficult elements	**Questions about family and private issues**
Subsequent dinner and bar or Karaoke bar	**Invitation home or private environment**
Ice Breakers (German: Eisbrecher) (Openers)	**Ice Bergs (German: Eisberge) (Barriers)**
Technology leadership	China´s rising role in Asia
Respect of the Japanese culture	Japans role in World War II
Event event, Japanese dinner and Karaoke	Overpacing in decision making

Fig. 7.6 Negotiations in Japan. (Source: Marc Helmold's own representation)

successful and unsuccessful strategies for negotiating with Japanese business partners (Helmold 2010). Although Japanese business partners prefer structured and systematic negotiations, business partners should be given time to understand proposals and arguments and discuss them within the group in the local language (Helmold 2010; Thomas 2001). Japanese decisions are always consensus-driven despite defined responsibilities and usually require long and extensive deliberations (Helmold 2010). Other strategies for success include mentioning Japan's technological leadership in the world and respecting the millennia-old Japanese culture and art (Helmold 2010). Physical closeness and loss of face, on the other hand, should be avoided (Helmold 2010). Japanese people work very long hours, including weekends if necessary, but family issues and personal relationships are not present in negotiations (Helmold and Terry 2016; Helmold 2010).

7.7 Negotiations in India

7.7.1 General Rules

Indian business people tend to be generalists rather than specialists, which makes business partners appear confident, flexible and optimistic (Frank 2006). The hierarchical nature of the Indian caste system—although officially abolished—demands that the superior is seen as the highest authority. The superior makes all decisions and takes full responsibility. Employees usually refuse to take responsibility, they carry out what they are told to do (Frank 2006). In the Indian caste system, there are the following castes:

1. Brahmins: priests and teachers
2. Kshatriyas: Warriors
3. Vaishyas: traders, craftsmen, farmers
4. Shudras: servants, farmhands

Furthermore, there are aspects that are atypical in our Western culture and can therefore seem very alienating. Indians are very relationship-oriented, even in business. People invest a lot of time in conversation and getting to know each other. Talking about friends and family is common and an important factor for a good business relationship. Indians see contracts as flexible and will try to renegotiate existing contracts and agreements periodically (Frank 2006).

7.7.2 Successful and Failed Strategies

Negotiations in India are personal, for this reason, an attempt should be made in advance to establish a personal and good relationship with the negotiating partner (Helmold 2018).

India	
Succesful Strategies	**Failing Strategies**
Involvement of a known mediator	Urging decisions and impatience
Personal contact and relationship to negotiation partner	Lack of respect for superiors or disapproval of superiors or hierarchical structure
Clear negotiations according to hierarchical structure (caste system in India)	Missing mediator and middleman
Patience and endurance. Negotiations can take weeks and months	Competitive negotiation style
Explanation of the interim results. Negotiations appear bureaucratic	Missing information on opposite side
Ice Breakers (German: Eisbrecher) (Openers)	**Ice Bergs (German: Eisberge) (Barriers)**
Haggling with negotiating partners (emotional but friendly haggling)	Mentioning conflict with Pakistan
Achievements of the Indian economy as an industrial nation	Criticism about India and situation of poverty
Personal gifts and appraisal of Mahatma Ghandi, sports like criquet	Wearing leather (devout Hindus worship cows as sacred)

Fig. 7.7 Negotiations in India. (Source: Marc Helmold's own representation)

Final decisions are always made in line with family, social group or company affiliation (Frank 2006). The ability to establish networks is often considered more important than competence or experience. Figure 7.7 shows these aspects.

It is also advisable not to enter into agreements too quickly or to make hasty concessions, as Indian business people are very fond of haggling. Patience is important, and planning should be pursued in the long term, as the Indian concept of time is very often not in line with the German concept of time (Indian Stretch Time). The Indian word "Kal" means "one day away" and stands as a term for a never-ending process (Helmold 2018). Many Indians are devout Buddhists and visit a temple daily. Negotiators are not infrequently asked to visit their own temple with them, which should be done enthusiastically and inquisitively (Helmold 2018). It can also be useful to find out about typical national sports such as cricket while still in Germany in order to impress your negotiating partners (Helmold 2018).

Topics like education can be good door openers. Meanwhile, many families send their children to university in European countries. Therefore, diplomas or certificates from German educational institutions are considered very important. Politics or addressing poverty can be icebergs and therefore should not be mentioned. India is carrying on a conflict with its neighbour Pakistan for many years, so this issue should not be brought up. Besides politics, sex or even current assaults on tourists are absolute taboo topics in a very conservative society.

7.8 Negotiations in Russia

7.8.1 General Rules

Negotiations in Russia are usually conducted in the context of a business dinner, as Fig. 7.8 shows (Frank 2004b). At a business dinner in Russia, one is usually invited to an exclusive restaurant. An invitation to one's home is rare, but an extraordinary honour. A bouquet of flowers for the host's wife is part of the welcome. The alcohol abuse of earlier years is dwindling in modern business life in Russia, but one should be careful about drinking habits in negotiations (Frank 2004b). Older Russians love vodka and can tolerate a lot of it. Those who are not used to it should only keep up with toasts. In this extremely important ritual, the first toast always belongs to the host. Afterwards, it is important to address the host in a toast of one's own and to highlight him or her or the overall situation in a positive way. This creates a good atmosphere for later negotiations.

Russians like to come to a conclusion quickly in negotiations. They are results-oriented and usually stick strictly to the agenda:

Russia	
Succesful Strategies	**Failing Strategies**
Patience and endurance during negotiation process	**Critique about Russia (social, political or ecosystem)**
Openness, directness and balanced competitive and collaborative style of negotiations. Russians like openness and toughness in conflicts	**Giving in too fast and not competing against demands (time consuming)**
Awareness of and respect to hierarchies	**Too competitive negotiations.**
Russian calendar and holidays	**Superficial negotiations**
Relationship with decision maker and small gifts	**Missing relationships with decision makers**
Ice Breakers (German: Eisbrecher) (Openers)	**Ice Bergs (German: Eisberge) (Barriers)**
Russische Literatur, Kunst etc.	Political conflicts , e.g. Crim coflict
Wodka drinking and speaking out toasts	Communsim or missing democratic strucutres in Russia
Russia and the patriotric war (World War II)	Critique about Russia, President Putin or the political system

Fig. 7.8 Negotiations in Russia. (Source: Marc Helmold's own representation)

- Straightforward negotiation does not mean that Russians are averse to small talk and privacy. What is important for them is to build a personal relationship with negotiating partners—for future talks.
- Beware of taboo topics such as crime and the national budget. The bad economic situation should be passed over just as generously as current catastrophes (such as the sinking of the submarine "Kursk" or the fire of the Moscow TV tower).
- Witty (not shallow!) humor is very much in demand among Russians.

  Most Russians are educated above average—not only politically and economically, but also culturally. One should adapt to this level—and occasionally let appreciative words flow in.

The time needed for negotiations in Russia should not be underestimated! People often talk about the "factor 4", which means that it takes four times as long to do the same business in Russia as in the West. Conversely, one should not trust that nothing will happen for a long time during the negotiations—sometimes very important decisions have to be made at great speed.

"It is helpful to make a complex subject of negotiation as transparent as possible. In addition to PowerPoint presentations, simple aids such as flip charts or blackboards are also useful. Furthermore, key terms should be defined together in advance in order to eliminate misunderstandings from the outset and to structure the course of the negotiation. In this context, a stringent agenda can also be useful," says the sales manager of a German automotive supplier, summarizing his experience. In principle, the same rules apply in Russia as everywhere else: "The simpler, the better" in language and "the more descriptive, the clearer" in explanations.

Without falling under the suspicion of wanting to bribe the other party, it is a good idea to do the Russian business partner a small favour. This should be done out of sympathy, but not from a position of weakness or even an emergency situation.

You Only Talk to the Boss

In Russia, there is a strong sense of authority, whether in politics or in business. This means that the CEO will not necessarily hand over his decision-making powers to subordinates and therefore, in his absence, a decision cannot be made.

This is also the view of the project manager of a German automotive supplier about a planned cooperation in Russia: "You can only do business if you talk directly to the general director." And he is right, managers, in the capacity of general directors or managing directors, unlike in Germany, do not delegate decision-making powers to their subordinates. And what the general manager doesn't direct, isn't carried out. In his absence, nothing happens.

7.8.2 Successful and Failed Strategies

See Fig. 7.8.

7.9 Negotiations in the United Kingdom

7.9.1 General Rules

Since Britain's entry into the European Union (EU) in 1972, the country has experienced a continuous economic boom and increased trade with countries in Europe (IPB 2018). Meanwhile, there is a lot of exchange between the main continent of Europe and the UK. Moreover, due to its history as a colonial power, Britain has relations in Commonwealth countries, which is also used by European countries and Germany (Meyering 2018). Recently, the UK has decided to leave the EU (Brexit). After Brexit, there will still be strong economic relations. These economic relations automatically lead to negotiations with ventures and managers from the UK. The British negotiation style differs from the German negotiation style and has its pitfalls from the German perspective. For example, some authors describe that typical German behaviour automatically triggers reluctance in a British person (IHK Rhein-Neckar 2018).

7.9.2 Successful and Failed Strategies

When negotiating in the UK, certain rules should be followed as icebreakers as follows (Marks 2006), Fig. 7.9 describes success and failure strategies as well as icebreakers and icebergs when negotiating in the UK:

1. Politeness and adherence to etiquette
2. Negotiations in the mother tongue: the language trap
3. Distance and no body proximity
4. Building relationships through "small talk"
5. Fairness and sportsmanship
6. Avoidance of exaggerations
7. Binding
8. Emotionless negotiations
9. Spontaneous pragmatism
10. Avoidance of political topics and no jokes about the monarchy

7.9.2.1 Courtesy and Observance of Etiquette

British politeness is recognized in the world and also plays a crucial role in negotiations with British business partners (Marks 2006). Meyering describes this politeness with a quote from Wiliam Horman, the famous head of the private school Eaton in the fifteenth century (Meyering 2018). "It is courtesy and good girth that make us human." This belief has not changed for many Britons to this day. In order not to offend their counterpart, Brits

Great Britain	
Succesful Strategies	**Failing Strategies**
Politeness and etiquettes	**Competitive and impatient negotiations**
Formal and smart business dresses	**Discourtesy and informal business dresses**
Punctuality and compliance with tea time etc.	**Non awareness of tea time**
Greeting cards (Christmas cards) etc. after negotiations	**Touching or being to close to the negotiation partner**
Sports topics and betting	**Sexism or jokes about monarchy**
Ice Breakers (German: Eisbrecher) (Openers)	**Ice Bergs (German: Eisberge) (Barriers)**
Small talk, appraisals of dress and small compliments	Jokes about monarchy and queen
Interests in sports like criquet, rugby, golf, football or tennis	Defeats in football against Germany
Humour of british people	Falkland war and other military conflicts. Topics like Brexit

Fig. 7.9 Negotiations in the UK. (Source: Marc Helmold's own representation)

like to express themselves indirectly. They usually hold back criticism, negative opinions and doubts. If at all, they express negative things "through the flower" or nicely packaged (Meyering 2018). With other things, on the other hand, they are very pragmatic and direct. For example, the British informally hand out business cards at the beginning of the conversation. Cards they receive themselves are usually pocketed quickly without this being perceived as impolite. These rules of British politeness should always be heeded in any case (Meyering 2018).

7.9.2.2 Negotiating in the Mother Tongue: The Language Trap

Even if British negotiators have a good command of English, from the point of view of the negotiator from the other country, English is usually only the second language. The subjunctive is a very often used and acceptable grammatical form in the English language to express requests, proposals, wishes or refusals (Would it be possible, Could it be possible). Experts therefore recommend the use of polite forms in the subjunctive. Direct addresses should be avoided (you must, you should). In the English language, little things can often put you in a bad position. For example, it does not go down well with high-ranking executives, who often include members of the aristocracy, if they are greeted with "Hello". Here, the old greetings such as "Good morning/afternoon/evening" are far from being obsolete. Colleagues on the same hierarchical level, on the other hand, can certainly greet you with "Hello" (Meyering 2018). Also, "How do you do?" is not the same as "How are you?" The former is far more formal and always requires the counter-question "How do you do?". This can be supplemented with a "very well, thank you" if necessary. "How are you?", on the other hand, is always answered with "fine, thank you" or "very well" before the counter-question is asked (Meyering 2018). It is particularly difficult to choose the correct form of address for female negotiators and business partners. Generally, one should choose "Ms", as this form of address is neutral. Married interlocutors can be addressed as "Mrs.". Just as much care should be taken in choosing the correct geographical designations in the British Isles. England is not the same as the United Kingdom, but only its southern part. Therefore, Scots, Welsh and Irish should not be referred to as English either. It is best to refer to all inhabitants of the main island and Northern Ireland as British (Meyering 2018).

7.9.2.3 Distance and No Body Contact

British negotiators dislike physical proximity and close contact in business situations. Therefore, unnecessary physical contact should be avoided. Britons also shake hands less frequently than continental Europeans, so greetings should be brief (Meyering 2018). People in the UK also do not shake hands when saying goodbye.

7.9.2.4 Building Relationships Through Small Talk

Of course, one can limit the small talk to the topic of weather. The location of the British Isles on the edge of the North Atlantic provides sufficient conversation material. But this does not achieve the actual goal of casual chit-chat. Small talk helps to build good and trusting relationships. After all, the Queen's subjects prefer to do business with people they trust. That's why they don't just want to talk about trivial topics during small talk, but often show genuine interest in their conversation partner (Meyering 2018).

7.9.2.5 Fairness and Sportsmanship

Britons have a sporting spirit and a keen sense of when and how everyone involved in a meeting or collaboration gets their money's worth. That's why, when negotiating, they consider all aspects of the matter and weigh them carefully. They are only really satisfied with the result achieved if both sides clearly benefit from the solution. Negotiation outcomes should therefore always be balanced and in the interests of both sides (Meyering 2018).

7.9.2.6 Avoidance of Exaggerations

Britain is the motherland of irony and humour, as Meyering describes (Meyering 2018). Britons also do not always take themselves seriously on the outside. Rather, they like to make others laugh by making jokes about themselves. The inhabitants of the kingdom do not like to put their own achievements in the spotlight. Know-it-alls, braggarts and people who proudly flaunt their own achievements are totally disliked by Brits. Those with real power, money or academic merit don't need to peddle it in the motherland of understatement. Instead, they are appreciated for their modesty (Meyering 2018).

7.9.2.7 Liability

Harmonious and respectful relationships are an inseparable part of life for the British. That's why they do everything in their power to preserve the dignity of their counterparts in every situation and to treat them with decency. Anyone who violates this imperative in business life by acting out of character, becoming angry or devaluing their counterpart and not letting them finish, destroys the relationship so profoundly that it can no longer be patched up. The following elements, which are insignificant for Germans, can show commitment and respect in the UK and can be seen as icebreakers (Meyering 2018):

- Sending greeting cards at Christmas or on birthdays
- Expressing thanks through greeting cards rather than e-mails
- Encounters with a positive, personal remark, for example, about the clothes of the interlocutor or the wonderful view from his office open up
- Apologize for even the smallest thing
- Thank sincerely and personally for small favors

7.9.2.8 Emotion-Free Negotiations

British people plan meetings and negotiations thoroughly. It is common practice to email the agenda and timetable of the talks to all participants in advance, so that everyone can prepare. The roles of the members of the individual negotiating teams are also clearly defined. If everyone is on the same hierarchical level, they exchange opinions equally (Meyering 2018). If there are differences in rank, the highest-ranking person leads the conversation or appoints someone to take over the task. In addition, there is often a minute-taker or secretary (Meyering 2018). Furthermore, it is common to record interim and discussion results as well as decisions on how to proceed in writing (Meyering 2018). The negotiation itself is always conducted by British people in a friendly manner, but without showing emotion. They closely control facial expression and body language and clearly withdraw them. Anyone who exerts pressure in negotiations, pushes their counterpart into a corner or tries to take advantage, damages the relationship with their interlocutor so fundamentally that it is usually beyond repair. This is because one violates the highest maxim of British business life: fairness. If, on the other hand, you occasionally give in and are prepared to compromise, you are behaving in the way that the British expect of you (Meyering 2018).

The Queen's subjects also always have an alternative in mind. Often, however, they only bring it up at the end of the negotiations and express themselves vaguely until then. Despite their politeness, this makes them difficult interlocutors. The same applies to the fact that the British take their time with decisions and stick to them unalterably once they have made them. Renegotiation should be avoided in the UK (Meyering 2018).

7.9.2.9 Spontaneous Pragmatism

British companies often have steeper hierarchies than German ones. In addition, areas of responsibility are usually clearly demarcated from one another, so that employees can usually only lead projects to success if they work in a very team-oriented manner and communicate efficiently. As a result, British people usually approach tasks in a very goal-oriented and pragmatic way. They often spontaneously make the decision that the situation requires at the moment. The British are also far less structured and detail-oriented than many German colleagues. British pragmatism also shapes the demands that employees and entrepreneurs make on how perfect a solution has to be. The British carefully weigh up whether 100% performance is worthwhile or whether 80% is also enough (Meyering 2018).

7.9.2.10 Avoidance of Political Topics and No Jokes About the Monarchy

Political topics and jokes about the Royal Family should be avoided in negotiations and business relationships. In principle, the British have a very positive attitude towards the Royal Family (Meyering 2018).

7.10 Negotiations in Denmark

7.10.1 General Rules

Although Germany and Denmark are neighboring countries, there are concise differences between Danes and Germans (Helmold 2018). Denmark is known to many as a holiday destination and is admired worldwide for its unique architecture. Moreover, the country is economically successful and an important trading partner of Germany. The most important German export goods to Denmark are machinery, food and feed, motor vehicles and motor vehicle parts. The most important German import goods from Denmark are foodstuffs and animal feed, machinery, agricultural products and hunting. According to OECD statistical data collection, Denmark is among the top 20 countries in the world for imports and exports to and from Germany (OECD 2018).

At first glance, doing business in Denmark seems easy, especially since people communicate in an easy-going, relaxed, direct and friendly manner. Danish business partners get to the point quickly, are often relaxed, quite informal and have a great sense of humour. But caution is needed here, as making contracts is not so easy (Helmold 2018). Throughout Scandinavia, communication tends to be unemotional, calm and with an "understatement". This is only partially true for Danes, although they are considered temperamental compared to Swedes and Norwegians and are often referred to as "the Italians of the North" (Helmold 2018). Nevertheless, extroverted rhetoric and hyperbole are generally not appropriate in Denmark. The body language of the Danes also expresses this. In particular, one should refrain from touching the arm of the counterpart when shaking hands for the first time. It is also advisable to keep a sufficient distance from the business partner (Helmold 2018).

Most Danes have a very good command of written and spoken English, and many also have a good command of German. You can start the correspondence in German, but a hint about the possibility to continue the correspondence in English makes the communication easier in most cases. At the beginning of negotiations, the Danish business partner is generally rather reserved. He underplays his own achievements, which is partly similar to the English culture of understatement, attaches importance to punctuality and a structured agenda (Helmold 2018).

7.10.2 Successful and Failed Strategies

When negotiating with German business partners, Danes are cool and distant (Helmold 2018). Danes like to understate things, which is partly similar to the British negotiation culture (Helmold 2018). Figure 7.10 summarises key characteristics in negotiations with Danish business partners (Helmold 2018).

Danish business partners also value punctuality and a structured agenda in negotiations (Helmold 2018). The social principle is summed up in a short formula: "Jante Lov", which translates as "Don't think you are more than your neighbour". Thus, in Denmark, there is

Denmark	
Succesful Strategies	**Failing Strategies**
Personal negotiation style (first name)	**Distance and too formal negotiations**
Acceptance of private invitations	**Arrogance and disrespect**
Unformal dress and unformal negotiations	**Untruth and exaggerations**
Equality between men and women	**Competitive negotiation style**
Lose and objective-oriented negotiation style	**Too much focus on hierarchies**
Ice Breakers (German: Eisbrecher) (Openers)	**Ice Bergs (German: Eisberge) (Barriers)**
Humour and friendliness	Jokes about Denish monarchy
Denish success in sports, e.g handball world cup in 2019	Negative statements about expensive social system and taxes
Denmark as open countries with traditions	Criticism about high tax on alcohol

Fig. 7.10 Negotiations in Denmark. (Source: Marc Helmold's own representation)

true equality between men and women. It is quite normal for male managers to take parental leave as well. And between business partners, a casual relationship is usually quickly established in which people address each other as “Du”. The style of dress is rather casual. At negotiations, you can wear jeans and a sweater. Pure business lunches and dinners are increasingly held in company-owned rooms. To build a personal relationship and to crown a successful negotiation, invitations to the private sphere of Danish business people are also not uncommon (Helmold 2018). To avoid misunderstandings: dinner is called “middag” in Danish.

The Dane can’t stand scorn and derision of the monarchy and the popular queen any more than he can criticism of his “welfare system”, which functions with high tax burdens. Otherwise, you can discuss “God and the world” with Danes. The Danes negotiate directly and openly. They expect clear conditions and presentations, calculate very precisely and are well prepared during negotiations. Whoever offers the best price and quality ratio usually makes the deal (Helmold 2018). It is important that offers and presentations are always clear and informative (Helmold 2018).

7.11 Negotiations in Italy

7.11.1 General Rules

Although Italy has been considered a euro crisis country for several years, Italian goods and commodities are enjoying ever-growing popularity in the world (OECD 2018). In the past two years, the country generated a large export surplus (OECD 2018). Due to increasing demand for Italian products from Japan Sect. 7.6 and the People’s Republic of China Sect. 7.4, Italy generated an export surplus of more than 50 billion EUR in 2017 (OECD 2018). In 2017, exports had exceeded imports by just under 42 billion EUR. After Germany Sect. 7.2 with more than 257 billion EUR and the Netherlands Sect. 7.12 with more than 60 billion EUR, Italy thus has the third highest trade surplus in the European Union. According to the OECD, an important reason for this is the increasing demand for “Made in Italy” from Asian countries (OECD 2018). Exports to Japan, for example, grew by almost 10%, and those to China by more than 6%. Export hits include luxury goods, food, vehicles and precision machinery. The EU Commission expects the gross domestic product in the southern European country to continue to grow in the coming years (Helmold 2018).

The most important rule in negotiations in Italy is to pay attention to a well-groomed appearance and the “good figure” (Italian: bella figura) (Kness-Bastaroli and Dahm 2006). As numerous as the regional characteristics of Italy are, the mentality of the people is just as different (Kness-Bastaroli and Dahm 2006). There are sometimes such great differences between northern and southern Italy that it is difficult to formulate generally applicable rules for dealing with business partners (Frank 2010a).

Italians insist on respecting hierarchical levels, so this aspect must be taken into account. Negotiations must be conducted with the boss and decision-maker (Italian: Padrone) (Frank 2010a). Those who miss the "padrone" or do not dress professionally have bad cards in northern and southern Italy, Frank describes as a potential failure strategy (Frank 2010a). To this day, the economic difference between the industrially underdeveloped Mezzogiorno in the south of Italy and the prosperous north is striking (Frank 2010a). One of the reasons for this is the different historical development: while the feudal system still prevailed in the south, the north, bordering France, Switzerland and Austria, was already economically advanced (Frank 2010a). In "polychronic" cultures, which also include South America and the Mediterranean region, human relationships are more important than abstract schedules, several tasks are managed in parallel, interruptions are frequent, flexibility is therefore important (Frank 2010a).

7.11.2 Successful and Failed Strategies

Anyone conducting negotiations in Italy must be prepared for long negotiations (Frank 2010a). As in other polychronic societies, personal business relationships and the development of a network are of central importance for business success in Italy (see Sect. 1.6.2.2). Characteristic of negotiations in Germany or Switzerland as monochronic societies are the formalisation of relationships and a negotiation style that is clear, unambiguous and systematic Sect. 7.2. In addition to the clear line, punctuality, structure and clear distribution of roles are visible (Helmold 2018).

In Italy, these negotiation patterns do not help, as Italy belongs to the so-called "high-context cultures" para. 1.6.2.1 (Hall 1976). In these cultural areas, as in other countries in Southern Europe or South America, signs of common ground and trust are fundamental (Frank 2010a). Therefore, good relationship building should be worked on before negotiations (Frank 2010a). Although Germans are expected to be punctual and straightforward, Italians can appear unpunctual. Also, deviation from the agenda is not uncommon (Frank 2010a). Negotiations in Italy need to be empathetic and also slightly emotional in order to convince the negotiating opponent (Frank 2010a). Impatience, lack of trust and an insufficient relationship with the decision maker are considered failure strategies (Frank 2010a). As with other countries, cultural achievements or sporting successes are icebreakers, although failures in football should rather not be mentioned (Frank 2010a). Figure 7.11 shows icebreakers, icebergs and successful strategies in negotiations in Italy (Frank 2010a).

Italy	
Succesful Strategies	**Failing Strategies**
Formal business dress for men and women (Bella Figura)	Arrogance and narrow minded behaviours
Awereness of hierarchies and decision makers (Italian: Padrone)	Urging decisions and competitive negotiations
Patience and endurance	Impatience and short-term oriented results or agreements
Mirroring behaviour. Rational emotional negotiations including signals of body language	Missing relationships
Flexible and dynamic negotiation execution	Missing trust
Ice Breakers (German: Eisbrecher) (Openers)	**Ice Bergs (German: Eisberge) (Barriers)**
Italy's success in football and other sports	Absence in football world cup 2018 in Russia
Italy's culture and innovations	Italy at the times of Mussulini
Italy's beauty (regional variances)	Topics like politics, religion or crime (Mafia)

Fig. 7.11 Negotiations in Italy. (Source: Marc Helmold's own representation)

7.12 Negotiations in the Netherlands

7.12.1 General Rules

The Netherlands (officially: Kingdom of the Netherlands) is famous as a seafaring nation and for its capable merchants. The country plays an important role in the past and present of the European Union (EU) and as a neighbour is one of the most important trading partners for Germany. Dutch people are born merchants with an extremely long and successful tradition. Their economy is highly dependent on foreign trade and is known for stable industrial relations, moderate inflation, a decent trade surplus. As a central country in the EU, the Netherlands represents one of the most important goods handling centres in Europe (Frank 2010b).

German business people like to come into a negotiation with a well-organised and structured agenda and want to work through the checklist point by point. The Dutch, on the other hand, approach business negotiations openly and flexibly. They are also happy to talk about private matters. Dutch people communicate in a very informal way and like to call their conversation and negotiation partners by their first names. English should be preferred to German (Frank 2010b).

7.12.2 Successful and Failed Strategies

Business negotiations usually take place in meeting rooms. However, for dinner the venue may be changed and a restaurant may be chosen. It is Dutch custom to pay separately (Let us go Dutch). This means that everyone pays for themselves. If you are invited home by a business partner, this is a very friendly gesture and should be accepted if possible. First impressions count and should be conservative in terms of dress. Extreme fashions and flamboyant appearances, such as those often seen in the centre of Amsterdam, are hardly met with approval in Dutch business life. A conservative, elegant style of dress, similar to that in the UK, is more recommended here. Structures and hierarchies are hardly visible in the Netherlands, so it is advisable to involve all members of the other party's negotiating team respectfully and politely (Frank 2010b) (Fig. 7.12).

Netherlands	
Succesful Strategies	**Failing Strategies**
Openness and addressing by first name	**Arrogance of negotiation partners**
Using first name and building a relationship	**Titles and insisting on hierarchies**
Respect to all hierarchical levels	**Formalities and static negotiations**
Involvement of all negotiation participants	**Speaking German**
Spontaneity and flexibility in negotiation	**Politics and history of colonies**
Ice Breakers (German: Eisbrecher) (Openers)	**Ice Bergs (German: Eisberge) (Barriers)**
Success in ice speed skating	Defeat in football world cup 1974 against Germanay and non participation in world cup 2018
Sportsmen like J. Cruff, show stars like R. Carell	Jokes about monarchy
Artists (Rembrandt) and Dutch innovations in history	Drugs, which are legal in the Netherlands

Fig. 7.12 Negotiations in the Netherlands. (Source: Marc Helmold's own representation)

7.13 Negotiations in Brazil

7.13.1 General Rules

Brazil (Portuguese: República Federativa do Brasil) is the largest country and the largest economy in South America. Brazil has more than 208 million inhabitants. Brazil is the eighth largest economy in the world (OECD 2018). It is the only country in South America besides Haiti where Portuguese is spoken. Brazil is a polychronic society according to Hall's cultural understanding, like Italy or Spain (Hall 1966). Brazilians are therefore used to doing several things at once, but in negotiations this can mean that each individual process takes longer and proceeds against a systematic agenda. German negotiators must therefore be prepared, when negotiating in Brazil, for their partners to jump around the issues and also to pick up aspects that are completely off the agenda, which they drop just as quickly (Anson 2013). German business partners, as a society of a monochronic culture based on systematics, punctuality and structure, therefore very often see the Brazilian approach as unstructured and with a lack of systematics (Anson 2013). Likewise, many managers understand this cultural difference as a low capacity for stringent action or even a low interest in the substantive issues. From a Brazilian point of view, however, this type of approach does have its advantages, as it prevents people from getting bogged down in one point and allowing controversy to cloud the negotiating climate. Brazilian business partners are much more relationship-oriented than issue-oriented (Anson 2013). Little happens on the basis of a 'right', a 'duty' or a written agreement. A personal 'obligation', on the other hand, motivates people to do their best for the other person. This, in turn, may mean complying with formal obligations or even going against them, depending on the situation (Anson 2013). People with whom it seems difficult to establish a personal relationship are considered outsiders in Brazilian society (Anson 2013). This is even more true when they deny them the sense of the "little twist" (Portuguese: jeitinho) that can be used to unravel and resolve entangled situations (Anson 2013). The proverbial Brazilian enthusiasm easily leads to situations in negotiations where ambition exceeds what is actually feasible. Especially when a positive and emotional mood is established, Brazilian partners like to make relationship-oriented rather than fact-oriented commitments. Deadline commitments or promises can be understood here as intentions through which the Brazilian negotiating partner emphasizes urgency (Anson 2013). On the one hand, it takes some experience to determine when a statement is predominantly relationship-oriented and when it is actually meant literally. On the other hand, Germans often lack the behavioral repertoire to deal with primarily relationship-oriented statements (Anson 2013). The following aspects must be taken into account when negotiating in Brazil:

- Respect for the decision-maker: strong hierarchical structures
- Haggling is part of the cultural understanding of the Brazilians

- Relationship building and patience
- Take into account delays of the other party
- Involve translator (Portuguese)
- Accept invitations to restaurants and clubs

7.13.2 Successful and Failed Strategies

Brazilian companies are clearly hierarchically structured. The middle management level is rather rare. Negotiations should be set as high as possible in the hierarchy. In most cases, only the managing director has decision-making power (Anson 2013). Contrary to German negotiation customs, haggling over prices, numbers or other aspects is part of daily life in Brazil (Anson 2013). Therefore, it is important to set your offer higher in order not to offend the counterpart from Brazil (Anson 2013). Patience and perseverance are key in this context, as one usually does not get concrete statements in the negotiations (Anson 2013). A "yes" in Brazil means "maybe" or "probably" at most. A "no" does not exist and is considered impolite (Anson 2013).

Pushing behaviour is perceived as aggressive. A good relationship should therefore be established first, and it is also advisable to ensure a friendly aura and to take an interest in the person, their attitudes, values and needs (Anson 2013). The form of address is usually "Senhor" (for men) and "Dona" (for women) plus first names, one then also quickly arrives at "Du" (Anson 2013). In view of the turbulent traffic situations in large cities such as Rio and Sao Paulo, but also because Brazilians have a different understanding of time, delays of up to an hour are not uncommon and are quite tolerated. Although many business people speak English, it is better to negotiate in Portuguese. Offers, technical documents and operating documents should generally be translated into Portuguese. Brazilians are very hospitable. Invitations usually lead to clubs or restaurants. Shared meals are used to maintain relationships, and business is discussed only after coffee (Anson 2013). Brazilians are fond of soccer and sports, so topics such as football, Pelé, or volleyball are ideal icebreakers. Carnival also enjoys a high reputation in the world, especially as a topic when inviting people to restaurants or clubs (Anson 2013). Brazil unfortunately also has negative sides such as crime, slums and poverty. These topics should not be discussed with business partners, after all Brazil is the eighth largest world economy (OECD 2018). Painful defeats can also tip the mood, especially the defeat against Germany in the home football World Cup in Brazil in 2014. Figure 7.13 shows successful and failed success strategies for negotiations in Brazil (Anson 2013).

Brazil	
Succesful Strategies	**Failing Strategies**
Professional and smart business dress style	**Pushing for negotiation results**
Set up of relationships by understanding the hierarchies	**Non understanding for unpunctuality**
Understaning of frequent breaks and delays	**Non compliance with decision making levels**
Involvement of a Portuguese translator and Brazilian middlemen in negotiations with public bodies	**Failure to take into account the complexity and bureaucracy of the administrative structures**
Patience and endurance	**Negotiations in German or English**
Ice Breakers (German: Eisbrecher) (Openers)	**Ice Bergs (German: Eisberge) (Barriers)**
Success in Football and idols like Pele	7:1 defeat in footbal at home world cup against Germany
Acceptance of invitation to restaurant, bar or club	Poverty and slums
Brazil´s carneval	Discrimination of native Brazilian indians

Fig. 7.13 Negotiations in Brazil. (Source: Marc Helmold's own representation)

7.14 Negotiations in Saudi Arabia and Arab Countries

7.14.1 General Rules

Visitors to Islamic countries sometimes move in modern and cosmopolitan societies, but also encounter rigid moral concepts and systems that are closed to strangers (Krachtowil 2018). Successful businesswomen and politicians may be confronted with women wrapped in full-body veils who are not allowed to leave home or court without male protectors (Krachtowil 2018). In numerous Arab countries such as Saudi Arabia, tolerant religious practice is in strong tension with fundamentalist beliefs. Negotiations in Arab countries are very much shaped by these beliefs (Krachtowil 2018). Alcohol, for example, is strictly forbidden for Muslims in strongly religious countries such as Saudi Arabia or Dubai (Krachtowil 2018). The family is considered a pillar within the Arab level of relationships and ranks above all other levels, so having an extensive network can be very useful (Thiel 2018). Similarly, women usually hold a subordinate role, which can affect negotiations (Thiel 2018). The following ten basic rules should be taken into account when doing business with partners in Saudi Arabia and Arab countries:

1. Maintaining the relationship level with decision makers
2. Personalized business relationships
3. Presence and networking
4. Use of intermediaries
5. Arab time management
6. Consideration of cultural customs
7. Consideration of religious customs
8. Compliance with hierarchical structures
9. Indirect and metaphorical style of negotiation
10. Respect for taboo subjects

7.14.2 Recommendations for Negotiations in Saudi Arabia

7.14.2.1 Maintaining the Relationship Level with Decision Makers

Arab culture is a strongly relational one (Krachtowil 2018). Often the education, qualification or competence is secondary in relation to the relationship of the decision maker, so the preparation of negotiations requires a thorough analysis of the relationship (Krachtowil 2018). A long-term successful business relationship with Arab partners requires a solid relationship level that needs to be built over several years (Krachtowil 2018). Figure 7.14 summarises the recommendations for successful negotiations in Saudi Arabia (Helmold 2018).

7.14.2.2 Personalised Business Relationships

In the Arab world, the motto "Family and friends first! Business is personal" also applies in business life (Krachtowil 2018). It is therefore crucial to build and sustain a solid relationship level with the Arab business partner, as the authors recommend (Krachtowil 2018; Thiel 2018). Several meetings with the business partner per year ensure a solid relationship maintenance in Saudi Arabia. The first priority here is always the personal meeting with the Arab business partner, after which contact should be consistently maintained by telephone, fax or e-mail. Continuity and steadiness in business contact are a central factor for success in the Arab region. A solid relationship comes before business. Although the national language is Arabic, the majority of business partners speak English. In order to establish social contacts, which are very important for business success, one should at least master the formal courtesies. It is helpful to learn idioms and other everyday phrases and weave them into the conversation. Just trying to speak Arabic will be honored by the person you are talking to. As the most traditional country in the Arabian Peninsula, Islamic commandments are strictly observed in Saudi Arabia. This is also required of foreigners. Violations can end up in court. A strict distinction is made between women and men, meaning that no reciprocal greetings are approved and normally no conversation between the sexes occurs (Hünniger 2018). Respect, honor, and reputation are very sensitive and elementary issues for Arabs. Strangers should not touch these guiding principles, as their

Saudi Arabia	
Succesful Strategies	**Failing Strategies**
Maintenance of relationships on decision maker levels	Competitive negotiations
Personalised negotiations	Negotiations with experts who know culture
Usage of respected and influencing middlemen who know culture, people and rituals	Impatience and pushing quickly for results
Network with authorities in economy and politics	Unawareness of hierarchy
Indirect negotiation style, using metaphers	Negotiations without decision maker
Ice Breakers (German: Eisbrecher) (Openers)	**Ice Bergs (German: Eisberge) (Barriers)**
Topics like family	Topics about political enemies like Israel or Quatar
Gifts, but no alcohol	Disrespect of religion and rituals
Acceptance of Arabian time management	Role of women in Saudi Arabia

Fig. 7.14 Negotiations in Saudi Arabia. (Source: Marc Helmold's own representation)

violation can lead to social ostracism of the person concerned. Central European manners, such as complimenting the wife or daughter of the interlocutor, are not customary and are better refrained from Hünniger (2018).

7.14.2.3 Presence and the Idea of Networking

Presence and regular business trips are imperative to maintain contacts and the network (Krachtowil 2018). One or two business trips a year to the target country is not enough if you are interested in long-term and sustainable business relationships in the Arab region. Being present on the ground is a competition-determining factor for success, which experience has shown is underestimated by Western partners (Krachtowil 2018). In a collective society where family, clan and tribal affiliations determine access to resources, it is crucial to build up appropriate local networks (Krachtowil 2018). Only in this way can business and negotiations be successful in the long term.

7.14.2.4 Use of Intermediaries

Middlemen with influential contacts help in negotiations and business dealings. It is usually advantageous to be introduced by a respected and influential person. The right recommendation can be decisive in initiating business. One should not be afraid of contact with regard to "patronage systems" or "nepotism", as these are part of the business culture in the Arab region (Krachtowil 2018). Host gifts also help to initiate business and negotiations (Hünniger 2018).

7.14.2.5 Arab Time Management

In the Arab world, the clocks sometimes tick differently; people and relationships take precedence over precisely observed schedules. Patience is therefore indicated, the business partner will come, "God willing" (Insha' Allâh). Paradoxical, but a fact: Conversely, Germans are expected to be punctual. It is generally advisable to plan plenty of time in advance. Schedules that are too tight and "clocked through" have little chance of success. "You have the clock, we have the time" is not an Arab proverb for nothing. Short-term, flexible time planning is more effective in the Arab world than long-term planning. "Time" is an important investment in business success. By the way, the phrase "I don't have time" is extremely impolite in Arabic and can be taken as an insult. You should use other, indirect formulations. You should always give your Arab business partner the feeling that you have time for him. Family commitments are always accepted as an "excuse" and are not considered unprofessional. But: Often, after a long time of waiting, Arab business partners suddenly can't move fast enough to advance a project. In such a case, everything has to be done immediately and with sometimes adventurous deadlines, which means that being flexible and prepared pays off (Hünniger 2018).

7.14.2.6 Consideration of Cultural Practices

Arab business culture is traditionally characterized by trade and mobility. "Buying and selling" is a matter of person to person. First you "sell" your personality, then the product. Business relationships are based on personal relations, the factual level is secondary. It is important to get to know the other person on a personal level first and to convince him or her of one's worth. In the Arab world, therefore, the professional is often combined with the private. There is no strict separation between professional and private life and it is advantageous to spend a lot of free time with Arab business partners in order to strengthen the relationship level. Sporting and cultural events are ideal for this. This also means that small talk is big talk! One should give his Arab business partners the feeling that he is more important than the business deal. People from less business-oriented cultures are very interested in good results and business deals. It's just that they don't see the possibility of achieving a good result when social relations are disturbed. So you should leave your personality first and foremost! And only then the first-class product (Hünniger 2018).

7.14.2.7 Consideration of Religious Customs

Islam permeates all areas of human life, it is not only a religion, but also a social order and economic factor and thus also affects business life. Therefore, inform yourself about the basics of Islam and the resulting rules of conduct for Muslims, such as the prohibition of alcohol and pork. The good Black Forest ham is just as unsuitable as a guest gift as the Franconian boxing bag (unless the Arab business partner expresses the corresponding wish. Taboo, but fact: Not all Muslims also adhere to the rules of Islam). If necessary practiced gender separation should be respected. The greatest possible physical distance should be maintained from the opposite-sex business partner, especially if this is signalled accordingly. Arab women, especially those from a traditional religious environment, should only be shaken hands with when asked to do so (react rather than act). With one's business partner, one should always inquire about the state of the family and not directly about the wife. Respect for Islam enables a climate of trust with Muslim business partners. Discussions about religion (Islam-Christianity) are to be avoided. They usually lead nowhere and can seriously damage the good relationship. Common ground should be emphasised. Atheism is usually met with incomprehension by devout Muslims and does not put the negotiating partner in a confidence-building light. Restraint is advisable in this respect. Incidentally, there are also Arab Christians in the Arab region (including Egypt, Lebanon, Iraq, Syria) (Hünniger 2018).

7.14.2.8 Compliance with Hierarchical Structures

As a rule, social advancement is still linked to membership of a particular family. It is therefore important to know the "right", i.e. influential, families. In clientelistic societies, this is crucial for competition. One should inform oneself about the important families (English: Leading Families) of the target country. Western business partners must therefore pay attention to internal rivalries between families, clans and tribes. In this context, investing in the right networks is a fundamental part of the negotiation strategy. An expert and intermediary who uses social occasions in the target country to initiate and maintain contacts can be helpful here (Hünniger 2018). The maintenance and strategy of the network can be a decisive advantage in negotiations, so it is advisable to constantly develop the network through one or more experts (Hünniger 2018).

7.14.2.9 Indirect and Metaphorical Negotiating Style

In Arab countries, one should use an indirect and paraphrased negotiation style. Direct demands or competitive negotiations usually have a negative effect on the negotiating partner and are considered extremely rude (Hünniger 2018). In addition, one should not discount a request of the counterpart by a direct "no", as this is also considered impolite. A "no" would hurt the counterpart and result in a disturbance on the relationship level. In the Arabic world, communication is indirect, and descriptive terms, metaphors or comparisons are used. Non-verbal signals also play a major role in communication. A generalizing but nevertheless often applicable rule of thumb is: when a diplomatic Arab says "yes" he means "maybe", when he says "maybe" he means "no" and when he says "no" he is undiplomatic. In collective societies, saving face is paramount. Honor and loyalty must always be protected, even in the face of controversy. But: the young generation of Arab businessmen in particular increasingly cultivates a direct communication style (Hünniger 2018).

7.14.2.10 Respect for Taboo Subjects

In order to keep the relationship level as trouble-free as possible, it is advisable to avoid politically or even religiously sensitive topics, especially at the beginning of business relationships. Politically sensitive topics include Israel (or a pro-Israeli stance), the Iraq war, the colonial era and, in the Arab Gulf states, the Arab-Iranian maritime border conflict. One should not underestimate this factor in one's business relations with the Arab world. The Arab partner could "engage" his negotiating partner in a politically explosive conversation. Restraint or rhetorically skillful expression of opinions are usually appropriate in the case of controversial views. In addition, it is advisable to inform oneself about the most important political, historical and cultural key data and personalities of the target country. A German business partner who knows who "Umm Koulthoum" is will make his Arab negotiating partners feel positive. Umm Kulthum was an Egyptian singer and musician. Her fame in the Arab world is comparable to that of Maria Callas and the Beatles in the Western world (Hünniger 2018). Figure 7.14 shows successful and unsuitable strategies for successful negotiations as well as icebreakers and icebergs.

7.14.3 Main Features of Islam

The term Islam means voluntary surrender to God, so Muslim means a person who "surrenders to God", "who professes Islam". Johann Wolfgang von Goethe put it this way: "If Islam means surrender to God's will, in Islam we all live and die" (Hünniger 2018). The word Allah is composed of: al (Arabic article) and illah (Arabic deity). So Allah means, "God, the one and only God." The concept of God in Islam states that God does not work solely in the extraordinary, in the miraculous, in His great deeds, but primarily in the everyday (Hünniger 2018). The Prophet Muhammad was born in Mecca in 570 AD. He was married to the wealthy merchant widow Khadidja, they had two sons and four daughters. 622 A.D. is the year of the transfer to Yathrib, later Medina, i.e. the year of the hijra (emigration) and the beginning of the Islamic calendar.

In the religious practice of Islam there are five pillars in total. A distinction is made between the duties that man owes to God and the duties to his fellow human beings and the community. The five basic religious duties (the pillars: arkan) refer to both areas of duty (Hünniger 2018). Table 7.2 describes the five pillars of Islam:

Table 7.2 Pillars of Islam

Column	Description of the basic duty
Pillar 1	The testimony of faith
Pillar 2	The ritual obligatory prayer
Pillar 3	The fast
Pillar 4	The compulsory levy
Pillar 5	The pilgrimage to Mecca

Source: Adapted from Hünniger (2018)

The Testimony of Faith—Shahada

Anyone who consciously and sincerely expresses the profession of faith in front of witnesses may consider himself a Muslim. The Shahada: "I testify that there is no deity but God (Allah) and that Muhammad is the messenger of God" (Hünniger 2018).

The Ritual Obligatory Prayer—Salat

Prayer expresses the inner attitude of humble submission and trust in divine mercy. It is a symbol of fraternity and solidarity, as believers gather together to pray. The prayer can be performed, for example, at home, at work, at school. On Friday, the prayer should take place in the mosque. It is prayed five times a day. The orientation, also of the prayer niche in the mosque, is towards Mecca. The place of prayer must be clean, the person praying needs a clean surface. The ritual cleansing of the body is a prerequisite.

Fasting in the Month of Ramadan—Saum

Ramadan is the ninth month of the Islamic (lunar) calendar. It lasts 29 or 30 days. According to the European calendar, Ramadan begins each year about eleven days earlier than the previous year. During the period of light, all adult, sensible and healthy Muslims abstain from food, drink, stimulants and sexual intercourse. Ramadan ends with a three-day festival of breaking the fast (Hünniger 2018).

The Compulsory Levy—Zakat

Besides the voluntary alms, there is the compulsory alms. Zakat is derived from the Arabic zaka—to purify. Compulsory donation is an act of purification from greed. It is an expression of gratitude to God for the opportunity to live in prosperity. The wealthy have a duty to allow poorer people to share in their possessions. The poor have a right to a share of the possessions of the better-off. As a rule, collection and distribution take place without state control (Hünniger 2018).

The Pilgrimage to Mecca—Hajj

Mecca, but above all the Kaaba itself, form the religious centre of the Islamic world. For all adult Muslims, the hajj is a religious duty. Participants must be "responsible", i.e. mentally and physically healthy, financially able to participate and not prevented from doing so by other reasons, such as war. The umra (small journey) is an individual action that is not bound to specific times. The hajj (major community journey) begins on the first day after the month of Ramadan. The pilgrimage focuses on equality and togetherness among Muslims (Hünniger 2018).

7.15 Summary of Country Examples

Negotiations of business partners in an international context are based on peculiarities that companies have to take into account (Obrien 2016; Helmold 2018; Dathe and Helmold 2018). Although salespeople or buyers cannot know all the idiosyncrasies, the line between

Table 7.3 International and intercultural negotiations

Recommendations for international negotiations
Thorough preparation (cultural awareness) through intercultural training or workshops by foreign chambers of commerce or trainers is advisable.
Successful strategies should be studied in advance, just like flawed strategies
Political topics should be avoided as a matter of principle
Specific country aspects should be used to advantage
In most cases, it is advisable to involve competent translators.
Intermediaries support the development of a network
Loss of face should be avoided
Agreements should always be ratified by lawyers
If possible, negotiations should take place in the home country with home advantage

negotiation successes and failures is usually narrow (Helmold 2018). Even though negotiators do not have to adapt 100 percent to the foreign culture or customs, some recommendations are helpful for international negotiations (Helmold 2018). In summary, it can be stated that negotiations with international business partners require detailed preparation (Helmold 2018; Helmold and Terry 2016). Country-specific aspects can be learned through training and are necessary when business negotiations have some and periodic regularity (Helmold 2018). In many cultural areas, it is imperative to involve experts who are perfectly familiar with the peculiarities and have a network in the country (Helmold 2018). Topics from politics as well as religion should generally be avoided. In the figures in Chap. 7, country-specific characteristics of a total of 13 nations are described (Helmold 2018).

Table 7.3 concludes Chap. 7 with recommendations for international and intercultural negotiations. In addition to thorough preparation through seminars and workshops offered by foreign chambers of commerce or by educational institutions, successful and appropriate strategies and tactics can be developed and used in the international arena. Negotiators who take country-specific aspects into account usually have more success than others. In many countries it is advisable to work with intermediaries who are familiar with the country, the language and the cultural customs.

References

AHK Japan (2018). Business-Knigge Japan. Abgerufen am 11.6.2018. http://japan.ahk.de/japan-tipps/auf-geschaeftsreisen/japanknigge/.

Anson, B. (2013). How to Negotiate with a Brazilian. The Brazil Business. 10.10.2013. Abgerufen am 22.6.2018. http://thebrazilbusiness.com/article/how-to-negotiate-with-a-brazilian.

Brooks, A. W. (2016). Verhandeln mit Gefühl. In: Harvard Business Manager. Abgerufen am 10.6.2018. http://www.harvardbusinessmanager.de/heft/d-141171019.html.

Bügner, T. (2017). Lost in Translation. Sind Sie fit für die Geschäftsverhandlung im Ausland? Durch Unkenntnis fremder Mentalitäten kann die Geschäftsreise zum Abenteuer werden. Diese Fehler sollten Sie bei internationalen Verhandlungen vermeiden. 15. Mai 2017. In: Wirtschaftswoche. Abgerufen am 22.6.2018. https://www.wiwo.de/erfolg/lost-in-translation-sind-sie-fit-fuer-die-geschaeftsverhandlung-im-ausland/19803368.html.

Dathe, T. & Helmold, M. (2018). Erfolg im Chinageschäft. Handlungsempfehlungen für kleine und mittlere Unternehmen (KMU). Springer Wiesbaden.

Frank, S. (2004a). Verhandeln in Frankreich. La Belle et la Bete. Veröffentlicht am 4.12.2004. In: Manager-Magazin. http://www.manager-magazin.de/unternehmen/karriere/a-331957.html.

Frank, S. (2004b). Verhandeln in Russland "Vielen Dank. Wir essen auch mit Messer und Gabel". In: Manager-Magazin. Abgerufen am 6.6.2018. http://www.manager-magazin.de/unternehmen/karriere/a-320837.html.

Frank, S. (2005). Verhandeln in Japan. Lächeln, auch wenn es weh tut. In: Manager-Magazin. Abgerufen am 11.6.2018. http://www.manager-magazin.de/unternehmen/karriere/a-371602.html.

Frank, S. (2006). Verhandeln in Indien. In: Manager-Magazin. Abgerufen am 11.6.2018. http://www.manager-magazin.de/unternehmen/karriere/a-448288-4.html.

Frank, S. (2010a). Weltspitze. Wie man in Italien Erfolg haben kann. In: Handelsblatt. Abgerufen am 11.6.2018. http://www.handelsblatt.com/unternehmen/management/weltspitze-worauf-man-in-holland-achten-muss/3656566.html.

Frank, S. (2010b). Weltspitze. Worauf man in Holland achten muss. In: Handelsblatt. Abgerufen am 11.6.2018. https://www.handelsblatt.com/unternehmen/management/weltspitze-wie-man-in-italien-erfolg-haben-kann-seite-2/3639484-2.html?ticket=ST-5338244-mV6BvUb4nKCdtfMvyojz-ap2.

Frank, S. (2016). Wie Sie in den USA Erfolg haben. Business Traveller. Abgerufen am 9.6.2018. https://sergey-frank.com/images/artikel-download/Business%20Traveller_USA.pdf.

Hall, E. (1966). *The Hidden Dimension.* New York: Garden City.

Hall, E. (1976). *Beyond Culture.* New York: Garden City.

Hall, E. (1983). *The Dance of Life: The Other Dimension of Time.* New York: Anchor Books.

Helmold, M. (2010). Best-in-Class Lieferantenmanagement in der Automobilindustrie. Shaker Aachen.

Helmold, M. (2018). Erfolgreiche Verhandlungen und Best-in-Class Empfehlungen für den Verhandlungsdurchbruch. Manuskript und Workshopunterlagen.

Helmold, M. & Terry, B. (2016). Lieferantenmanagement 2030. Springer Gabler Wiesbaden.

Helmold, M., Dathe, T. & Büsch, M. (2017). Praxisbericht aus der Bahnindustrie – Bombardier Transportation. Veränderte Anforderungen durch Global Sourcing. In Beschaffung aktuell. 4.5.2017. Abgerufen am 17.5.2018. https://beschaffung-aktuell.industrie.de/einkauf/veraenderte-anforderungen-durch-global-sourcing/.

Hofstede, G. (1980). Culture's Consequences: International Differences in Worked-Related Values. Beverly Hills: Sage Publication.

Hofstede, G. (1991). Cultures and Organizations: Software of the Mind. McGraw-Hill Maidenhead.

Hünniger, (2018). In. Welt Online. A.H. Sängerin Umm Kulthum. Die Araberin, für die Gaddafi sogar seinen Staatsstreich verschob. Veröffentlicht am 08.06.2018. Abgerufen am 26.6.2018. https://www.welt.de/kultur/kino/article177151680/So-ewig-wie-die-Pyramiden-die-Saengerin-Umm-Kulthum.html.

IHK Rhein-Neckar (2018). Business-Knigge für das Ausland. Abgerufen am 22.6.2018. https://www.ihk.de/rhein-neckar/international/maerkte-international/mena-subsahara-afrika/maghreb/maghreb-business-knigge-3632310.

IPB (2018). Institut für politische Bildung. Zeitleiste Großbritannien und Europa. Abgerufen am 22.6.2018. http://www.bpb.de/internationales/europa/brexit/229985/zeitleiste.

Jansen, M.B. (2000). The Making of Modern Japan. Harvard Press, London.

Kness-Bastaroli, Th. & Dahm, K.H. (2006). In: Handelsblatt. In Italien auf die Bella Figura achten. Abgerufen am 22.6.2018. https://www.handelsblatt.com/unternehmen/mittelstand/verhandlungspraxis-in-italien-auf-die-bella-figura-achten/2717452.html.

Krachtowil, G. (2018). Business—Etiquette Arabische Welt. Die 10 Lieblingsfehler im Umgang mit arabischen Geschäftspartnern. Dr. Gabi Kratochwil, CrossCultures Frechen/Köln. https://www.osnabrueck.ihk24.de/blob/osihk24/international/Downloads/1201512/fbde074b93ba16d5240c23fb1a167fe4/Business-Etikette-Arabische-Welt-data.pdf.

Marks, M. (2006). Verhandlungen in Großbritannien Bei der „teatime" ist das Geschäft tabu. In: Handelsblatt online. https://www.handelsblatt.com/unternehmen/mittelstand/verhandlungen-in-grossbritannien-bei-der-teatime-ist-das-geschaeft-tabu-seite-6/2698386-6.html.

Meyering, G. (2018). Business-Knigge für Großbritannien. 9 Verhandlungstipps für Einkäufer. In: Technik und Einkauf. https://www.technik-einkauf.de/ratgeber/business-knigge-grossbritannien-im-mutterland-des-understatement-9-verhandlungstipps-einkaeufer/.

Nitobe, I. & Keller. G. (2004). Bushido. Die sieben Tugenden des Samurai. New and completely translated Edition from the American language to German by G. Keller. Piper. München.

Obrien, J. (2016). Negotiations for Procurement Professionals. 2nd Edition. Kogan Page Croyden.

OECD (2018). Die OECD in Zahlen und Fakten. Die wichtigsten Volkswirtschaften nach dem Bruttoinlandsprodukt. Abgerufen am 17.6.2018. http://www.oecd.org/berlin/statistiken/.

Panasonic (2018). Panasonic Verhaltensregeln. Panasonic Code of Conduct. Abgerufen am 11.6.2018. https://www.panasonic.com/global/corporate/management/code-of-conduct/pdf/code-of-conduct/06_coc2008German.pdf.

Schulz, U. (2017). Verhandeln und Auseinandersetzen. Die deutsche und die schwedische Art auf einen Nenner zu kommen. Abgerufen am 20.3.2018. http://www.schwedenkammer.de/fileadmin/user_upload/3_Business_interkulturell/SA2_12_verhandeln_und_auseinandersetzen.pdf.

Thiel, S. (2018). Kulturschock Islam. Alltagskultur, Traditionen, Verhaltensregeln. Verlag Peter Rump Bielefeld.

Thomas, G. (2001). Reisegast in Japan. Fremde Kulturen verstehen und erleben. (Edited. By Simon, G.) Iwanowski Reisebuchverlag. 3rd Edition. Dormagen.

Thomas, A. (2011). Interkulturelle Handlungskompetenz- Versiert, angemessen und erfolgreich im internationalen Geschäft. In: A. Thomas, Interkulturelle Handlungskompetenz- Versiert, angemessen und erfolgreich im internationalen Geschäft (S. 80). Gabler Verlag Wiesbaden.

Winkels, U. & Schlütermann, Y. (2013). Verhandeln mit Japanern: Das japanische Businessverhalten besser verstehen und nutzen. Gabler Verlag Wiesbaden.

8 Negotiations in the Event of Performance Disruptions: Demand Management

He who knows the goal can decide He who decides finds peace He who finds peace is certain He who is certain can consider He who considers can improve
Confucius (551 B.C.–479 B.C.)

Contents

Summary

Non-conformities are non-conformities of the contractually agreed specification features and properties of a product (Dathe and Helmold, Erfolgreich im Chinageschäft. Strategien und Handlungsempfehlungen für kleinere und mittlere Unternehmen (KMU). Springer Gabler, Wiesbaden 2018). In this context, claim management or supplement management have a central role in negotiating these missing properties (Helmold and Terry, Lieferantenmanagement 2030, Springer Gabler, Wiesbaden 2016). Subsequent claim management is also called claim management or regression. Unless specified and agreed in contracts, subsequent claims are usually made after services have been rendered and deliveries have been made due to deficits in quality, quantity, time, type of delivery or due to other deviations from the originally agreed condition. However, they can also be made by the supplier (delivering company).

M. Helmold et al., *Successful Negotiations*,
https://doi.org/10.1007/978-3-658-35701-6_8

8.1 Performance Disruptions and Subsequent Claims Management

Defects in performance are characteristics or performance features of the product which have been contractually agreed by the customer and supplier but which have not been provided. In German legal terms, this is referred to as a material defect. Material defects are usually defective design, defective manufacture or defective materials. In addition to material defects, there are other performance defects such as early or late deliveries, deliveries to a place not agreed upon or missing functions (Helmold 2013). Performance failures are often called non-conformities (English: Non Conformities, (Vidogah and Ndegukuri 1988) in companies (Dathe and Helmold 2018). In this context, claim management or supplement management have a central role in negotiating these missing features (Helmold and Terry 2017). Subsequent claim management is also called claim management or regression (Helmold 2013). Unless specified and agreed in contracts, subsequent claims are usually made by the customer (the procuring company) after the service has been provided and delivery has been made due to deficits in quality, quantity, time, type of delivery (customer subsequent claims). However, subsequent claims can also be made by the supplier (delivering company) (supplier subsequent claims). Claim management is a discipline that has so far been little described in research or teaching, as numerous authors describe (Helmold 2013; Wenxin et al. 2017).

In supplier management, the aim of supplement management is to clarify by mutual agreement the consequences of events in the course of the project that could not be foreseen when the contract was concluded. After an order has been placed by the client with the contractor, changes, supplements or extensions usually occur, especially in large projects. Possible reasons are usually delivery failures, delays or quality deviations (Vidogah and Ndegukuri 1988). In their study, Hendricks and Singhal found out that performance problems in the supply chain can reduce the value of a company by up to 40% (Hendricks and Singhal 2005), so that the primary goal of claim management is prevention, as numerous authors state (Helmold 2013; Wieland and Wallenburg 2012; Hendricks and Singhal 2005).

Delivery failures due to force majeure such as floods and earthquakes are also regressed. In cases of force majeure, subsequent claims are also legally enforceable under certain conditions (Helmold 2013). In particular, claims for damages can be asserted in the case of deficiencies in coverage and prevention, for example in the case of gross negligence. Changes or extensions covered by the contract do not lead to subsequent claims. If this is not the case, the contractor can make a subsequent claim for the additional costs incurred by him to the party causing the change or extension (Vidogah and Ndegukuri 1988; Helmold 2013). Examples include:

- Lost profits due to production downtime
- Costs of removal of defects and repair
- Costs incurred in connection with troubleshooting (including shunting costs)
- Damages due to a default in performance

- Late or premature delivery
- Storage costs for early deliveries
- Transport costs for returning the goods for repair
- Packaging costs for new packaging
- Administrative costs for processing the subsequent claim

8.2 Demand Manager (Contract Manager)

In principle, the goal of every company should be to avoid subsequent claims, but studies show that in national and international companies, performance characteristics are often not fulfilled 100% in goods transactions, so that disputes arise (Helmold 2013). This is where a contract or claim manager can be used to assist with contracts and negotiations of buyers or sellers (Helmold 2013). His task includes the creation of contracts in cooperation with purchasing and sales staff.

In addition, the contract manager is responsible for the preparation of claims from a technical and commercial point of view, including the determination of contractual and legal bases for claims and the securing of claims against suppliers, customers or insurance companies. The contract manager supports the purchasing or marketing department in the execution of claim management from the settlement to the warranty phase, especially in the area of delivery disruptions and checking the contractual and legal basis for claims. The requirement profile and the necessary competencies of a contract manager are shown in Fig. 8.1. In addition to knowledge of national and international contract law, it is usually necessary to understand technical issues and translate them into a subsequent claim (Helmold 2013). In addition to legal training (academic training as a lawyer or business lawyer), contract managers should have moderation and project management skills, as subsequent claims are usually drawn up and checked on an interdisciplinary basis, i.e. with the knowledge of several departments (Helmold 2013).

8.3 Phases in Subsequent Claims Management

In the case of performance failures, the phase model shown in Fig. 8.2 can be used, which suggests a structured and systematic way of dealing with subsequent claims (Helmold 2013). In the case of non-delivered performance characteristics and notification by purchasing or sales, subsequent claims can be made as follows: In phase 1, the supplementary claims manager is involved and consulted. In phase 2, this manager examines the extent to which performance characteristics deviate from the purchase contract through discussions with the functions involved, such as purchasing, sales, development or quality management (Helmold 2013). He also documents the facts. In addition to elements such as the purchase contract, specification, performance description, date of occurrence of the event, evidence of deviations, description and justification, the documentation includes the evaluation of

Fig. 8.1 Requirement profile of the contract manager. (Source: own representation)

the subsequent claim and the probability of a subsequent claim success from a legal perspective (Helmold 2013). Here, invoices, witness statements, photographs, correspondence or expert opinions can serve as evidence. Modern organisations have centralised and electronic recording of additional expenses on a separate cost account, whereas conventional organisations choose the paper route. Phase 3 then deals with the post-claim strategy. Often executives want to be compensated for all expenses and therefore make claims for all associated costs such as lost production, rework and administration of the additional claims. This can lead to millions of dollars in expenses in the case of production line outages and can economically bankrupt suppliers, so a strategy becomes necessary (MIK 2017; Helmold 2013). Subsequent claims can be made in different ways:

- Replacement deliveries after assertion of the subsequent claim
- Conversion of the purchase contract and refund of the purchase price
- Claims for compensation for all the costs of replacement
- Claims for compensation of all direct costs such as replacement or repair
- Claims for compensation of all associated costs such as production downtime, rework and administration of subsequent claims
- Offsetting a subsequent claim against future orders
- Offsetting a subsequent claim against existing orders

Fig. 8.2 Phase model in demand management. (Source: own representation)

Phase 4 starts with the assertion of the subsequent claim with the customer or supplier with the transmission of the subsequent claim and the setting of a deadline to react to the subsequent claim. Here it is important to consider deadlines and hierarchical levels so that the subsequent claim is also legally valid (Helmold 2013). Phase 4 is therefore a step that requires expert legal knowledge.

Phase 5 is the actual negotiation of the subsequent claim with the other party. After successful negotiation, phase 6 must then ensure that the agreement is ratified. With ratification, the monetary or material compensation takes place (Helmold 2013).

8.4 Recommendations for the Management of Subsequent Claims

Subsequent claims management is a central issue for many companies, but should always be implemented with a sense of proportion. Therefore, it is advisable not to involve lawyers, who have a negative impact on the relationship management between customer

Table 8.1 Subsequent claims management

Recommendations for innovative demand management:
Claims or subsequent demands always have the goal of improving performance, and not to achieve ostensible savings.
Companies should employ contract managers who are active in supplementary claim management. A position of 80,000 EUR p.a. is expected to pay for itself within a short period of time
Companies should pursue their claims far-sightedly in their strategy. Example: Waiving a claim in order to achieve cost reductions and savings in the next project
Subsequent claims are used as a strategic tool in negotiations
Subsequent claims and the negotiations must not burden the business relationship
Claims should be evaluated and analysed realistically, and in relation to the actual damage
Lawyers, especially external lawyers, should remain in the background and not intervene in the negotiations
Companies should take out insurance to protect themselves against subsequent claims

and supplier, when negotiating subsequent claims. The use of lawyers causes high costs, so this step should be well weighed (Helmold 2013). Claims or subsequent claims are always aimed at improving performance and not at making ostensible savings. Companies should employ contract managers who are involved in post-claims management. A position of 80,000 EUR p.a. is likely to pay for itself within a short period of time. Companies should be far-sighted in their receivables strategy. For example, waiving a claim in order to reduce costs and make savings in the next project. In this context, other concessions are also negotiable, e.g. provision of service personnel or free replacement. Post-claims are used as a strategic tool in negotiations and should therefore be well documented so that sufficient evidence and material is available in the negotiations. Subsequent claims and the negotiations should not be a burden on the business relationship. Lastly, it is recommended that claims and post-claim values are evaluated and analysed realistically, and in a reasonable proportion to the actual damages (Helmold 2013). Table 8.1 summarises the recommendations for innovative claims management.

References

Dathe, T. & Helmold, M. (2018). Erfolgreich im Chinageschäft. Strategien und Handlungsempfehlungen für kleinere und mittlere Unternehmen (KMU). Springer Gabler Wiesbaden.

Helmold, M. (2013). Claim-Management in der Praxis. Was tun bei Leistungsstörungen in der Lieferkette. In: FM-Logistik. Ausgabe 1–2/2013. S. 76–77.

Helmold, M. & Terry, B. (2017). Global Sourcing and Supply Management Excellence in China. Springer Singapur.

Hendricks, K.B., & Singhal, V.R. (2005). An empirical analysis of the effect of supply chain disruptions on long-run stock price performance and equity risk of the firm. In: Production Operations Management, 21 (5), 501–522.

MIK (2017). In: Spiegel Online. Lieferausfälle BMW und Bosch verhandeln über Schadensersatz. Die Lieferprobleme Ende Mai haben für Bosch ein teures Nachspiel. Denn BMW will den Schaden ersetzt haben, der durch den dadurch erzwungenen Stopp der Produktion entstanden ist. Es geht um Millionen. Abgerufen am 26.5.2017. http://www.spiegel.de/wirtschaft/unternehmen/bmw-und-bosch-verhandeln-ueber-schadensersatz-wegen-lieferausfaellen-a-1156486.html.

Vidogah, W. & Ndegukuri, I. (1988). Improving the management of claims on construction contracts: Consultant's perspective. In: Construction Management and Economics 16(3):363–372. February 1998.

Wenxin, Shen et al. (2017). Causes of contractors' claims in international engineering-procurement-construction projects. In: Journal of Civil Engineering and Management 23(6):727–739. August 2017.

Wieland, A. & Wallenburg, C.M. (2012). Dealing with supply chain risks: Linking risk management practices and strategies to performance. In: International Journal of Physical Distribution & Logistics Management, 42 (10), 887–905.

Negotiations in the Event of Financial Difficulties

9

Beautiful things can also be built from stones that are placed in one's path
Johann Wolfgang von Goethe (1749–1832)

Contents

M. Helmold et al., *Successful Negotiations*,
https://doi.org/10.1007/978-3-658-35701-6_9

Summary

Companies in financial difficulties are in a crisis situation. The word crisis is a word with negative connotations and has something to do with danger and threat. According to the "Gabler Wirtschaftslexikon", crisis is defined as the most diverse manifestations or phenomena of an enterprise, from the mere disruption in the course of operations to conflicts to the destruction of the enterprise (Gabler Wirtschaftslexikon, Unternehmenskrise. Abgerufen am 26.5.2018. https://wirtschaftslexikon.gabler.de/definition/unternehmungskrise-49331, 2018). If a company is in an economic enterprise crisis, the functionality and stability can be impaired to such an extent that there is a threat of a company collapse—insolvency (insolvency). From the point of view of the affected company, these manifestations can be described as a financial crisis or catastrophe, which substantially threatens the continuation of the company and its existence (Gabler Wirtschaftslexikon, Unternehmenskrise. Abgerufen am 26.5.2018. https://wirtschaftslexikon.gabler.de/definition/unternehmungskrise-49331, 2018). The authors Krystek and Moldenhauer define three types of crisis for companies (Krystek, Moldenhauer, Handbuch Krisen- und Restrukturierungsmanagement, Kohlhammer, Stuttgart, 2007): non-existence-threatening crisis situation, existence-threatening crisis situation and existence-destroying crisis situation.

9.1 Signs of Financial Difficulties

9.1.1 Phases of a Financial Crisis

Companies in financial difficulties are in a crisis situation. The word crisis is a word with negative connotations and has something to do with danger and threat. According to the "Gabler Wirtschaftslexikon", crisis is defined as the most diverse manifestations or phenomena of a company, from the mere disruption in the course of operations to conflicts to the destruction of the company (Gabler Wirtschaftslexikon 2018). If a company is in an economic enterprise crisis, the functionality and stability can be so impaired that the danger of a company collapse, which means the insolvency (insolvency), threatens. From the point of view of the affected company, these manifestations can be described as a financial crisis or catastrophe, which substantially endangers the continuation of the company and its existence (Gabler Wirtschaftslexikon 2018). The authors Krystek and Moldenhauer define three types of crisis for companies (Krystek and Moldenhauer 2007):

- Crisis situation not threatening existence
- Existentially threatening crisis situation
- Existentially destructive crisis situation

Table 9.1 Reasons for company crises

Exogenous causes	Endogenous causes
Changing customer requirements	Management error
Economic changes	incompetence of staff
Socio-political changes	Inefficiency in processes
Governmental causes	Deficits in the area of production
Crises caused by suppliers	Owner-induced crises
Competitor	Lack of capital
Other external influences	Wrong strategy alignment

Own illustration based on Helmold (2018)

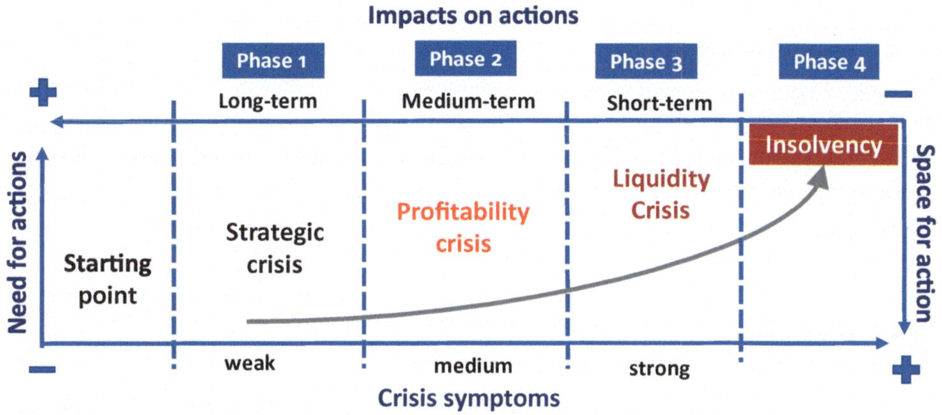

Fig. 9.1 Phase model of corporate crises. (Source: own representation based on Müller 1986)

Reasons for crises are manifold and can be divided into exogenous (external) and endogenous (internal) causes (Table 9.1):

One model for describing corporate crises is the four-phase model by Müller, who is a renowned scientist in the field of business administration and has published numerous papers in the area of corporate and financial crises (Müller 1986). In his model, he characterizes a total of four phases of corporate crises, as Fig. 9.1 shows. In his model, he assumes that the different crisis phases also require a certain period of time to find effective countermeasures to overcome the crisis. Müller calls the four phases the strategic crisis, profitability crisis, liquidity crisis and insolvency.

9.1.2 Strategic Crisis

At the beginning of a company crisis there is always the strategic crisis. This means that one or more strategic mistakes lead to a higher cost structure or declining revenues. This can be, for example, changes in demand, increased operating costs or failure to take market changes into account. Strategic crises can be identified by an early warning system so that countermeasures can be taken.

9.1.3 Profitability Crisis

This is followed by the balance sheet crisis. In this phase, the crisis is already reflected in negative figures in the balance sheets or profit and loss accounts. Important features here are the decline in sales or the deterioration of the return on investment.

9.1.4 Liquidity Crisis

This is followed by the liquidity crisis. Phase 4 is characterized by the use of supplier credits, permanent utilization of the overdraft facility or even foreclosure. Up to this phase, the company can still recover by acting quickly and correctly, but not in the next phase of insolvency.

9.1.5 Insolvency

Phase 5 is insolvency or over-indebtedness. This is the beginning of insolvency proceedings. "Insolvency" means inability to pay. This always occurs when the debtor is no longer able to meet his payment obligations. This is usually the case when he no longer has the funds he needs.

9.2 Recommendations for the Elimination of Financial Difficulties

9.2.1 Restructuring

Most often, latent corporate crises slip through the perception system in the company, as they are very difficult to detect and do not yet send out strong signals. In the case of a company's profit and liquidity crisis, it is obvious that there is a crisis because the key figures, profit and loss accounts or finances are clearly affected. In the case of weak signals of a latent company crisis, a crisis cannot be diagnosed so quickly, because the consequences will only be visible in the future. The significance of these weak signals is often underestimated and therefore they then develop into major problems. This also shows that crises cannot just occur suddenly, but develop slowly and gradually. Therefore, it is important for the crisis manager not to let crises become acute, but to recognize them early in order to be able to act. It would be best to identify the crisis at the stage of potential crisis, as this could prevent a crisis.

Early warning systems are of great importance when it comes to perceiving crises. Early detection or early warning is not only used to identify threats and risks to the company, but also points out for opportunities and chances that this may present to the company. Some early warning concepts are ratio analysis, financial statement analysis, and forecasting and portfolio techniques. Constant checks and balances within the company are part of the process. Various methods help in making better and effective controls. The most common ones are liquidity control, profitability control, equity investigation, SWOT analysis and value in use analysis. These methods encompass the entire company and its environment, therefore it is easier to identify negative influences. This book will not go into detail on how to handle each method, but early warning and its methods are important for crisis management in business management. The most common early warning methods are ratio analysis and financial statement analysis, which reveal important facts for the company. Here, accounting provides the necessary basic data and data external to the company is included. In ratio analysis, the entire ratios, such as equity or debt, are analyzed and a balance sheet is created. In this balance sheet, the profits or losses become clear and it can be seen whether the company is in danger or not.

9.2.2 Measures to Increase Liquidity

9.2.2.1 Immediate Measures

In the following, measures for bridging financial bottlenecks will be presented on the basis of the balance sheet Fig. 9.2 and the income statement Fig. 9.3. The measures can be divided into those that increase cash and/or short-term receivables and those that reduce short-term liabilities. In this context, it is crucial that the measures are implemented immediately, otherwise liquidity bottlenecks will lead to insolvency. Figure 9.2 shows the simplified balance sheet with the assets and liabilities side. On the asset side, financial resources can be booked through different steps in fixed or current assets, whereas on the liability side, activities in equity or debt (increasing equity through equity providers or rescheduling debt through negotiations with the bank) are necessary to eliminate a financial crisis (Olfert 2013, 2015).

9.2.2.2 Equity Increase

One step to improve liquidity immediately is the use of new funds by the shareholders or equity investors (Olfert 2013, 2015). With a capital increase through cash contributions, liquid funds are injected into the company, which can be used to repay due liabilities. However, it should be noted that the shareholders only agree to a capital increase as long as the earnings prospects of the company are positive and the shareholders can expect a return on their contribution in the form of a dividend, which is usually higher than the interest rate for debt capital (Olfert 2013, 2015).

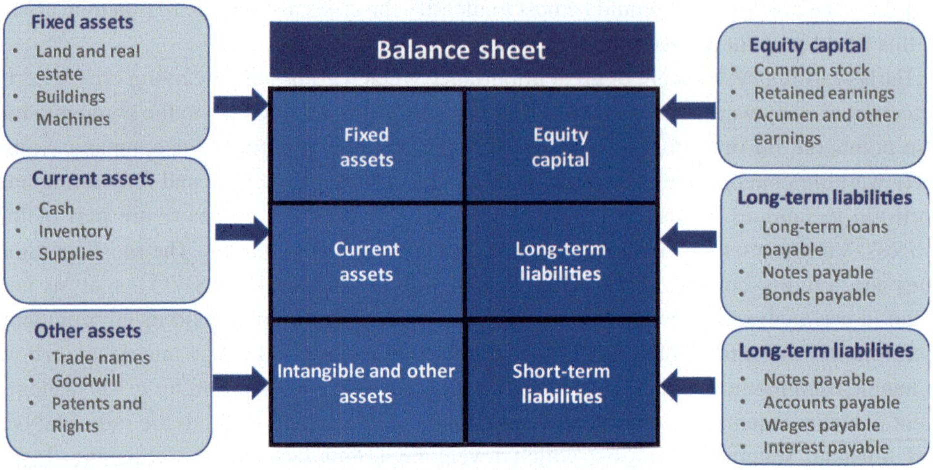

Fig. 9.2 Effects on the balance sheet. (Source: own representation)

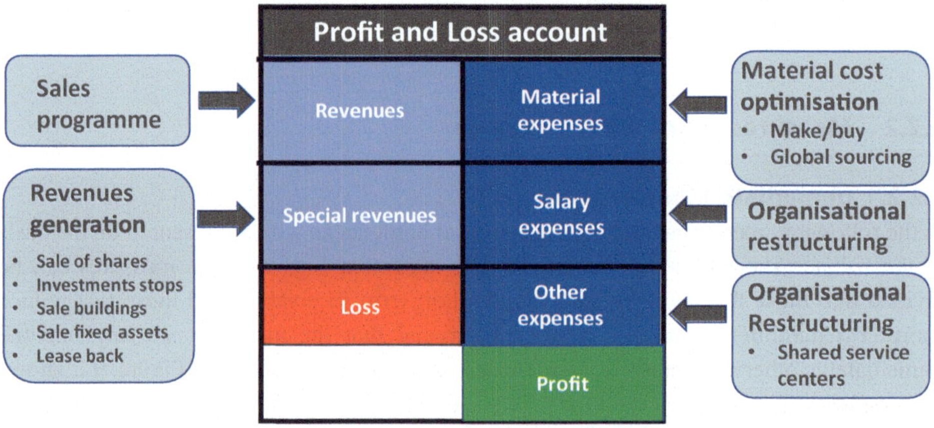

Fig. 9.3 Effects on the profit and loss account (P&L). (Source: own representation)

9.2.2.3 Increase in Long-term Liabilities

Another step is to increase debt capital (Olfert 2013, 2015). A company's liquidity can also be improved in the short term by taking out long-term loans to repay short-term liabilities. However, it should not be overlooked here that this measure is only suitable for a short liquidity squeeze, as the payment problem is merely shifted into the future (Olfert 2013, 2015). It should also be noted here that creditors are only willing to grant new loans to a company with liquidity difficulties if the company's earnings prospects are positive (Olfert 2013, 2015).

9.2.2.4 Sale of Fixed Assets and Leaseback

A popular method used by companies is the sale of fixed assets. To improve liquidity in the short term, it is possible to sell fixed assets (usually land and buildings), which are then leased back (so-called "sale-and-lease-back"). The sale leads to a high inflow of cash, while the payments for rental expenses are shifted into the future (Olfert 2013, 2015).

9.2.2.5 Factoring

The liquidity effect of the sale of receivables (so-called factoring) must be viewed in a differentiated manner. While the sale of receivables increases first-degree liquidity, it has a negative effect on second-degree liquidity. Although the sale of receivables increases the cash position, the receivables position is reduced at the same time. Since the factoring bank retains a discount on receivables for its financing function, the increase in the stock of cash is less than the decrease in the stock of receivables, so that the second-degree liquidity decreases (Olfert 2013, 2015).

9.2.2.6 Inventory Optimisation

Another activity is the reduction of inventories. A high level of inventory leaves particularly inventory-intensive businesses groaning under the cost burden. For example, a lot of warehouse staff is needed, which quickly adds up not only the expenses for wages and salaries, but also for ancillary wage costs. In addition, extra costs are incurred for personnel administration. But the storage facilities themselves also generate costs for rent, energy and water, maintenance, loss of value of the equipment, expansion of the storage facilities, interest on invested capital, insurance and cleaning. A high inventory level itself also creates burdens that are not yet taken into account here. Immense amounts of dead capital, the interest accruing on it and a lack of liquidity result in further high losses. And of course, insurance premiums are also incurred for the goods, be they finished or intermediate products. In addition, however, factors that are hardly tangible should also be considered. Spoilage, overstocking, obsolescence, damage, enormous inventory effort and theft—all these losses can be quantified in a rough approximation at best. Worse, further expenses can result from any of these components. Video cameras because of thieving colleagues or suppliers, extra work in plant security, sickness costs due to an above-average number of employees under heavy physical strain—the list goes on and on. In such a situation, there is a constant danger of losing track of expenses. A high level of inventory carries serious risks that can unexpectedly put even successful companies in a precarious position.

9.2.3 Measures to Reduce Current Liabilities

9.2.3.1 Conversion of Debt Capital into Equity Capital

By converting debt into equity, the company no longer has to make the repayments due. Here too, the existing creditors will only agree to this project if the earnings prospects are positive. The disadvantage for the company is that dividend payments must be made in the future and that the previous creditors now have a say in the management (Helmold and Terry 2016).

Table 9.2 Negotiations and actions in case of financial difficulties

Recommendations for negotiations in a precarious financial situation
Sales programs
Opening up new markets
Liquidity improvement plans through advance payments from customers
Increase in contributions from equity investors
Negotiation with lenders
Adding new investments
Liquidity improvement plans by extending the payment terms of suppliers
Cost-saving programs
Renegotiations with all suppliers
Supplementary claim management
Process improvements
Inventory minimization through the introduction of Vendor Managed Inventory (VMI)
Divestment of non-vital divisions
Closure of non-profitable plants and business areas
Discontinuation of non-profitable lines of business
asset disposal
Global sourcing activities

9.2.3.2 Debt Rescheduling

Liquidity can also be improved in the short term by rescheduling short-term liabilities into long-term loans. However, here too the payment problem is merely shifted into the future.

Table 9.2 summarises the recommendations for negotiating with different stakeholders in the event of financial distress.

References

Gabler Wirtschaftslexikon (2018). Unternehmenskrise. Abgerufen am 26.5.2018. https://wirtschaftslexikon.gabler.de/definition/unternehmungskrise-49331.

Helmold, M. (2018). Erfolgreiche Verhandlungen und Best-in-Class Empfehlungen für den Verhandlungsdurchbruch. Manuskript und Workshopunterlagen im Master- und MBA-Studium.

Helmold, M. & Terry, B. (2016). Lieferantenmanagement 2030. Springer Gabler Wiesbaden.

Krystek, U. & Moldenhauer, R. (2007). Handbuch Krisen- und Restrukturierungsmanagement. Kohlhammer Stuttgart.

Müller, R. (1986). Krisenmanagement in der Unternehmung: Vorgehen, Massnahmen und Organisation. Peter Lang Verlag Bern.

Olfert, K. (2013). Investition. 13. Auflage. NWB Verlag Herne.

Olfert, K. (2015). Finanzierung. 15. Auflage. NWB Verlag Herne.

Negotiations in Complex Projects

10

If you want to build a ship, do not gather men together to procure wood, prepare tools, assign tasks and divide up the work, but teach men to long for the vast endless sea
Antoine de Saint-Exupéry (1900–1944)

Contents

Summary

A project is a purposeful and usually unique undertaking that is carried out under specifications of time, resources, costs, and other elements, such as the use of human or operational resources (PM, http://www.pm-handbuch.com/begriffe/, accessed July 7, 2018, 2018). Within projects, there are start and end dates set by the client within

M. Helmold et al., *Successful Negotiations*,
https://doi.org/10.1007/978-3-658-35701-6_10

which the project must be completed. Project derives from Latin (Latin: proiectum, thrown forward). In the seventeenth century, the meaning "construction project" became accepted as the project definition in Germany (PM, http://www.pm-handbuch.com/begriffe/, Accessed July 7, 2018, 2018). Due to their growing complexity, projects place special demands on both the client and the contractor or order processor in terms of project management and thus also negotiation management. There are often multiple groups or departments involved in complex projects. Due to their complexity, projects involve significant negotiations with customers, suppliers, banks or other stakeholders. Examples of projects include the construction of a railway station in one of the metropolitan areas such as Stuttgart, e.g. Stuttgart 2, and the construction of an airport, e.g. construction and completion of the Williy Brandt Airport BER.

10.1 Definition and Characteristics of Projects

A project is a goal-oriented and usually one-time undertaking that is carried out under specifications regarding time, resources, costs and other elements, e.g. deployment of personnel or operating resources (PM 2018). Within projects, there are start and end dates set by the client within which the project must be completed. Project derives from the Latin language (Latin: proiectum, thrown forward). In the seventeenth century, the meaning "construction project" became accepted as the project definition in Germany (PM 2018).

Due to their growing complexity, projects place special demands on project management and thus also on negotiation management, both for the client and the contractor or order processor. There are often several groups or departments involved in complex projects. Due to their complexity, projects involve significant negotiations with customers, suppliers, banks or other stakeholders. Examples of projects include:

- Construction of a railway station in one of the metropolises such as Stuttgart, e.g. Stuttgart 21
- Construction of an airport, e.g. construction and completion of the Williy Brandt Airport BER
- Renovation of a museum, e.g. Neues Museum in Berlin
- Construction of a high-speed train, e.g. construction of the ICE by Siemens and Bombardier
- Construction and completion of an opera house, e.g. the opera in Hamburg

According to the project management manual, projects fulfil certain criteria (PM 2018). Essential criteria for projects can be defined as shown in Table 10.1. If these project criteria are not met, there is normally no real project. This does not mean that project management

Table 10.1 Project criteria

Time limit	Projects are limited in time, which means that both the beginning and the end are defined in terms of deadlines.
Uniqueness	Projects are unique, they are not suitable for reproducing things that already exist (process management is much better suited for this)
Resource scarcity	Projects have limited resources
Targets	Projects pursue a clearly specified and positively formulated objective
Organization	Projects require their own project management organization
Risk	Projects imply the risk of deviations and failure
Interdisciplinarity	Projects work interdisciplinarily and interdepartmentally
Novelty	Projects break new ground. They realise solutions that do not yet exist in the form envisaged
Project phases	Projects are handled in defined phases
Project negotiations	Projects include internal and external negotiations

Own representation

methods cannot be usefully applied beyond project work. However, one should not speak of project work in order not to confuse the terms.

Projects always include an organizational structure and a process organization (Helmold 2018). The organizational structure forms the hierarchical framework of the project organization and defines the organizational framework, i.e. which tasks are to be handled by which functional units and sub-departments. In contrast, the process organization regulates the processes that take place within this framework (flow and information processes within the project phases). Companies usually have a line organization or a project matrix organization, although in many cases there is a combination or hybrid of both organizational forms (Helmold 2018).

Projects usually take place under cost, manufacturing, and performance pressures, so they involve numerous negotiations. To carry out projects, project teams are formed that consist of different functions (PM 2018). These teams then perform control and steering tasks as part of project management (PM 2018). Projects go through four phases as shown in Fig. 10.1. Projects start with a feasibility review. If the feasibility is given, the next phase starts with the preliminary project planning. In this context, it is recommended to have a project brief that clearly defines key performance indicators, such as quality, cost, time or resources (PM 2018). After confirming all performance measures, the project can be started in phase 3, the project implementation. After successful project completion, project validation takes place with a target-performance comparison. In particular, deviations will have to be negotiated via the supplementary management Chap. 8 (Helmold 2018).

Projects are executed in interdisciplinary functional groups, as Fig. 10.2 shows. Figure 10.2 shows projects A, B and C, which consist of different functions such as procurement, production, marketing, quality, finance or human resources (Helmold 2018). Advantages of a project organization are:

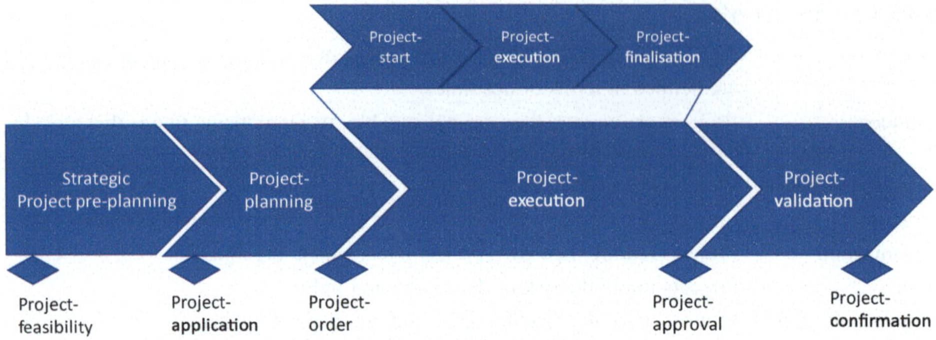

Fig. 10.1 Project phases. (Source: own representation based on PM 2018)

Funktion	Projekt A	Projekt B	Projekt C
Procurement	O	O	O
Production	O	O	O
Marketing & Sales	O	O	O
Quality	O	O	O
Finance	O	O	O
Huma Resources	O	O	O

Fig. 10.2 Project organization. (Source: own representation based on PM 2018)

- Short decision-making processes through co-allocation
- Representation of all functions
- Operational orientation leads to quick decisions for the implementation of measures
- Project-specific material budgets create transparency about the real purchasing costs for all products
- Group dynamic advantages through cooperation of all areas (no "silo thinking" or autonomous thinking of departments or functions, but joint project thinking)

10.2 Critical Success Factors in Projects

10.2.1 Key Criteria in Projects

The project management manual defines key criteria and success factors for controlling and steering projects (PM 2018). These criteria include a total of nine categories that must be considered for successful project completion.

10.2.2 Integration Management

Integration management in project management describes the procedures and processes required for good coordination and integration of the various activities of a project. It includes project plan development, project plan execution and change management (PM 2018).

10.2.3 Scope and Performance Management

Project scope management deals with the ongoing planning and control of the progress of performance in the project. Scope management involves checking at regular intervals whether the project is within the targets defined in the project order or whether there are any deviations. Project scope management includes project initiation, content and scope planning, performance definition, performance verification, and performance control (PM 2018).

10.2.4 Time and Schedule Management

Time and schedule management is to ensure that a project is completed on time. Time and schedule management includes task definition, task sequence definition, task duration estimation, schedule development, and schedule monitoring (PM 2018).

10.2.5 Cost Management

Cost management describes all the processes required to ensure that the project is completed within the planned and approved budget. Cost management includes resource planning, cost estimation, budgeting and cost monitoring (PM 2018).

10.2.6 Quality Management

Quality management in projects should ensure that the quality requirements defined by the client are met or even exceeded. This includes quality planning, quality assurance and quality control (PM 2018).

10.2.7 Personnel Management

The main task of personnel management is to ensure that the employees involved in the project are deployed as efficiently as possible. The following functions and tasks can be assigned to human resource management: Project organization, personnel acquisition and team development (PM 2018).

10.2.8 Communication Management

Project communication management aims to create, collect, disseminate, file, and define all project information in a timely and appropriate manner. This includes the development of an information and reporting system, the distribution of information, the determination of progress and the administrative closure (PM 2018).

10.2.9 Risk Management

Risk management describes all iterative processes necessary to identify, analyze, and respond to project risks. This includes risk identification, risk assessment, the development of measures to address risks, and risk tracking (PM 2018).

10.2.10 Procurement Management

The knowledge field of procurement management includes the procurement of goods and services outside the organization and the associated contract design. This area includes procurement preparation, bid preparation, solicitation of bids, supplier selection, contract design and contract performance (PM 2018).

10.3 Recommendations for Project Negotiations

Projects with complex objectives require a competent project leader or manager. This person needs both hard skills (e.g. project management skills) and soft skills (e.g. emotional intelligence) in order to be convincing both internally and externally. In addition to a good and sustainable relationship with the management level, one of the key components of project managers is to successfully lead a team. Project managers need to select their people in such a way that there is a healthy mix between expertise and people skills. Projects should be projected through a robust project brief where performance parameters are clearly defined and scheduled (PM 2018). Targets must have specific attributes and be specific, measurable, acceptable, realistic and timely (SMART

Table 10.2 Negotiations in projects

Recommendations for successful project management
Leadership and management
Social skills and expertise
Project planning by project order
Targets according to SMART aspects
Sustainability of project activities
Success control and validation
Incentive system and career planning
Return to the line department
Internationality and diversity
Use of digital media

methodology: English: specific, measurable, achievable, realistic, timely). Sustainability as well as a permanent and regular success control round off the SMART goals. An incentive system is recommended here so that employees are sufficiently motivated by material or immaterial benefits for project success. Internationality and diversity strengthen project teams and help to successfully implement projects in an international context. The use of digital media supports networking, especially across national borders and time zones. Finally, organizations should enable project members to return to line functions. Table 10.2 summarizes the most important recommendations (PM 2018).

References

Helmold, M. (2018). Erfolgreiche Verhandlungen und Best-in-Class Empfehlungen für den Verhandlungsdurchbruch. Manuskript und Workshopunterlagen im Master- und MBA-Studium.

PM (2018). Abgerufen am 7.7.2018. http://www.pm-handbuch.com/begriffe/.

Negotiations in the Services Sector

11

Having money is beautiful, as long as you haven't lost the joy of things that money can't buy
—Salvador Dali (1904–1989)

Contents

Summary

The 4 Ps (product, price, place and promotion) are known from conventional marketing theory (Heskett, Sasser, Schlesinger, The Service Profit Chain: How Leading Companies Link Profit and Growth to Loyalty, Satisfaction, and Value, Free Press, New York, 1997). Product is about product and program policy decisions; price is about price policy decisions; place is about distribution policy decisions, and promotion is about communication policy decisions (Meffert, Burmann, Kirchgeorg, Marketing: Grundlagen marktorientierter Unternehmensführung, Gabler, Wiesbaden, 2012).

M. Helmold et al., *Successful Negotiations*,
https://doi.org/10.1007/978-3-658-35701-6_11

However, the concept of the 4 Ps of marketing cannot be transferred one-to-one to services marketing, as there are special challenges in marketing services that result from the nature of the services.

11.1 Characteristics of Services

The *4 Ps (product, price, place* and *promotion) are* known from conventional marketing theory (Heskett et al. 1997). *Product* is about product and program policy decisions; *price is* about price policy decisions; *place is about* distribution policy decisions, and *promotion is about* communication policy decisions (Meffert et al. 2012). However, the concept of the *4 Ps of* marketing cannot be transferred one-to-one to services marketing, as there are special challenges in marketing services that result from the nature of the services.

11.1.1 Special Features of Services Marketing

Such special challenges in the context of service provision relate in particular to the fact that services can only be experienced when they are provided (Scheuer 2015). A service can therefore only be claimed and consumed at the moment it is provided. The customer must be actively involved in the service creation process in order for the service to be provided at all (Haller 2015). The participation of the consumer in the creation process is therefore referred to as the *integration of the external factor* (Haller 2015; Meffert et al. 2012). Thus, the service provider is dependent on the customer and his participation; the customer participates in the service process as a "co-producer" (Haller 2015). This complicates any kind of standardization of services because "[d]a the customer participates in the service production, the process is unpredictable" (Haller 2015), as is the outcome. This can lead to problems in service delivery, as customers may behave unexpectedly, making service delivery difficult or even impossible (Haller 2015).

Services are also "characterised by the feature of immateriality" (Meffert et al. 2015), because the service as such cannot be represented materially (Scheuer 2015). This results in two further characteristics of services: Non-storability and non-transportability (Meffert et al. 2012, 2015).

Services are neither storable nor transportable, as they are created or produced at the point of use only at the moment of use, which is referred to as the "Uno-Actu principle" (Meffert et al. 2012, 2015).

Contrary to the characteristics of other products that can be grasped with the human senses, services are initially an abstract product that can only be illustrated initially and prior to its use by means of service descriptions and promises (Scheuer 2015, p. 83). Services are thus intangible and difficult to grasp, as they practically do not exist at all before their creation and simultaneous use and cannot be tested before purchase (Haller

2015). Service providers can counteract this problem by materialising services, for example through external, tangible factors such as personnel or equipment (Meffert et al. 2015), because "[t]angibles help convey the value of the service transaction's intangible aspects" (Thomas and Applegate 2010).

11.1.2 The 7 Ps

The concept of the *4 Ps of* marketing is heavily discussed as well as criticized especially in the field of services marketing and extended by additional components, since the dimensions of the *4 Ps do* not do justice to the special characteristics of services marketing (Rafiq and Ahmed 1995).

Rafiq and Ahmed (1995) therefore introduce the concept of *7 Ps*, where the original *4 Ps (product, price, promotion, place)* are extended to include the additional dimensions of *personnel, physical facilities* and *process* (Beibst 2011).

Managers in all industries today should heed these *7 Ps* because every company, regardless of product, provides service to the customer in some way, and impeccable service delivery continues to become a differentiator, whether in new customer acquisition, sales, or after sales or support (Goldsmith 1999).

Personnel policy is aimed at the internal customers, the employees of a company, and includes topics such as personnel recruitment, personnel development, employee satisfaction and internal communication (Beibst 2011). In the context of service provision, human resources policy plays a central role, as services can usually only be experienced through personal, interpersonal interaction. On the part of the employees, a pronounced customer and service orientation is therefore a prerequisite for performing convincingly in the context of service provision and achieving a high quality of service.

Physical facilities, the equipment policy, is another relevant dimension in the context of service marketing, through which the otherwise invisible and intangible services at the service location can be materialized through tangible equipment or visible design and thus made more accessible (Beibst 2011). The inclusion of the service environment in the marketing of services plays an important role here, because services that are not visible and intangible can stand out from the competition by working on this component accordingly (Beibst 2011).

The process policy *(process) refers to* the business processes within a company and includes, among others, the service and relationship process (Beibst 2011). Since the customer is usually part of the creation process when providing services, efficient, targeted and customer-oriented business processes should be the focus of every company, since the quality of the business processes is decisive for the service quality to be expected (Beibst 2011). This results in a simple chain of effects: the more efficient the processes on the company side, the higher the perceived service quality on the customer side, the greater the customer satisfaction, the more recurring business, the more personal recommendations, the larger the customer base and the more revenue.

Goldsmith (1999) names "personalisation" (p. 178) as an *eighth P*, since personalised service is becoming increasingly important and is becoming more and more the focus of marketing decisions. In fact, personalisation should be seen as the most important component in the future and therefore firmly anchored in the marketing mix (Goldsmith 1999). In product development, decisions regarding the other *Ps* should be aligned with the desired degree of personalization in order to meet today's customer needs (Goldsmith 1999).

On the other hand, *after a* product has been used or a service has been provided, it is too late to take the customer's opinion into account because the product has already been developed or the service has already been defined and provided. The customer's point of view should therefore be obtained, researched and taken into account *before* the product or service is developed, so that customer wishes and expectations can be adequately taken into account during product or service development (Goldsmith 1999).

11.1.3 The 3 Rs

Heskett et al. (1997) supplement the conventional *4 Ps of* marketing with the "three Rs of lifetime customer value" (p. 60): *retention, related sales* and *referrals* (p. 59). Central to this is Reichheld and Sasser's (1990, p. 105 f.) assumption that customers become increasingly profitable the longer the business relationship with a company lasts, also referred to by Heskett et al. (1997, p. 60) as the "lifetime customer value" concept. As a result, market share is no longer the sole criterion for defining the success of a company, but rather "market share quality" (Heskett et al. 1997), i.e. how many profitable customers a company has and how profitable these customers are calculated over the entire time they are in contact with the company.

Retention is defined as a "continuing, active relationship with a customer that yields a stream of revenue from the sale of the initial product or service" (Heskett et al. 1997) and represents the first pillar of increased customer profitability. The longer a customer is in a business relationship with a company, the more profitable the customer becomes over time from a marketing perspective, as marketing costs are allocated over a longer period of time and not as much marketing effort is needed to get the customer excited about the product or service. Especially at the beginning of a customer relationship, marketing costs are much higher to attract customers to a company and to familiarize them with the product or service specifications (ibid). In this context, Heskett et al. (1997) also speak of the "get acquainted marketing effort", which is the largest expenditure at the beginning of a business relationship.

In many companies, however, the main focus is still on the acquisition of new customers and not on retaining and binding existing customers, although the costs of customer loyalty measures are considerably lower than the costs of acquiring new customers (Heskett et al. 1997). By aligning employee reward systems appropriately, the wrong incentives are sometimes set and all efforts are focused only on acquiring new customers. The negative effects of churning customers on the overall performance of a company are thus neglected at this point and opportunities for securing long-term success are neither considered nor perceived (Reichheld and Sasser 1990).

Heskett et al. (1997) therefore recommend focusing on customer loyalty measures to be able to realize *lifetime customer value* over time.

Related Sales is based on the assumption that it is easier to sell new products and services to existing customers than to new customers (Heskett et al. 1997) and represents the second pillar of increased customer profitability. Again, much less *get* acquainted *marketing effort is* required because the company is already known with its products and services. By selling new products and services to existing customers, higher margins can be achieved, as these customers are not quite as price sensitive as new customers (Heskett et al. 1997; Reichheld and Sasser 1990). Another effect is that additional sales can also reduce unit operating costs (Heskett et al. 1997; Reichheld and Sasser 1990).

Feedback management plays a central role, especially in the area of *related sales*, since product and service improvements can be achieved much more easily thanks to customer feedback, new products and services can be developed much more specifically for the target group, and customers can be served more efficiently (Heskett et al. 1997; Reichheld and Sasser 1990). Feedback from existing customers enables the company to identify up-selling and cross-selling potentials and to react accordingly.

Referrals refers to the additional business generated by recommending the product or service to others (Heskett et al. 1997; Reichheld and Sasser 1990) and forms the third pillar of increased customer profitability. However, the basic prerequisite for this is satisfied customers, so that a recommendation takes place at all (Heskett et al. 1997; Reichheld and Sasser 1990). A study by McKinsey & Company showed that satisfied customers who are emotionally attached to a company are three times more likely to recommend or repurchase a product (Bhattacharjee et al. 2016).

The *3 Rs* are interdependent: If the customer is satisfied with the service provision and service quality, he or she remains loyal to the company or service provider *(retention)*. This makes the customer more receptive to other products from the same provider *(related sales)*. If the service provider convinces the customer at several touchpoints and throughout the entire *customer journey* (Maechler et al. 2016), the customer will recommend the product to others *(referral)*. Customers thus remain with the company for longer and continuously generate sales, which increases lifetime customer value (Reichheld and Sasser 1990).

The optimization of existing performance is becoming increasingly relevant due to higher operational costs, for example caused by wages (Ernst & Young 2017). Through the targeted use of the *3 Rs*, such optimization can be achieved and made sustainable.

11.1.4 Negotiation of Services

The special characteristics of services have already been presented. These have a particular impact on negotiations of services, since such negotiations are usually conducted in the abstract about those services that have not yet been provided and that therefore do not yet exist in fact.

In the context of negotiations, tangible framework conditions can also be used to draw conclusions about the quality of service to be expected. The initiation of negotiations, the communication beforehand, the quantity and quality of any preparations made, the premises of the negotiations and, finally and decisively, of course, the competence and professionalism of the negotiating partner are just some of several possible indicators that can be used as additional evaluation criteria alongside the content of the negotiations.

11.1.5 Negotiations in Purchasing

When purchasing services, it is also important to estimate the expected service quality as accurately as possible, especially because the purchase of services involves large order values (e.g. wholesalers in tourism). When negotiating the purchase of services, it is advisable to define a catalogue of criteria of obligatory and optional negotiation points in advance. Due to the intangibility of services, the obligatory criteria in particular should be contractually assured in the course of negotiations. Since the services purchased in the wholesale trade are passed on to a large number of end customers, there is often no direct feedback between the expected and the actual service, since the purchaser does not always obligatorily use the products himself or test them before purchasing. It is therefore recommended that the responsible purchaser obligatorily tests the negotiated service before purchasing it in large quantities and passing it on to the end customers. This is particularly useful for sustainable quality assurance, as it allows the seller to detect and correct any discrepancies between the expected and actual service before passing it on to the end customer. This approach is particularly worthwhile in view of the fact that wholesalers can demand certain service characteristics due to the size of the order. For example, a service buyer may require a hotel to set up and offer 24-h room service, otherwise the buyer will not purchase contingents for the next season. By improving quality accordingly, existing customers can be retained and new customers can be attracted. However, this presupposes that the purchasing department is also aware of the customer's needs and takes these into account in the negotiations. The importance of customer feedback in the context of service negotiations is described in detail at the end of the chapter. At this point, reference is made only to the relevance of regular communication and to the importance of a close exchange between the purchase of the relevant service and the opinion of the users. Through feedback from customer feedback management, purchasing can take better account of customer needs in order to offer services that are better accepted, thus leading to higher customer satisfaction, a higher recommendation rate and sustainably secured sales.

11.1.6 Negotiations at Events

Similar to purchasing, event negotiations are also primarily about communicating expectations prior to using the service. This plays a key role as there is often only one opportunity for the supplier to provide the service, for example weddings in a hotel. The importance of feedback in purchasing negotiations has already been highlighted, but in purchasing customer feedback can be taken into account for the next purchases. If a wholesaler buys a room contingent at a hotel where customer feedback indicates that it is not well received by guests, either the hotel can be renegotiated to remedy guest-identified criticisms for the next season, or purchasing can contract with another hotel. If the guest books the hotel through the buyer a second time, they can benefit from the improved service. However, for a wedding, if the expectations of the bride and groom were not communicated clearly enough to the hotel, or if the hotel did not diligently note the expressed wishes and does not implement some points at the event, the actual service provided differs from that expected and unintended differences arise. In this case, however, the possibilities of redress are limited, because the hotel, unlike when purchasing hotel rooms, is unlikely to be able to offer the bride and groom to rectify the mistakes at the next wedding celebration. Thus, negotiations are of particular importance for events in order to establish a clear horizon of needs and expectations in the run-up to the event, if possible.

11.1.7 Negotiations in the Context of Customer Feedback Management

Customers can express their dissatisfaction after buying a product or using a service in a variety of ways, such as making complaints directly to the company or a *third party*, moving to a competitor, negative word of mouth, or continuing to use the product or service but being dissatisfied or becoming increasingly dissatisfied.

In a study by Svari and Olsen (2012), the two authors investigated the influence of emotions on the complaint behaviour of customers who have experienced a negative service irregularity. In doing so, they identified three distinct complaint behaviors: "complaining to the company, switching, and engaging in negative word-of-mouth communication" (Svari and Olsen 2012). These three behaviors represent the overarching main complaint behaviors of dissatisfied customers.

Following the three behaviours identified by Svari and Olsen (2012) in relation to complaint behaviour, these are visualised again in Fig. 11.1 and supplemented by the two dimensions "chance of success of redress" and "impact on the company".

Figure 11.1 shows that, compared to the alternative complaint behaviours, the chances of success of redress are highest and the impact on the company is lowest when the customer complains directly to the company. Therefore, management should always encourage customers to direct their feedback to the company. If the customer has already switched providers, the chances of success in making amends are already lower and the impact on the company more noticeable. If the customer has already switched to a

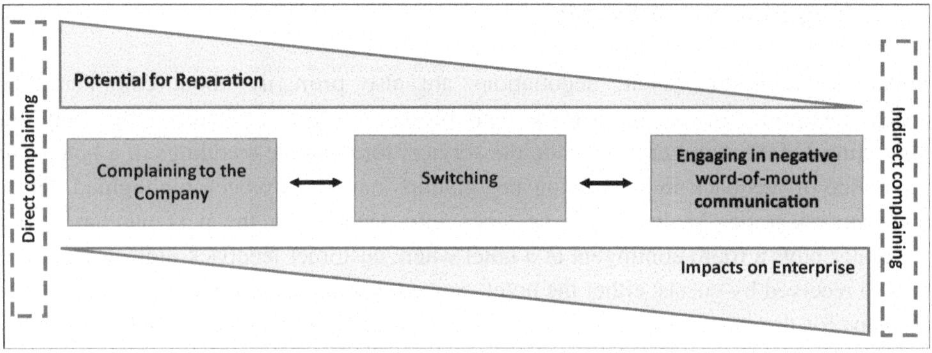

Fig. 11.1 Different complaint behaviour

competitor and then spreads negative word-of-mouth, the chances of success in making amends are the lowest and the impact on the company the greatest, because in addition to lost sales, there is also bad word-of-mouth, which not only damages sales but also the company's image.

In their study, Svari and Olsen (2012) also investigated the relationship between the cause of the complaint and complaint behaviour. They found that the likelihood of customers making a complaint directly to the company or telling family and friends about it is correspondingly lower if the customers are (at least proportionally) partly to blame, as in such a case the likelihood of the contributory negligence being discovered and a loss of face is much greater Svari and Olsen (2012). Nevertheless, the emotions in connection with the negative service experience must be ventilated (ibid., p. 276, 278), for which the form of the online complaint is often used, since these can be expressed anonymously on the web (ibid.) and complainants can thus express themselves negatively but save face Svari and Olsen (2012).

Consequently, online complaint behavior plays a special role, especially via social media channels and on relevant online portals, which enable ratings and thus a comparison of providers. Because these reviews can influence potential future buyers in their purchasing decisions, companies must not only respond to complaints *on property*, but increasingly also develop a strategy for *online service recovery*, even if not every online complaint is based exclusively on the fault of the company. Nevertheless, a company must respond to such online complaints because of the involvement of the digital public (Svari and Olsen 2012). This is because the report of a negative experience can reach thousands of potential customers in real time via social media, who may reconsider their purchase decision as a result.

The processing of online feedback and online complaints can, in turn, also be seen as an opportunity, since successful complaint processing signals to potential buyers that the feedback is taken seriously and responded to accordingly—also online. The focus should nevertheless be on obtaining, recording, processing and reacting to the feedback directly on site, as the chances of success are greatest on *property*.

11.1.8 Salary Negotiations in the Service Sector

The special features of the service sector have already been presented in more detail at the beginning. Unlike in the manufacturing sector, labour success in the service sector is much more difficult to measure. If factors such as costs and productivity can be determined in the primary and secondary sectors on the basis of, for example, unit numbers, material consumption and directly attributable costs, comparable key figures for determining the position within the service sector are difficult to apply across the board.

Employees in the manufacturing industry can thus fall back on tangible and tangible key figures in salary negotiations, for example, in order to push through a higher wage. Instead of sewing ten pairs of jeans per day, the worker can now sew twelve pairs of jeans per day through increasing experience and skill. If the target is ten jeans per day, her performance gives her the opportunity to negotiate a higher salary.

In the service sector, on the other hand, an increase in productivity is possible, but not easy to measure. First of all, key figures must be defined with which the service provided can be measured in the first place. This raises the question of the immediacy of the influence of the service provided on those indicators. In the manufacturing sector, the influence of the labour used is direct; in the example of the jeans mentioned above, an employee sews X amount of trousers per unit Y (hour, day, etc.). In the tertiary sector, on the other hand, the impact of the service provided is usually not directly identifiable or traceable and usually still represents the sum of various services provided.

If an employee wants to negotiate a better salary in a hotel, for example, he or she cannot justify this wish by saying that more guests will come back thanks to his or her commitment, because the guest usually has to deal with more than one employee during his or her stay, so that from this point at the latest the allocation or traceability becomes difficult and the wish for a higher salary is invalidated due to the lack of a direct influence of work performance on success.

When negotiating salaries in the service sector, it is therefore advisable to always take the overall picture into account and to attribute it to the entire workforce or to a specific team. A reduction to individual employees is difficult and therefore does not make much sense, especially since the motivation of the entire team may suffer as a result.

11.1.9 The Importance of Feedback in Service Negotiations

It was pointed out that negotiations are usually conducted in the abstract about those services that have not yet been provided and do not even exist. This makes feedback meetings after the agreed service has been provided all the more important. Only then can a comparison be made between expected and actual quality. At this point, the relevance of realistic expectation management should be mentioned, through which a company can already influence how a service is perceived by the consumer from the moment it is used. It is essential that all departments of a company work together cross-functionally so that there are no unwanted divergences between expected and actual service quality.

For example, if the marketing department runs an advertising campaign highlighting a particular feature of the service, but the campaign is not agreed with the operational departments, they may not be able to fully meet customer expectations regarding that one particular service feature, expectations will not be met, customers will be disappointed, which in turn will affect customer satisfaction, referral rates and in the long run the performance of the respective company.

By implementing a holistic feedback management system, companies can succeed in reflecting on and retrospectively evaluating the service that was initially negotiated and finally provided. In this way, any discrepancies can be identified and eliminated for future service provision.

Hatz (2018) has developed a twelve-step model for this purpose, in which he uses the example of the luxury hotel industry to show how a sustainable competitive advantage can be achieved through holistic customer feedback management.

The model is based on the customer process of perceived complaint handling by Stauss and Seidel (2007, p. 192) and consists of three phases: *pre-complaint, complaint* and *post-complaint*. In the main phase of the model, the *Complaint phase*, feedback is provided on the service provided. In this phase, the focus is on how the company responds to the feedback and what solution it presents. At this point, it is important to place this main phase in the overall model, because "[w]hile handling individual complaints is an important part of complaint management, it tends to address symptoms rather than causes." Only by placing it in this larger, superordinate context can the feedback received be processed further. In particular, complaints should be investigated so that they are not only treated symptomatically, but the main causes are identified. Thus, the model of Hatz (2018) represents a holistic approach and presents in the two other phases *pre-complaint* and *post-complaint* respectively the upstream and downstream phases to the actual core phase *Complaint*.

Figure 11.2 takes into account the necessity of such a holistic handling of feedback in negotiations and depicts the individual interrelationships of effects. By integrating feedback into the negotiation process, it can be supplemented by the component of the continuous improvement process (CIP).

In conclusion, Chap. 11 can be summarised to the effect that negotiations in the service sector are partly subject to other determinants. These are taken into account by the 7P model, as Table 11.1 shows. Finally, a feedback system should be supplemented with a continuous improvement process for the constant improvement of performance and customer satisfaction.

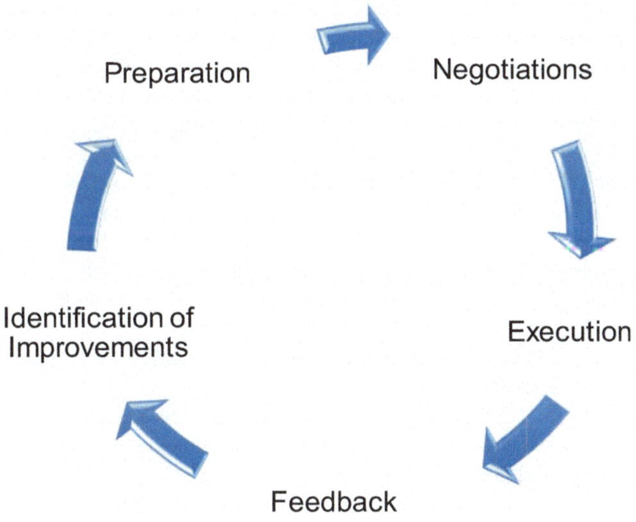

Fig. 11.2 Integration of feedback into the improvement process

Table 11.1 Negotiations in the services sector

Recommendations for negotiations on services
Consideration of special features in the service sector by 7 Ps or 3 Rs
Use of social media
Implementation of a holistic feedback management system
Identification of improvement potentials
Introduction of a performance measurement system

References

Beibst, G. (2011). Dienstleistungsmarketing (2. Aufl.). Studienbrief 2-033-0009. Brandenburg: Hochschulverbund Distance Learning.

Bhattacharjee, D., Moreno, J., & Ortega, F. (2016): The secret to delighting customers: Putting employees first. McKinsey&Company Article (März 2016). Abgerufen am 4.1.2018. Online unter: https://www.mckinsey.com/business-functions/operations/our-insights/the-secret-to-delighting-customers-putting-employees-first.

Ernst & Young [EY] (2017): Global hospitality insights: Top 10 thoughts for 2017. Abgerufen am 4.1.2018. Online unter: www.ey.com/Publication/vwLUAssets/EY-global-hospitalityinsights-2017/$FILE/EY-global-hospitality-insights-top-10-thoughts-for-2017.pdf.

Goldsmith, R. E. (1999). The personalised marketplace: Beyond the 4Ps. Marketing Intelligence & Planning, 17(4), 178–185. https://doi.org/10.1108/02634509910275917.

Haller, S. (2015). Dienstleistungsmanagement: Grundlagen – Konzepte – Instrumente (6. Aufl.). Wiesbaden: Springer Gabler.

Hatz, N. (2018). Wettbewerbsvorteil durch exzellenten Service: die optimale Gestaltung von Kundenfeedback-Management in der Luxushotellerie als nachhaltiges Differenzierungsmerkmal (Master-Thesis). Donau-Universität Krems, Krems an der Donau, Österreich.

Heskett, J. L., Sasser, Jr., W. E., & Schlesinger, L. A. (1997). The Service Profit Chain: How Leading Companies Link Profit and Growth to Loyalty, Satisfaction, and Value. New York: The Free Press.

Maechler, N., Neher, K., & Park, R. (2016): From touchpoints to journeys: Seeing the world as customers do. McKinsey&Company Article (März 2016). Online unter: https://www.mckinsey.com/business-functions/marketing-and-sales/our-insights/from-touchpoints-to-journeys-seeing-the-world-as-customers-do [Zugriff am 22.10.2017].

Meffert, H., Burmann, C., & Kirchgeorg, M. (2012). Marketing: Grundlagen marktorientierter Unternehmensführung (11. Aufl.). Wiesbaden: Gabler Verlag.

Meffert, H., Bruhn, M., & Hadwich, K. (2015). Dienstleistungsmarketing: Grundlagen – Konzepte – Methoden (8. Aufl.). Wiesbaden: Springer Gabler.

Rafiq, M., & Ahmed, P. K. (1995). Using the 7Ps as a generic marketing mix: An exploratory survey of UK and European marketing academics. In: Marketing Intelligence & Planning, 13(9), 4–15. https://doi.org/10.1108/02634509510097793.

Reichheld, F. F., & Sasser, Jr., W. E. (1990). Zero Defections: Quality Comes to Services. In: Harvard Business Review, September-Oktober 1990, 105–111.

Scheuer, T. (2015). Marketing für Dienstleister: Wie Sie unsichtbare Leistungen erfolgreich vermarkten (3. Aufl.). Wiesbaden: Springer Gabler.

Stauss, B. & Seidel, W. (2007). Beschwerdemanagement: Unzufriedene Kunden als profitable Zielgruppe. Hanserverlag Berlin.

Svari, S. & Olsen L.E. (2012). The role of emotions in customer complaint behaviors. International Journal of Quality and Service Sciences, 4(3), 270–282. https://doi.org/10.1108/17566691211269585.

Thomas, A., & Applegate, J. (2010). Pay Attention! How to Listen, Respond, and Profit from Customer Feedback. Hoboken, New Jersey: John Wiley & Sons.

Summary and Recommendations for Negotiation Success

12

He who has never made a mistake has never tried anything new.
—Albert Einstein (1879–1955)

Contents

Summary

Negotiations are a form of communication about a controversial issue, which are characterized by conflicting needs, interests and motives. In principle, negotiations aim to achieve a balance of interests by weighing one's own motives against those of the other party in the negotiation and arriving at a negotiated outcome by making concessions (Obrien, Negotiations for Procurement Professionals. 2nd Edition. Kogan Page Croyden, 2016). In business, negotiations usually take place in the international trade of goods between a selling (supplier or vendor) and a buying (buyer or customer) company. Buyers have the desire and need to obtain the lowest purchase price in a transaction, whereas sellers seek the highest selling price. Thorough preparation is a prerequisite for a successful negotiation Sect. 12.4. In addition to the scope, minimum and maximum objectives (Least Desired Outcome, LDO; Most Desired Outcome, MdO) to be negotiated and achieved, the secret lies in thorough preparation and analysis of the negotiating opponents and their motives and interests.

M. Helmold et al., *Successful Negotiations*,
https://doi.org/10.1007/978-3-658-35701-6_12

12.1 Preparation and Analysis as a Prerequisite for Negotiation Success

Negotiation is a form of communication, usually verbal and conversational, about a controversial issue characterized by conflicting needs, interests, and motives (Obrien 2016; Helmold 2018). Basically, negotiations aim to achieve a reconciliation of interests by weighing one's own motives with those of the other party in the negotiation and reaching a negotiated outcome by making concessions (Obrien 2016). In business, negotiations usually take place in the international trade of goods between a selling (supplier or vendor) and a buying (buyer or customer) company (Helmold 2018). Buyers have the desire and need to obtain the lowest purchase price in a transaction, whereas sellers seek the highest selling price. Thorough preparation is a prerequisite for the negotiation breakthrough para 12.4. In addition to the scope, minimum and maximum objectives (Least Desired Outcome, LDO; Most Desired Outcome, MdO) to be negotiated and achieved, the secret lies in thorough preparation and analysis of the negotiating opponents and their motives and interests. Furthermore, negotiation scopes, roles, strategies and tactics must be defined and made transparent before negotiations begin in order to successfully reach the goal. The negotiation manuscript/scriptwriting serves as a preparatory aid here Sect. 12.4. The classic W-questions help with preparation Fig. 2.3. Table 12.1 shows the elements that need to be considered in the preparation phase. The table describes and summarizes categories and the relevant questions for a successful negotiation breakthrough (Helmold 2018):

Table 12.1 Preparation and detailed analysis for negotiation success

Category	Question
Subject matter and scope of negotiations	What should be negotiated? What are important successes for your own and the other side?
Analysis of the negotiating partners	With whom do I negotiate? Who is the decision-maker on the other side? Who is the influencer?
Motives and interests of the negotiating party	What are the interests of the other party? How can I convince the negotiating partner?
Strategies and tactics	How can I get my points across? What strategies and tactics can I use to achieve a breakthrough in negotiations?
counterarguments	What counterarguments does my opponent have? How can I react and respond to them?
Intercultural elements	What are the intercultural specifics?

Own representation based on the A-6 concept (Helmold 2018)

12.2 Key Competences for International and Intercultural Negotiations

International and intercultural negotiations require different key competences, as various authors state (Helmold 2018; Obrien 2016; Erbacher 2018; IUBH 2018; Dathe and Helmold 2018). Key competences are described as special knowledge, characteristics and skills in a certain field. Key competences can be divided in the context of negotiations into factual, methodological, self, language and intercultural competences IUBH 2018. Table 12.2 shows the most important key competences.

Study results from the German Institute for Sales Research (Deutschen Instituts für Vertriebsforschung) show that, again, misjudgements on the part of salespeople and a lack of qualifications or characteristics often result in excessive price discounts being granted in favour of customers (DIV 2018; Guba 2016). Furthermore, the results show that in terms of personality structure, salespeople turn out to be comparatively less intercultural, conscientious, risk-taking and less team-oriented, which may counteract the key competencies listed in Table 12.2 and promote misjudgements in international negotiations and business cases. Alongside this, however, it can also be surmised that the pressure to close deals among salespeople often leads them to by all means exhaust their own leftover negotiating leeway and thus once again grant a price reduction or other concessions in favour of the customer (DIV 2018; Guba 2016). Numerous companies see their qualified employees and their negotiation skills in the international context as a competitive advantage and an opportunity

Table 12.2 Key competences for negotiations

Non-cash Competencies	Methods-Competencies	Self-Competencies	Language and intercultural skills
Contracts	Analytical skills	Endurance	Foreign languages
International Law	Learning methods	Motivation	Country knowledge
Commercial arithmetic	Moderation techniques	Solution Orientation	Cultural understanding
Affinity for numbers	Presentation techniques	Self-confidence	Behavior
Business Knowledge	Information Retrieval	Respect for other people	Demographic trends
Technical understanding	Rhetorical skills	Patience	Knowledge about important people
IT knowledge	Argumentation skills	Agility	Historical understanding
Lean methods	Structured way of working	Flexibility	Knowledge of the respective political system
Incoterms 2010	Project management	Openness	Thinking patterns

Own representation based on IUBH (2018)

for differentiation and performance leadership. Therefore, sustained and continuous training in the area of key competencies is imperative.

There are also various deficits in key competencies in purchasing, as study results show. In recent years, the guiding principle of many companies has been "the cheaper the better" and the focus has been on "squeezing costs", i.e. achieving the lowest cost price. The role of purchasing was trimmed to the generation of savings (cost savings) (BME 2017). Purchasing was primarily perceived as an uncomfortable interlocutor. However, purchasing is not unaffected by global changes. Topics such as globalization, scarcity of resources and environmental awareness, Industry 4.0 as well as rapid advancements in information technology are knitting a new matrix of requirements for high-performance purchasing. In addition, purchasing is confronted with increasing multidimensional volatility. Not only currencies and commodities, but entire markets are exposed to fluctuating developments. Against the backdrop of these challenges, the role of purchasing is taking on a new form. The focus of this new function and objective is essentially on five elements: monitoring, controlling and continuously improving overall costs, ensuring quality, improving performance with value-added partners, implementing innovations and identifying and implementing partnership activities for sustainable improvement along the entire value chain. It is the task of purchasing to look for alternative solutions in order to generate a sustainable value contribution for the company. In this strategic and long-term orientation, purchasing provides essential support throughout the entire value chain as a cooperative partner. Through the use of new tools and innovative strategy changes, purchasing will become even more important in the future, namely as a pacesetter and guarantor of success for the market position and the economic success of the company. This interactive workshop will show how to prepare your purchasing organization and purchasing tools for changing requirements. Concrete approaches for the development of a corresponding strategy will be worked out and the essential key factors and new requirements for purchasing that need to be taken into account will be identified (BME 2017).

12.3 Success Factors for a Breakthrough in Negotiations

Both negotiation success and negotiation breakthrough can be achieved through systematic and thorough preparation and sustainable implementation, as described by numerous authors (Dathe and Helmold 2018; Schranner 2018). Here, Dr. Marc Helmold's A-6 model represents an innovative, systematic and sustainable negotiation model that has proven itself in practice in an international context and is divided into six phases (Helmold 2018; IUBH 2018). In this context, preparation within the first phase includes the determination of the scope of the negotiation, the identification of target corridors, the analysis of the counterparty in terms of decision-makers and influencers, and the selection of the appropriate environment. The negotiation model focuses on target corridors and not on purely static targets (maximum and minimum targets). Attention combined with the right questioning technique usually lead to the identification of the opponent's motives and interests. One's own arguments, on the other hand, should be presented in a well-considered manner and in the right order. As a rule from psychology, the following is recommended: the most important argument first, then the least important argument followed by the second most important argument Schranner 2018. Other authors recommend using the strongest argument at the end, as it will be immediately remembered by the negotiation opponent (Werkstatt für Führung und Vertrieb 2018). In the A-6 model, Dr. Helmold recommends naming the most important and strongest arguments at the beginning, followed by less important arguments, but one should not use all arguments at the beginning and "shoot one's powder" (IUBH 2018). Strong arguments need to be framed by strong reasoning, this can also be done emotionally (IUBH 2018; Erbacher 2018; Helmold 2018).

Negotiations may and can be emotional, however Helmold speaks of planned and rational emotionality (Helmold 2018). In negotiation, it is advisable to let the negotiating partner speak first and wait for opposing statements or questions to respond (Helmold 2018; Erbacher 2018). Similarly, if you have nothing to say, you should not say anything true to the motto "talk is silver, silence is gold". In difficult negotiations, one can mirror the language, gestures, and facial expressions of the negotiating opponent by repeating the statements or gestures of the negotiating partner Chap. 6. To rebut opposing arguments one should always attack the weakest argument of the negotiating opponent. Similarly, weighting and prioritizing the other party's arguments is an ideal tool for negotiation success. In this context, the previously described tools are ideal means for the ultimate negotiation breakthrough. Table 12.3 summarizes the six phases of Dr. Marc Helmold's A-6 negotiation model Chap. 4 (Helmold 2018).

Table 12.3 The A-6 negotiation model according to Dr. Marc Helmold

Phase	Brief description and summary
A-1	Analysis of the negotiating partners and determination of one's own starting position with minimum and maximum targets, taking into account intercultural aspects and determinants
A-2	Selection of appropriate strategies and tactics that will lead to negotiation success
A-3	Structured structure and argumentation of negotiations through prioritization of arguments
A-4	Execution of negotiations through strong and logical argumentation with a clear distribution of roles
A-5	Defending against counter-arguments and combating resistance by identifying the weakest arguments of the opposing side and one's own strength in the argumentation through prioritization and sequencing
A-6	The results of the negotiations and the observance of the agreements by means of a written agreement.

A-6 Negotiation Concept by Dr. Marc Helmold

12.4 Success Factors for International Negotiations

International trade is growing steadily, as the Federal Statistical Office states in its annual report (Statistisches Bundesamt 2018). Despite current and temporary trade restrictions from the direction of the United States of America and an "America first" policy, free trade and liberalisation, e.g. free trade agreements between the European Union (EU) and Canada, South Korea or Japan, are trends that will continue to increase international trade (Federal Statistical Office 2018). Foreign trade is one of the most important pillars of the German economy. Looking at the trade balance Figs. 1.4 and 1.5, it becomes clear that both European and non-European countries such as the United States or China are important trading partners from a German perspective (Federal Statistical Office 2018). Business relations and thus negotiations in an international context therefore play a central role for companies (BME 2017). Success factors for international negotiations therefore imply that companies need to further imperatively align themselves strategically and operationally with this trend. Table 12.4 summarises the most important recommendations for international negotiations.

In summary, it can be stated that international negotiations and the determinants associated with them are attracting an increasing amount of interest in all sectors of the economy (Federal Statistical Office 2018). Negotiations across cultural boundaries have become a commonplace and fundamental part of business (Helmold and Terry 2016). In the era of globalization, national borders play less and less of a role, thus transactions and business connections in an international context increase significantly. The world economy has become internationalized in unprecedented ways in recent decades. This also leads to the fact that employees have to be trained in order to acquire the necessary competences.

Table 12.4 Elements in international negotiations

Brief description and summary
International awareness of own employees through competent training and education
Long-term development of an own organization in the target country, e.g. international sales office
Strategic promotion of international talents as internal experts as well as promotion of internal networks (English: Insider)
Knowledge of country specifics and intercultural peculiarities such as religion, customs or holidays
Analysis of hierarchical levels, motives, influencers and decision-makers on the negotiating counterparty
Maintaining relationships with business partners and decision makers through regular and periodic meetings
Establishment of a network with different interest groups in the respective country in business, associations and government organisations
perseverance and patience in international negotiations through cautious approaches to the envisaged outcome
compliance with and respect for the negotiated results through a contract and a "watertight" agreement in the language of the country concerned

Numerous experts, associations (Bundesverband Materialwirtschaft, Einkauf und Logistik, BME) or educational institutions such as the International University of Applied Sciences Bad Honnef (iubh, Campus Studies) offer negotiation training in an international context. In addition to skills, a structured and systematic approach is a guarantee for successful negotiations. Standardized methodologies in negotiation help in this regard (Knapp 2017). Strategies and tactics must be used dynamically and flexibly, whereby these must be carefully weighed in the international and intercultural context. The negotiation scope must be defined, quantified and made transparent in order to clearly understand the impact of negotiation options (total cost of ownership, TCO).

Flexibility and creativity help to create added value in negotiations that is beneficial for both sides. Negotiations take place in the interpersonal sphere and must be conducted respectfully. Finally, when making demands and in all negotiation situations, it should be avoided that the negotiating partner loses face Chap. 8. Consideration of the eleven principles and recommendations for action in Table 12.5 will help companies to achieve a sustainable competitive advantage and thus the ultimate success and breakthrough in negotiations.

Table 12.5 Eleven recommendations for successful negotiations

Principles	Recommendation for action and description:
Qualification	Decision-makers and employees must be trained in international negotiations
Structuring	Negotiations need a structure. The A-6 model by Dr. Marc Helmold shows six important phases for successful negotiations
Standardization	Negotiations should be standardised so that all stakeholders can follow their progress.
Strategy & tactics	Strategies and tactics should be well chosen and used flexibly
Professional tools	Tools for analysis or prioritization are a foundation for negotiation breakthroughs
Internationality	Exports and imports shape negotiations internationally, so that foreign language skills and internationality are necessary
Total cost of ownership (TCO)	Negotiators must design the scope of negotiations according to the TCO principle
Flexibility	Decision-makers should be able to react flexibly to offers or make proactive offers
Adding value	Companies should encourage employees to identify and negotiate added value.
Additional claims	Preventive use of supplementary claims in the event of deficiencies in performance or other bad listings
Respect and avoidance of loss of face	Respect and face value are a knock-out criterion for all negotiations.

References

BME (2017). 7. BME-Forum Der Einkauf 2025 Vernetzt. Flexibel. Zukunftsorientiert. 15–16. Februar 2017 Köln.

Dathe, T. & Helmold, M. (2018). Erfolgreich im Chinageschäft. Strategien und Handlungsempfehlungen für kleinere und mittlere Unternehmen (KMU). Springer Gabler Wiesbaden.

DIV (2018). https://div-vertriebsforschung.de/.

Erbacher, Ch. (2018). Grundzüge der Verhandlungsführung. VDF Hochschul-Verlag Zürich.

Guba, J. H. (2016). Sollen Verkäufer individuelle Preise bei Ihren Kunden durchsetzen dürfen? 4.5.2016. In: Deutsche Vertriebszeitung. Abgerufen am 7.7.2018. https://vertriebszeitung.de/verkaeufer-wissen-sie-wie-wichtig-ihren-kunden-der-preis-ist/.

Helmold, M. & Terry, B. (2016). Lieferantenmanagement 2030. Springer Gabler Wiesbaden.

Helmold, M. (2018). Erfolgreiche Verhandlungen und Best-in-Class Empfehlungen für den Verhandlungsdurchbruch. Manuskript und Workshopunterlagen im Master- und MBA-Studium.

IUBH (2018). Negotiations in the international Context. Master-Studiengänge. Abgerufen am 18.5.2018. https://www.iubh-fernstudium.de/modul/negotiation-dlmnege/.

Knapp, P. (2017). Verhandlungs-Tools. Effiziente Verhandlungstechniken im Business-Alltag. managerSeminare Verlags GmbH Bonn.

Obrien, J. (2016). Negotiations for Procurement Professionals. 2nd Edition. Kogan Page Croyden.

Schranner, M. (2018). Schranner Negotiations Institute. Abgerufen am 19.5.2018. https://www.schranner.com/de/institute/matthias-schranner-ceo.

Statistisches Bundesamt (2018). Pressemitteilung Nr. 039 vom 08.02.2018: Deutsche Exporte im Jahr 2017: +6.3 % zum Jahr 2016. Exporte und Importe erreichen neue Rekordwerte. Abgerufen am 15.3.2018. https://www.destatis.de/DE/PresseService/Presse/Pressemitteilungen/2018/02/PD18_039_51.html.

Werkstatt für Führung und Vertrieb (2018). Führung und Rhetorik—Argumente wirksam platzieren. Abgerufen am 7.7.2018. http://www.mitarbeiter-fuehren.de/category/rhetorik-fuehrung.

Suitable Tools and Attachments 13

Imagination is more important than knowledge, because knowledge is limited.
—Albert Einstein (1879–1955)

Contents

Summary

Chapter 13 includes tools and forms for successful negotiations: the Manuscript, Priority Matrix, 5-Forces Analysis, SWOT Analysis, Argument and Counterargument Form, A-6 Negotiation Concept, PESTEL, Balance Sheet, Profit and Loss Statement (P&L), and Demand Matrix.

M. Helmold et al., *Successful Negotiations*,
https://doi.org/10.1007/978-3-658-35701-6_13

13.1 Annex 1: The Manuscript

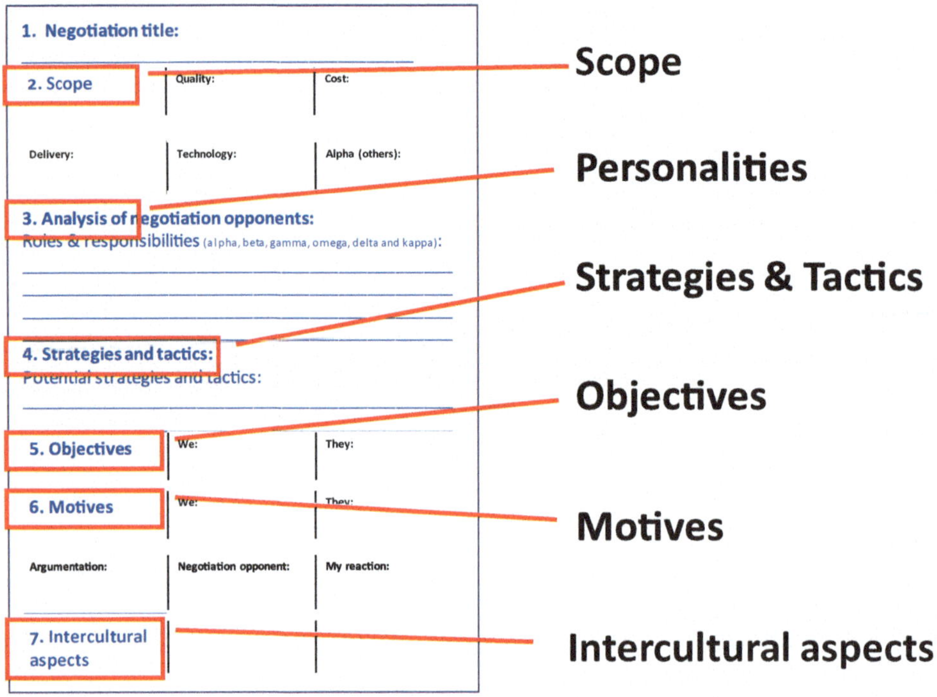

13.2 Annex 2: Priority Matrix

No.	Negotiation Catgeory	Very high Priority	High Priority	Medium Priority	Low Priority
1.					
2.					
3.					
4.					
5.					
6.					
7.					
8.					
9.					
10.					

13.3 Annex 3: 5-Forces Analysis

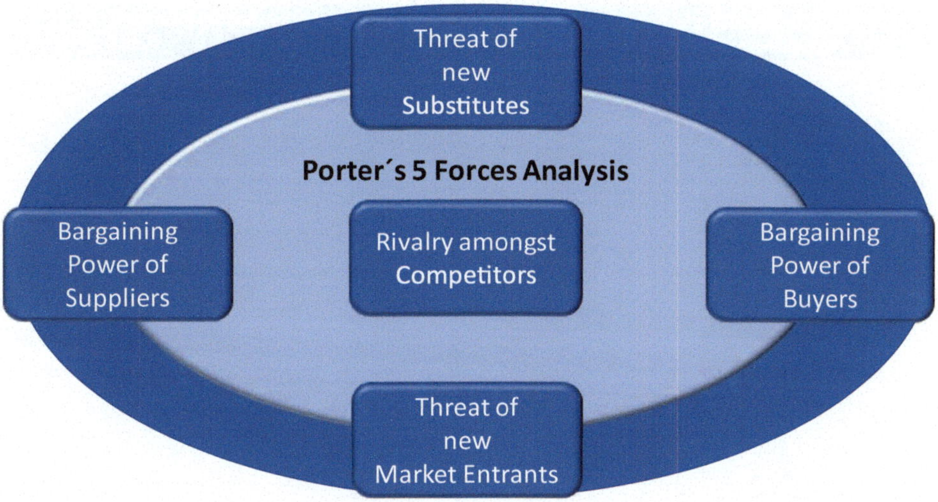

13.4 Annex 4: SWOT Analysis

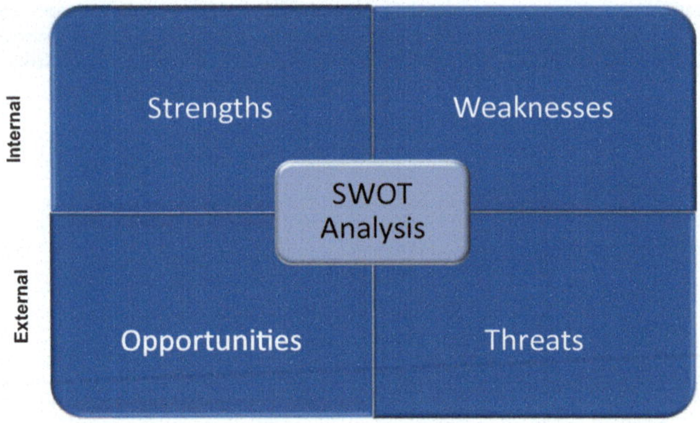

13.5 Annex 5: Priorities and Arguments

Priorität:	Meine Argumente: Argumente für die Verhandlungsführung	Mögliche Gegenargumente und Reaktion
1.		
2.		
3.		
4.		
Priorität:	**Verhandlungsgegner: Argumente für die Verhandlungsführung**	**Schwachstellen der Argumente**
1.		
2.		
3.		
4.		

13.6 Annex 6: A-6 Model by Dr Marc Helmold

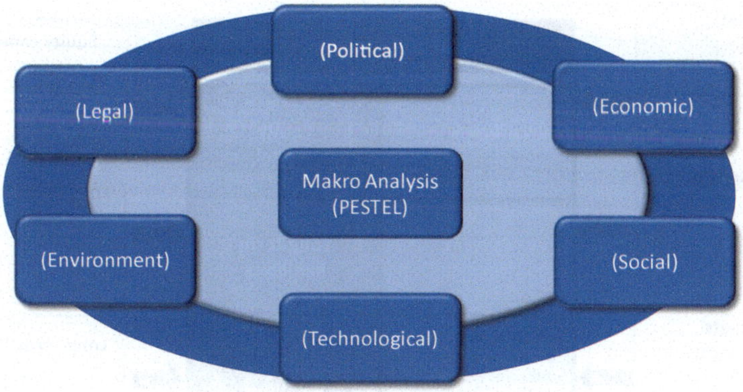

13.7 Annex 7: PESTEL Analysis

13.8 Annex 8: Balance Sheet

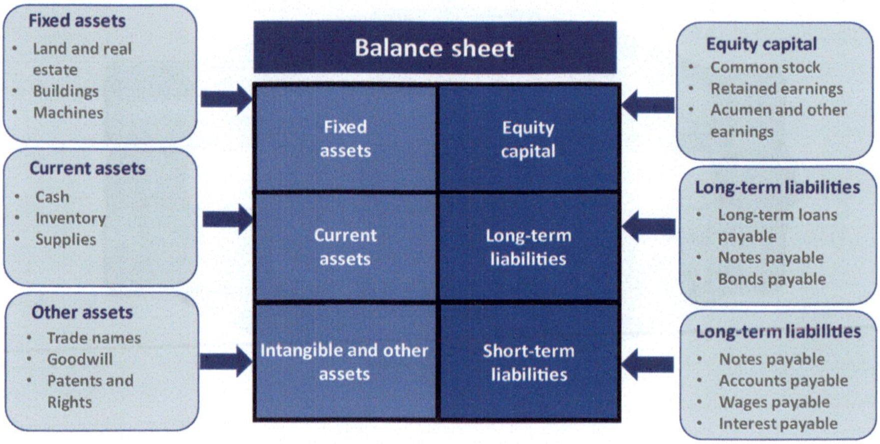

13.9 Annex 9: Profit and Loss Account (P&L)

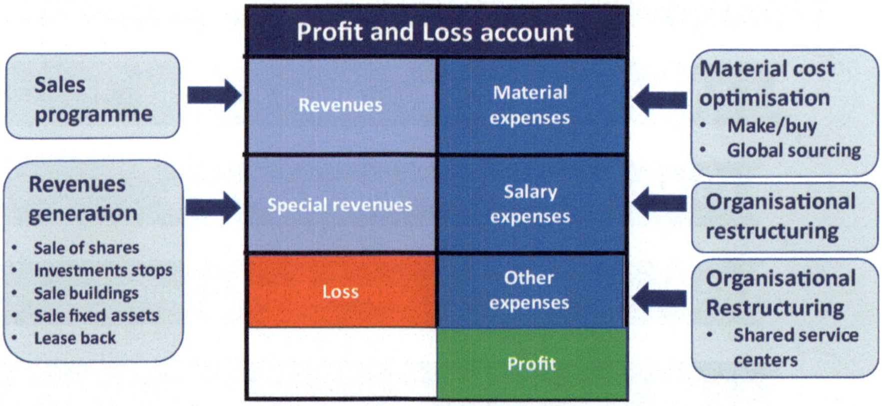

13.10 Annex 10: Demand Matrix

Claim Nr.	Amount	Reason	Minimum-Claim	Maximum-Claim	Probability	Negotiation Strategy
1.						
2.						
3.						
4.						